MODERN LEGAL STUDIES

The Legal Profession: Regulation and the Consumer

Professor Mary Seneviratne

Professor of Law, Nottingham Trent University

SWEET & MAXWELL

GENTIUM LEX

LUX

200 YEARS

1799 1999

London
Sweet & Maxwell
1999

Published in 1999 by
Sweet & Maxwell Limited of
100 Avenue Road London NW3 3PF.
http://www/smlawpub.co.uk
Typeset by Tradespools Ltd
Printed in England by MPG Books Ltd, Bodmin

A CIP catalogue record for this book
is available from the British Library.

ISBN 0421 587407

No natural forests were destroyed to make this product,
only farmed timber was used and re-planted.

The Legal Profession: Regulation and the Consumer

AUSTRALIA
LBC Information Services Sydney
Sydney

CANADA and USA
Carswell
Toronto—Ontario

NEW ZEALAND
Brookers
Auckland

SINGAPORE and MALAYSIA
Sweet & Maxwell Asia
Singapore and Kuala Lumpur

To the memory of Chris and Winnie Seneviratne

Preface

My interest in addressing the issues in this book developed from my wider enquiries into complaints procedures, particularly the role of ombudsmen as alternative dispute resolution mechanisms. Having examined a number of ombudsman schemes in the public and private sectors, a colleague, Rhoda James, and I turned our attention to the work of the Legal Services Ombudsman. This scheme is particularly interesting because it does not conform to the accepted model of ombudsman schemes. It does not fit the accepted taxonomy of public or private, but is a hybrid category embracing both the private and public spheres. It is a state-funded, public body, accountable to the Lord Chancellor. However, the function of the Ombudsman is to oversee the self-regulatory complaints mechanisms of the legal profession, which operate mainly in the private sector. The Legal Services Ombudsman is thus a part of the regulatory framework of the legal profession, an independent watchdog over the way the profession regulates itself.

It is clear that, in order to evaluate the effectiveness of the Legal Services Ombudsman, account must be taken of the professional bodies' complaints mechanisms too. Any study of the Ombudsman will only be coherent if it takes these mechanisms into account. It is only by examining the whole scheme for complaint handling against the legal profession, together with other regulatory mechanisms for protecting the interests of consumers, that it becomes possible to evaluate whether the structure successfully marries the self-regulatory and independent forms of control. This book is therefore an attempt to present these regulatory mechanisms in a coherent form, in order to inform the debate about the appropriate mechanisms for protecting the interests of consumers of legal services.

In researching and writing this book, I have been fortunate in receiving advice and assistance from a number of people, whose help I would like to acknowledge here. I would like to thank Rhoda James, for the useful collaborative work which we have undertaken in relation to the Legal Services Ombudsman and the legal profession. Without this collaboration, this book would never have been written. My thanks also go to those who gave up their time to be interviewed, or who have read and commented on draft chapters. They are as follows: Ann Abraham, Ian Brownlee, Michael Gunn, Peter Kunzlik, Diane Longley, Nick O'Brien, Martin O'Reilly, John Peysner, Bob White, Kevin Williams, and Tessa Williamson. I would also like to thank Hugh Beale for his helpful suggestions. Finally, my biggest thanks go to my family: to Anna, Sarah and Christopher for reminding me that there are more important things in life than writing books; and especially to Ian for his immense help, support and encouragement.

Mary Seneviratne   January 29, 1999
Centre for Legal Research
Nottingham Trent University

Contents

Table of Cases

Table of Statutes

Table of Statutory Instruments

Introduction

Lawyers in England and Wales have, in the last decade, been subject to criticisms and attacks from a number of quarters. Although not the object of disparaging jokes to the same extent as in the United States, they are often viewed as providing services which are too expensive, and which take them an unnecessarily long time to deliver. Barristers are perceived as greedy "fat cats", growing rich at public expense on the legal aid budget. Solicitors are criticised for the ever-increasing number of complaints against them, and the perception that these are not being satisfactorily resolved through the system of regulation set up by the Law Society. In the past, a deference to professionals probably protected lawyers from too much adverse criticism, and from too much investigation into their work. This is no longer the case. Consumer organisations, departments of Government, and academics are becoming concerned to know what lawyers do, what they charge for doing it, and what accountability and redress mechanisms are available to consumers when a problem occurs with the services they provide. This book addresses the last concern.

There is no doubt that the legal profession is in a state of change. It has been subjected to monumental changes in the delivery of legal services during the last decade. Conditional fees, extended rights of audience, new providers of legal services, changes to legal aid provisions, are all operating to change radically the nature of the legal profession. In 1990, the Courts and Legal Services Act was passed. This legislation was described at the time as one of the "great reforming statutes of the second half of this century" and one of the "most important pieces of legislation affecting the delivery of legal services".[1] The intention of the (then) Government in enacting this legislation was to improve access to good quality legal services at a price which consumers could afford. There was to be more choice in legal services, which would have the effect of making delivery more efficient and cost-effective. This was the rhetoric of the market and competition, and not surprisingly, it was resisted by the profession. The 1990 Act made a direct attack on the profession's traditional and restrictive practices, by opening up the market for legal services.

---

[1] R. White, *A Guide to the Courts and Legal Services Act 1990* (1991) [London: Format].

Less than 10 years later, this Act is now being followed with even more far-reaching legislation,[2] in turn described as "unquestionably the greatest shake-up of legal services since the original Legal Aid Act 1948".[3] The present Government is also concerned to provide access to justice at an affordable price, and is preparing to make further inroads into the self-regulatory mechanisms of the legal profession in order to achieve this. However, this widening of choice is not to be paid for by a decrease in standards. The Government remains concerned that professional bodies maintain appropriate standards for the profession and that the interests of consumers are protected.

The purpose of this book is to describe and evaluate the mechanisms which do exist to protect the interests of consumers of legal services. It focuses on the traditional providers of these services, solicitors and barristers. Despite the fact that new professionals are now able to provide some legal services, barristers and solicitors still constitute the legal profession as we know it. The book examines both the statutory and self-regulatory provisions which are available to protect the interests of consumers. It also considers the role of private law in this respect. It will look at general issues of professionalism and self-regulation and how these impact on the consumer of legal services. It focuses on individual, private clients, who may have infrequent dealings with the legal profession throughout their lifetime. There are different issues as regards accountability and redress for corporate clients, which are not the subject of this book. In particular the book will examine the way the redress mechanisms work and will draw some conclusions on how well the present regulatory arrangements operate in the consumer interest. Any system of regulation involves a balancing act between the interests of clients and the general public interest and those of the profession. This book is an attempt to inform the debate about whether the present balance is appropriate.

---

[2] The Access to Justice Bill, which was given its second Reading on December 14, 1998, and is, at the time of writing, passing through the Parliamentary process.

[3] Lord Goodhart, H.L. Deb., col. 1119, December 14, 1998.

Chapter 1

Regulation, Self-Regulation and Professionalism

At first glance, recent developments in the opening up of the market for legal services may suggest a relaxation of the regulatory mechanisms which control the work of the legal profession. Certainly the reform of the system for the regulation of the profession which took place under the Courts and Legal Services Act 1990,[1] was designed to deregulate the provision of legal services by allowing for the abolition of many of the legal profession's traditional and restrictive practices. However, it would be a mistake to assume that deregulation of the *supply* of legal services has resulted in a relaxation of regulation of the legal profession itself, as the supplier of these services. In part, the thrust for the regulatory reforms was a result of concerns that the legal profession, through its monopolies and privileges, was acting in its own interests, rather than in the interests of the consumers it was supposed to serve. The profession was seen as operating cartels, which restricted choice and enabled price fixing and over-charging. There was widespread public perception that the self-interest of lawyers was masquerading as a public service.[2]

The new regulatory framework aimed, therefore, to provide the widest range of choice in legal services, compatible with the maintenance of standards.[3] In order to widen choice, the supply of services was to be expanded, but in order to maintain quality and access to justice, some regulation was deemed to be necessary. These developments have subjected legal services to some of the rigours of the market, and have not been entirely welcomed by the whole

---

[1] This is discussed in detail in Chapter 3
[2] R. Cranston, "Legal Ethics and Professional Responsibility" in *Legal Ethics and Professional Responsibility* (R. Cranston ed., 1995), at p.32 [Oxford: Clarendon Press].
[3] *Legal Services: A Framework for the Future.* White Paper, Cm 740 (1989), at p. 4 [London, HMSO].

profession. Indeed, some of the changes have been interpreted as an attack on the very concept of a profession and professionalism, and dire warnings have been given of the consequences, not just to individuals, but to society as a whole, if professional autonomy is attacked in this way.[4]

Such interpretations are not new. When the legal profession was subjected to investigation and inquiry into its work in the 1960s and 1970s, not only did it react negatively to the adverse criticism, but it also exhibited some resentment that there should be such investigation at all, on the ground that it equated the professional relationship of solicitor and client with that of the market place.[5] This was perceived as detrimental to the profession and to its clients, as the profession was not motivated "merely by monetary reward", but rather had a "moral right" to be paid properly for its skills and services.[6] The majority of the legal profession did not consider law to be a business and felt that a concern with markets and greater productivity would kill the idealism of the legal profession.[7]

Implicit in these statements is the view that the legal profession, and professions in general, have characteristics which set them apart from other occupations, and that therefore the state should afford them some protection from the rigours of the market. In addition, the state should play little part in controlling the profession, and it should be for the profession itself to decide on the quality of the services it delivers. Such claims necessitate some elaboration of the concept of a profession.

Professions and professionalism

Much of the recent change to the regulatory structure of the legal profession has been driven by the modern rhetoric of "consumerism", and the view that the profession is a service industry. However, a profession has traditionally been seen as different from a business enterprise. While a business may be defined as "a commercial

---

[4] A. Crawley and C. Bramall, "Professional Rules, Codes, and Principles Affecting Solicitors (Or What Has Professional Regulation to do with Ethics?)" in *Legal Ethics and Professional Responsibility* (R. Cranston ed., 1995), at p. 106 [Oxford: Clarendon Press].

[5] G. Mungham and P. Thomas, "Solicitors and Clients: Altruism or Self-Interest?" in *The Sociology of the Professions* (R. Dingwall and P. Lewis eds., 1983), at p.133 [London: Macmillan].

[6] Leader (1972) *The Conveyancer* 81–82

[7] E. A. Williams, "The Solicitor and his Social Conscience" (1973) 117 *Solicitor's Journal* 199

enterprise designed for profit", definitions of a profession usually include the notion of a "vocation", particularly one which involves some branch of learning or science, and some sense that this knowledge is applied to the affairs of, and for the benefit of, others. A profession is an occupation, but a discrete category of occupation, which is "based on advanced, or complex, or esoteric, or arcane knowledge".[8] The concept of a profession implies a discipline which is capable of study, and which has to be mastered before membership of the profession is available.[9] There is, however, no definition which is unequivocal and uncontested, and undoubtedly the term "profession" is controversial and value-laden.

The debate about the problem of a suitable definition for professions has raged over a number of decades.[10] Sociologists, practitioners and commentators have attempted to construct lists of characteristics which are essential to the definition of a profession. Against these lists of characteristics, or traits, a particular occupation could be measured and assessed as professional or not. Thus, according to a past president of the Law Society, a profession is identified by three characteristics. It puts its clients' interests before its own, it has the highest standards of training and integrity, and it accepts, so far as it reasonably can, responsibility for its members' failures.[11]

One of the major inquiries into the work of the legal profession identified the following five characteristics of a profession.

1. It should have a governing body, or bodies, to represent it, and to exercise powers of control and discipline over its members.

2. It should have a specialised field of knowledge, acquired by education and training and also by practical experience and continuing study.

3. Admission to the profession should be dependent upon a period of theoretical and practical training, competence being assessed by means of examinations.

4. There should also be some self-regulation, to ensure that members of the profession will observe higher standards than could be successfully imposed from without.

---

[8] K. Macdonald, *The Sociology of the Professions* (1995), at p.1 [London: Sage].
[9] M. Zander, *Lawyers and the Public Interest* (1968), at p.21
[10] E. Freidson, "The Theory of Professions: State of the Art" in *The Sociology of the Professions* (R. Dingwall and P. Lewis eds., 1983), at p.21 [London: Macmillan].
[11] M. Mears, "Foreword" in *The Guide to the Professional Conduct of Solicitors* (7th Edition, 1996) [London: The Law Society].

5. Finally, there must be a professional ethic which requires that the practitioner's first and particular responsibility is to the client.[12]

The characteristics of a profession, therefore, have included the idea of selflessness, service to the community, and the common good, as well as the sacrifices necessary to obtain the relevant qualifications and skill. The distinguishing attributes of a profession have emphasised the trust between the professional and client, and the existence of controls to guarantee competence in the delivery of services. It was these characteristics which differentiated the professions from other occupations, and therefore, for an occupation to be given the status of a profession there had to be some notion of training, ethics, disciplinary action and self-regulation. This approach, an idealised view of the professions, has been criticised as reducing sociological analysis "to little more than professional apologetics".[13] It accepts without question the view that professions are concerned to protect the public, and that professionals will always put the clients' interests before their own.

As well as presenting an idealised view, another problem with this approach is that it implies that it is possible to list exhaustive criteria for distinguishing professions from other occupations.[14] Such characteristics, however, can be present to a greater or lesser extent in a variety of occupations, and they are differences of degree rather than kind.[15] It also implies that the characteristics of a profession are somehow immutable, ignoring the fact that professionalism is a dynamic concept which is capable of change. The trait approach restates the professionals' own definitions of themselves, while using apparently neutral characteristics.[16] It does not however address the question of why it was that some occupations became professions, and how they managed to do so.

Another approach to the concept of professions is to examine the role or function they play in society. Durkheim,[17] who was concerned for social order, saw the professions as meeting a certain function in

---

[12] *Royal Commission on Legal Services*, Final Report, Volume 1, Cmnd. 7640 (1979), at pp.23, 30. [London: HMSO].
[13] R Abel, *The Legal Profession in England and Wales* (1988), at p.7 [Oxford: Blackwell], commenting on the definition used by the *Royal Commission on Legal Services*, Final Report, Cmnd. 7640 (1979).
[14] R. Dingwall, "Introduction" in *The Sociology of the Professions* (R. Dingwall and P.Lewis eds., 1983), at p.8 [London: Macmillan].
[15] E. C. Hughes, *Men and Their Work* (1958), at p.5 [New York: The Free Press].
[16] T. Johnson, *Professions and Power* (1972), at p.25. [London: Macmillan].
[17] E. Durkheim, *The Division of Labour in Society* (1964) [New York: Free Press]

society. They were an antidote to selfish materialism, a community within anomic society. He emphasised the function of professions as saving modern society from breakdown in moral authority, because of their intermediatory status between the individual and the state. They played a significant role within the system of stratification which unites the extremes of society. The functionalist tradition emphasises the homogeneity of particular professions in terms of background, training, and clientele. An important aspect of functionalist theory is that the professions will use their knowledge for social cohesion. These characteristics, particularly those concerned with altruism and special skill, were the justification for the privileged status of the professions. Implicit in this approach, therefore, is the idea of a bargain between the state and the profession. The state will afford some degree of protection to those who take the trouble to qualify for, and adhere to the discipline imposed by, a particular profession.

The functionalist analysis of professionalism was subject to criticism, because it ignored questions of power and the role of the state. It was largely superseded, in the 1970s, by the "power" approach to the study of the professions, and the analysis moved from an inquiry about the characteristics of professions, and the role they play in the established order of society, to studies of the circumstances in which an occupation could be turned into a profession. This follows the Weberian tradition, as it seeks to discover how it is that certain occupations managed to persuade the state to grant them a privileged position in society. For Weber,[18] society is a collection of individuals pursuing their own interests. These groups attempt to exclude others from the group in order to establish monopolies and privileges for the group, a practice known as social closure. The purpose of exclusion is not only to attain and maintain certain monopolies, but also to achieve the upward social mobility of the group as a whole.[19]

The work of Larson[20] and Johnson[21] are important in this Weberian context, and mark a break from the traditional approach. For Johnson, the essence of a profession is that it is an occupation which has control over the producer-consumer relationship. The profession defines the needs of the consumer and how these needs should be met. Professionalism arises where certain conditions exist. First, there has to be effective demand for certain skills from a large and relatively heterogeneous consumer group. This will ensure that

---

[18] M. Weber, *Economy and Society* (1968), at p.341–343 [University of California Press].

[19] K. Macdonald, *The Sociology of the Professions* (1995), at p.29 [London: Sage].

[20] M. Larson, *The Rise of Professionalism: A Sociological Analysis* (1977) [University of California Press: Berkeley].

[21] T. Johnson, *Professions and Power* (1972) [London: Macmillan].

consumers are unorganised, dependent and exploitable. Second, the occupational group has to be homogeneous in outlook and interest, with a low degree of specialisation, and recruiting those with similar social backgrounds. In Britain, the conditions for professionalism developed in the second half of the nineteenth century, with the rise to power of the urban middle class, which resulted in an expanding market for services based on individual needs.[22]

For Larson, the singular characteristic of professional power is that the profession has the exclusive privilege of defining both its knowledge base, and the legitimate conditions of access to it. The fact that this knowledge is unequally distributed means that the power of professions could be protected and enhanced.[23] Larson calls this the "professional project", that is, the striving by the professions for both economic power, through market control, and social power, through status by using the claims to special knowledge and skills.[24]

The professions, then, have sought economic control, by restricting the numbers entering the profession, and by demarcating and protecting areas of work which were their sole preserve. Such practices ensured their economic power, and the imposition of rules of etiquette and ethics enhanced their social status.[25] Social closure and exclusion are therefore important, as is the idea of exclusivity of knowledge, and the special skills necessary to apply this knowledge. Particularly important is the idea that some types of knowledge would be dangerous in untrained and unqualified hands, because of risks to life, property, or third-party interests.

No monopoly, however, can be obtained and guaranteed without the co-operation of the state, or at least its benign neglect,[26] and therefore the profession must have a special relationship with the state.[27] In return for the licence from the state to carry out some of the dangerous and important tasks for society, the professions have claimed a mandate to define and control their own work, and to influence its content and delivery.[28] Professions therefore struck a bargain with society, in which they exchanged competence and integrity in return for trust, freedom from interference, protection

[22] ibid., at p.52.
[23] M. Larson, The Rise of Professionalism: A Sociological Analysis (1977), at p.48 [University of California Press: Berkeley]
[24] ibid., at p.xvi.
[25] M. Burrage, "Revolution and the collective action of the French, American and English legal professions" (1988) 13(2) Law and Social Enquiry: the Journal of the American Bar Foundation 225–77.
[26] K. Macdonald, The Sociology of the Professions (1995), at p.xii [London: Sage].
[27] ibid., at p.34.
[28] E. C. Hughes, Men and Their Work (1958), at pp.78–80 [NewYork: The Free Press].

against unqualified competition, and substantial remuneration and higher social status.[29] The professions are enabled to carry out their side of the bargain by means of careful recruitment and training, codes of ethics, and professional bodies which enforce the code. This then is the "regulative bargain",[30] which is a feature of all professional conduct. A central issue for the discussion which follows is whether the "regulative bargain" struck between the state and the profession is being, or should be, renegotiated, and whether this indicates the demise of the profession.

The legal profession

Although we talk about the legal profession, in fact, barristers and solicitors are two separate professions, each with its own separate governing body, separate rules of conduct and discipline, and different systems of entry and training. Although both are subject to the provisions of the Courts and Legal Services Act 1990, they are governed by a separate statutory framework. The reasons for the division are historical. Before 1895, training to become a barrister was only available in the four Inns of Court: the Inner Temple, the Middle Temple, Gray's Inn and Lincoln's Inn. The professions of attorney, conveyancer and proctor developed independently of the Inns of Court, and they merged to form the solicitors' branch of the profession. As a result, the two separate functions of preparing a case and presenting it became established, and with it the rule which required a barrister to be instructed by a solicitor, thus preventing instruction directly by a lay client.

The continuation of the two separate professions is said to reflect the difference in the type of work done by each branch. For example, solicitors give advice, and have day-to-day contact with clients. Barristers, often considered to be the senior branch of the profession, give specialist advice, draft documents, and act as advocates in the higher courts. They do not have direct contact with clients, and have to be approached through a solicitor. Although it appears that solicitors are the generalists, and that barristers are the advocates and

---

[29] D. Rueschemeyer, "Professional Autonomy and the Social Control of Expertise" in *The Sociololgy of the Professions: Lawyers, Doctors and Others* (R. Dingwall and P. Lewis eds., 1983), at p.41[London: Macmillan].

[30] D. Cooper, A. Lowe, A. Puxty, K. Robson and H. Willmott, "Regulating the UK accountancy profession: episodes in the relation between the profession and the state" (1988). Paper presented at Economic and Social Research Council Conference on *Corporatism*. Policy Studies Institute , London.

the specialists, this distinction between the two branches of the profession is often artificial. No legal tasks are exclusive to one branch. Solicitors do appear as advocates in the lower courts, and are increasingly appearing in the higher courts. Not all barristers are advocates. Many rarely appear in court, but spend their time writing opinions on the law.

The artificial nature of this distinction has been recognised for some time. Thirty years ago, one commentator noted that "the two sides of the profession are more and more doing the same things and are increasingly in direct competition with each other".[31] Although the Benson Commission[32] in 1979 had concluded that the division should remain, a minority of the Commission did not agree, on the basis that the system was inefficient, and resulted in delay. The continued existence of the two branches of the profession continues to be debated in both academic and professional circles. There has been a gradual erosion of the monopoly on advocacy rights enjoyed by barristers, and the distinction is being blurred, leading some to conclude that eventually there will be fusion between the two branches of the profession.[33] The continued separation is becoming particularly hard to justify in view of the Government's recent proposals that all qualified solicitors and qualified barristers should, in principle, have the right to appear in any court.[34]

SOLICITORS

The larger of the two branches of the profession is the solicitors' branch, with over 95,000 on the roll of solicitors, approximately 75,000 of whom are practising solicitors.[35] In the early 1960s, there were 20,000 solicitors. The yearly increase in the numbers began to accelerate in the 1960s, with the largest rate of increase taking place in the 1970s. The Law Society predicted that unless this growth was halted, there would be 80,000 practising solicitors by the end of the century.[36] There is some concern as to whether future demand for the

---

[31] M. Zander, *Lawyers in the Public Interest* (1968), at p.3 [London: Weidenfeld and Nicolson].

[32] *Royal Commission on Legal Services.* Final Report, Cmnd. 7648 (1979) [London: HMSO].

[33] R. White, *The Administration of Justice* (2nd ed., 1991), at p.298 [Oxford: Blackwells].

[34] *Rights of audience and rights to conduct litigation in England and Wales: the way ahead* (1998). Lord Chancellor's Department Consultation Paper. See also the Access to Justice Bill, which is discussed in Chapter 3.

[35] On July 1, 1998 there were 95,521 solicitors on the roll, 75,072 of whom had practising certificates.

[36] *Annual Report of the Law Society 1995/96*, at p.5.

services of solicitors will be sufficient to sustain this growth.[37] The increase in numbers has been accounted for by the numbers of women now entering the profession. In 1985, there were approximately 40,000 men and fewer than 10,000 women in the profession. Ten years later, the number of men had risen slightly, but the number of women had more than doubled.[38]

The 75,000 practising solicitors form a disparate profession. A number are employed in-house for organisations in the private and public sectors. Within the public sector solicitors are employed by local government, magistrates' courts, the Government Legal Service and the Crown Prosecution Service. However, the majority of solicitors is in private practice, working as sole practitioners, partners in firms, or employees in firms. Most of the higher fee paying work is concentrated in a few large firms, mainly in London, which employ a significant percentage of the profession. For example, the 10[39] largest firms in London together employ just under 10 per cent of all solicitors in private practice.

This is a significant change for the profession. In 1950, there were only five firms of solicitors which had six or more partners, and the largest had ten. By 1977 this had increased to 217 firms with six or more principals, and 25 with more than 20 principals.[40] At the end of the 1990s, the largest firm had 775 solicitors, consisting of 287 partners and 488 assistants, plus a further 381 other fee earners. The smallest of the top 50 firms had 67 partners, 46 assistants, and 93 other fee earning staff.[41] These large firms have standard formats for delivering complex, high-quality services. It is understandable if the lawyers there see themselves more as paid servants of their clients, rather than as officers of the court and an integral part of the scheme of justice.[42]

The rise in the numbers and size of large firms has not meant that there has been a decrease in the number of small firms. The number of small practices has increased every year since 1990, and more than

---

[37] *Directory of Solicitors 1993*, at p.ix. The Law Society: London.

[38] In July 1998, there were 49,633 men and 25,139 women with practising certificates. Of those admitted onto the roll in 1998, 51 per cent were women. 57 per cent of law students enrolled with the Law Society are women (*Annual Statistical Report of 1998*, The Law Society).

[39] On July 1, 1998, there were 8,764 firms of solicitors.

[40] M. Burrage, "From a gentlemen's to a public profession: status and politics in the history of English solicitors" (1996) 3(1/2) *International Journal of the Legal Profession* 45–80, at p. 69

[41] Chambers and Partners, *A Guide to the Legal Profession 1997–98*.

[42] M. Galanter and T. Palay, "Large Law Firms and Professional responsibility" in *Legal Ethics and Professional Responsbility* (R. Cranston ed., 1995), at p.189 [Oxford: Clarendon Press]

one-third of solicitors in private practice work in firms with fewer than five partners. The number of solicitors working on their own, too, is far from insignificant, with about 45 per cent of firms being sole practitioners. The interests and needs of large practices and small ones are very different, and there is thus an increasing gulf between sole practitioners and their counterparts in large firms.[43] There is also a growing disparity in the earnings of solicitors.[44] This polarisation may make it unrealistic to talk about a single profession. It also makes it more difficult to govern the profession, as rules are easier to instil and enforce among those who are doing roughly the same work in similar work settings.[45]

The nature of much of the work of solicitors has also changed. At one time, solicitors used to serve mainly private clients, and their work was concerned with transferring property, administering estates, and litigating personal claims. Now the clients are companies, and the government, through state-funded legal aid schemes.[46] There is increasing specialisation, which has led to a differentiation within the profession of its knowledge base. The market for legal services has changed, and deregulation and the removal of monopolies is blurring the boundaries between different professional disciplines. Solicitors are also facing competition from outside the profession, from new providers of legal services.

These changes have caused some to observe that the solicitor's branch of the profession "is at a watershed facing considerable challenges from inside and outside".[47] It is less homogeneous, both in relation to the characteristics of solicitors themselves,[48] and in relation

---

[43] Y. Dezalay and D. Sugarman, "Forward" in *Professional Competition and Professional Power: Lawyers, Accountants and the Social Construction of Reality* (Y. Dezalay and D. Sugarman eds., 1995) [London: Routledge].

[44] There has been a reduction in real income in small firms. It is estimated that 25 per cent of sole practitioners generated gross fees of less than £46,000, and 50 per cent generated less than £80,000. In two to four partner firms, there was an average of £52,000 profit per partner. 25 percent of these partners earned £30,000 or less. In five to 10 partner firms, the average profit was £66,000, which increased to £88,000 for 11 to 25 partner firms (*Trends in the Solicitors Profession* (1997) Law Society: Research and Planning Unit).

[45] M. Burrage, "From a gentlemen's to a public profession: status and politics in the history of English solicitors" (1996) 3(1/2) *International Journal of the Legal Profession* 45–80, at p.73

[46] R. Abel, *The Legal Profession in England and Wales* (1988), at p.307 [Oxford: Blackwell].

[47] K. Bahl, "Solicitor's profession—slow decline or golden future" (1998) June 19 *New Law Journal* 920.

[48] For example, there are more females in the profession, and they are younger, on average. The average age of women in practice is 35, compared to 43 for men. The average age of all solicitors in private practice is 40. Sole practitioners have an average age of 48, and partners, 44. Solicitors are also drawn from a wider social base than in the past.

to their working experience once in practice. Certainly the rise of large firms presents a challenge to the profession, as does the opportunity (or threat) to practise as multi-disciplinary partnerships. This latter development has caused concern that solicitors' firms could be taken over by firms of accountants. For smaller firms challenges are presented by the proposals for legal aid reforms, increasing specialisation, and competition from other professionals in their traditional areas of work, notably conveyancing and probate. Many firms will only survive by establishing cost-effective niche markets for their services, especially from business clients.

BARRISTERS

In comparison to solicitors, the Bar is a small profession, with less than 10,000 barristers in independent practice in England and Wales.[49] The Bar has always been the smaller branch of the profession, but it, too, has grown dramatically over the last 40 years. In 1950, for example, there were only about 2,000 barristers in independent practice. There are no precise figures available for the number of employed barristers, although it has been estimated[50] that in 1994 there were about 2,500, of whom 656 worked for the Crown Prosecution Service. This figure appears to have remained fairly constant.[51]

Barristers still remain a more homogeneous profession than solicitors. The vast majority work in independent practice, and are self-employed. They do not work in partnership with other barristers.[52] They usually work from chambers, which are shared with other barristers, and where there are common resources, such as clerks and office facilities. The clerk performs the role of office administrator, accountant, business manager and agent for the barristers in a set of chambers. The clerk allocates work from solicitors to barristers, and negotiates their fees.[53]

Although the number of barristers has increased, the nature of their work remains basically the same. They act as advocates in courts and tribunals, and they give specialist advice in the form of opinions. They

---

[49] On October 1, 1998, there were 9,698 barristers in independent practice.
[50] R. Cranston, "Legal Ethics and Professional Responsibility" in *Legal Ethics and Professional Responsibility* (R. Cranston ed., 1995), at p.6 [Oxford: Clarendon Press].
[51] In 1998, the figure for employed barristers was 2,472.
[52] There are proposals to allow barristers to work in partnerships. These are discussed in Chapter 3.
[53] Senior clerks receive between 5 and 10 per cent of the barrister's fee as commission. The earnings of some clerks can exceed that of many barristers.

still have referral status,[54] that is, they receive their work from solicitors. This system evolved from the formal system of pleading required by the courts prior to the changes in court practice which took place in the nineteenth century.[55] The traditional area of barristers' work, advocacy, is now being threatened as a result of rights of audience in the higher courts being granted to solicitors. This represents a considerable challenge for barristers

The end of the legal profession?

Do these demographic changes, together with the regulatory changes, herald the end of the legal profession? Abel's work[56] provides a useful starting point in addressing this question. In his thorough analysis of the work of the legal profession, he adopts a market theory approach, his thesis being that an occupation becomes a profession by mobilising state power to control entry. His approach to theories of professions and the market is Weberian, an approach that was also adopted by Larson.[57] The essence of this is that professions are engaged in the control of supply and creation of demand. As professions produce services rather than goods, consumers must be persuaded to acknowledge the value of these services, and must be convinced that they cannot produce the services themselves. Because services are not embodied in a physical form, there is no opportunity to control the supply of the product. Therefore, in order to ensure scarcity, there has to be control over the production of producers.[58]

The essence of a profession, therefore, is the ability to control the production of producers. This does not, however, explain how it is that some occupations have been successful in achieving this. Abel believes that the success of this depends upon the strength of the value that the professional service ostensibly promotes. Thus, it is no accident that the traditional professions of medicine and law are concerned with health and justice, which are high-ranking values in society. Also important is the fact that these services are given to

---

[54] There are proposals to change this. These are discussed in Chapter 3.
[55] See generally A. Thornton, "The Professional Responsibility and Ethics of the English Bar" in *Legal Ethics and Professional Responsibility* (R. Cranston ed., 1995) [Oxford: Clarendon Press].
[56] R. Abel, *The Legal Profession in England and Wales* (1988) [Oxford: Blackwell].
[57] M. Larson, *The Rise of Professionalism: A Sociological Analysis* (1977) [Berkeley: University of California Press].
[58] R. Abel, *The Legal Profession in England and Wales* (1988), at pp.8–11 [Oxford: Blackwell].

isolated individuals, so there is a direct personal relationship.[59] Professional status is enhanced and social respect is accorded because of the lengthy training involved. This sacrifice is considered necessary to justify future privilege.

Abel provides empirical evidence to demonstrate how the legal profession controls the production of producers. For example, in the case of barristers, entry is limited because a barrister has to be admitted to one of the four Inns of Court, and keep the necessary terms there. There is a financial cost in qualifying, and not only must an intending barrister obtain the necessary academic and professional qualifications, but he or she must also obtain pupillage, and then a tenancy in order to practise. All these hurdles maintain the relatively small numbers at the bar, and this scarcity ensures that the rewards for practice are high. As well as controlling the supply of producers, the producers control production by their monopoly of certain legal services, for example, the right to act as advocates in court. Other monopolies were conveyancing and probate.

As well as controlling supply, the professions also need to create demand. This is more difficult as there are a number of factors which influence the demand for legal services. For example, the demand for such services in property matters depends on factors such as the distribution of income and wealth. The rise of home ownership, and the demand for financial services will create a demand for legal services. As Galanter has noted, there are differences between societies and across time in the extent to which using the law is culturally approved or discouraged.[60] Legal services can also be displaced by administrative arrangements, the demand for law rising and falling according to the prominence of other forms of social control. For example, the legal regulation of marriage and of its dissolution, gives rise to the demand for legal services.[61]

The profession can create demand for legal services. It does this by offering a particular world view of conflict and its resolution, and by generating a sense of rights and entitlements.[62] It can, for example,

---

[59] *ibid.*, at p.14.

[60] M. Galanter, "Reading the landscapes of disputes: what we know and don't know (and think we know) about our allegedly contentious and litigious society" (1983) 31 *U.C.L.A. Law Review* 4–71.

[61] R. Abel, *The Legal Profession in England and Wales* (1988), at p.20 [Oxford: Blackwell]. Other examples include family conferencing in New Zealand, which reduces the role of the juvenile courts (see G. Maxwell and A. Morris, *Family, Victims and Culture: Youth Justice in New Zealand* (1993) [Wellington: Social Policy Agency and Institute of Criminology]. There are similar mediation schemes in the United Kingdom (see T. F. Marshall and S. Merry, *Crime and Accountability: Victim/Offender Mediation in Practice* (1990) [London: HMSO].

[62] J. McCahery and S. Picciotto, "Creative Lawyering and the dynamics of business

persuade private clients to make wills. Where business clients are concerned, a lawyer will not be used unless the lawyer adds value to the business transaction in question.[63] Demand for legal services can also be created by public subsidy. Although the legal profession operates in a private market, demand for legal services can be stimulated by the availability of state funded legal aid and assistance. The profession has also been able to stimulate demand by the relaxation of the rules on advertising.[64] However, even when lawyers succeed in creating demand, they may lose it to other providers, through alternative dispute resolution techniques, for example mediation, self-help, and ombudsmen. Another problem with demand creation, and the subsequent moves into wider markets, is that it affects the homogeneity of the profession. If the profession has different markets, clients and methods of operation it is less coherent, and becomes less powerful.[65]

Abel concluded that legal profession, at the end of the 1980s, had lost control of its market. This was due to a number of factors. First, there were some major attacks on the profession's restrictive practices. Market control was thus lost through deregulation of legal services, with the resulting loss of immunity from competition. In addition, there was an erosion of the control the profession once had over the production of producers, because control of the supply of producers had been surrendered to the universities. This had resulted in a more heterogeneous and larger profession. The increase in the numbers of salaried lawyers had also caused the profession to be less homogeneous. One of the strengths of a profession is claimed to be its homogeneity, and the loss of this could herald its decline.

Other factors which have contributed to the transformation of the profession include the increase in internal competition within the profession. Lawyers now have different clienteles. Rather than

---

regulation" in *Professional Competition and Professional Power: Lawyers, Accountants and the Social Construction of Reality* (Y. Dezalay and D. Sugarman eds., 1995), at p.254 [London: Routledge]. See also N. Christie's formative article "Conflicts as Property" (1977) 17(1) *British Journal of Criminology* 1–15, on the role of the state and lawyers in "stealing" conflicts from the parties to a crime. See also M. Cain "The General Practice Lawyer and the Client: Towards a Radical Conception" in *The Sociology of the Professions: Lawyers, Doctors and Others* (R. Dingwall and P. Lewis eds., 1983) [London: Macmillan].

[63] J. McCahery and S. Picciotto "Creative Lawyering and the dynamics of business regulation" in *Professional Competition and Professional Power: Lawyers, Accountants and the Social Construction of Reality* (Y. Dezalay and D. Sugarman eds., 1995), at p.243 [London: Routledge].

[64] Solicitors can advertise provided that it does not impair their independence and integrity, and does not bring the profession into disrepute.

[65] R. Abel, "Lawyers in the Civil World" in *Lawyers in Society: the civil world* (R. Abel and P. Lewis eds., 1988) [University of California Press: Los Angeles].

working for private individuals, as the profession did in the past, major sources of work come from companies, the government, and other organisations. In particular, public funding of legal services gives the government tremendous power over the legal profession. Many lawyers in private practice are now financially dependent on the state, which makes non-negotiable payments in the form of legal aid.[66] Within this climate of market forces and state regulation to protect clients, ideas of professionalism may be harder to preserve.[67]

The evidence thus suggests that the legal profession has lost, or is losing, control of its market. Increasing state intervention has eroded the profession's independence and autonomy. Since the market control thesis argues, crucially, that the essence of a profession is how successful it is in controlling its market, the above factors indicate a transformation of the legal profession to an extent so great, that it may result in its eventual demise.[68] The lawyer will become either an entrepreneur in a competitive market, or an employee, and all lawyers will come to depend on the state or business organisations. The ideal of professionalism may remain as an "anachronistic warrant of legitimacy", but the profession as an economic, social and political institution will be "moribund".[69]

The new professionalism

This gloomy prediction has been challenged. Abel's thesis of a decline cannot account for the huge expansion in the profession in the 1980s. Glasser, for instance, has argued that, while it is true that many of what were thought to be essential characteristics of the professional lawyer have been "challenged, amended or abandoned",[70] most of the changes have been happening internally. These changes are not universally perceived as heralding the end of the legal profession, but a

---

[66] The Government recognises its power in this respect. In the White Paper *Modernising Justice* (1998), it spoke of its intention to use its position as a major purchaser of legal services to achieve its aims of wider access to justice and better value for money (para.2.2). In the Second Reading of the Access to Justice Bill, the Lord Chancellor spoke of the Government "as a major purchaser of legal services" playing a role in raising standards (H.L.Deb. Col 1107, December 14, 1998).

[67] R. Abel, *The Legal Profession in England and Wales* (1988), at p.306 [Oxford: Blackwell].

[68] R. Abel, "The Politics of the Market for Legal services" in *Law in the Balance. Legal services in the 1980s* (P. Thomas ed., 1982), at p.44 [Oxford: Martin Robertson].

[69] ibid., at p.48

[70] C. Glasser, "The legal profession in the 1990s—images of change" (1990) 10(1) *Legal Studies* 1, at p.1.

change in the nature of the profession rather than its decline. The main feature of this transformation is the rejection of an outdated ideology of professionalism, not the concept of professionalism itself. This internal re-ordering of the power relationship within the profession could strengthen the position and status of some groups of lawyers.[71]

Paterson, too, disagrees with Abel's analysis that the decline in market control has led to a decline in the professions and professionalism. He challenges Abel's conclusion on a number of fronts. First, although there is no doubt that there has been an increase in the size of the profession, it is far from clear that the profession's ability to control the supply of producers has greatly changed over the years. Although there is no control by the profession over the number of law graduates who are produced, or even the numbers passing professional examinations, actual entry into practice depends upon training contracts (in the case of solicitors) and pupillages and tenancies (in the case of barristers). These are controlled by the professions. Nor is it problematic that many in the profession have employee status, rather than being self-employed. In the past, large numbers of practitioners were employees, and this did not affect the status as a profession.[72] In other professions, for example medicine, many practitioners are employees. The fact that their clinical freedom has, to some extent, been eroded does not call into question their professional status.

The idea that the traditional characteristics of a profession have always been present in the legal profession is also challenged. It is questionable whether solicitors had the traditional characteristics of a profession until comparatively recently.[73] Certainly, as far as self-regulation was concerned, it was only "slowly and haphazardly" that the Law Society assumed responsibility for dealing with complaints against solicitors,[74] nor did this increasing self-regulation result in a tougher regime for professional regulation and conduct. The introduction of a compensation fund and the strict insistence on separate accounts for clients' money are comparatively recent. In the

---

[71] ibid., at p. 9.

[72] A. Paterson, "Professionalism and the Legal Services Market" (1996) 3(1/2) International Journal of the Legal Profession 137–168.

[73] Paterson argues that the traditional concept of professionalism for the legal profession is a comparatively recent construct, probably dating from the 1930s ("Professionalism and the Legal Services Market" (1996) 3(1/2) International Journal of the Legal Profession 137–168, at p.137).

[74] D. Sugarman, "Bourgeois collectivism, professional power and the boundaries of the State. The private and the public life of the Law Society, 1825 to 1914" (1996) 3(1/2) International Journal of the Legal Profession 81–135, at p.106.

early nineteenth century there was no restricted competition, and there was widespread advertising.

The market control theory exaggerates the profession's control over its market, and assumes that there was greater homogeneity within the profession in the past than was actually the case. It also underestimates the extent of state control that existed. The market control theory of professionalism also understates the importance of the pursuit of status. Certainly for solicitors, the pursuit of status in the past was more important than market control.[75] Indeed, it has been claimed that rather than trying to extend the market for legal services, the legal profession has been withdrawing from many services. For example, there is evidence that solicitors in the eighteenth and early nineteenth centuries were persuaded to withdraw from a great variety of managerial, financial and clerical tasks, which attorneys had previously performed.[76] Nor was the profession traditionally concerned to increase income within a protected and sheltered market, but was primarily concerned with honour, reputation and status.[77]

Professionalism is a socially constructed, contingent and dynamic concept that is capable of evolution. Paterson calls for a different interpretation of the changes that are taking place within the profession. For him, the changes in the profession reflect a renegotiation rather than a decline, a renegotiation which has involved the profession, the state and consumer movements. Accounts which see the process of change as a process of decline are thought of as misconceived.[78] According to the traditional model, the essential feature of professionalism was a balance, or a bargain. On one side of the balance, the client expects competence, access to the legal system, a service ethic, and public protection. In return, the lawyer expects high status, reasonable rewards, restricted competition and autonomy.

There is an implicit contractualism in the model, which reflects the "enduring tension between service orientation and self-interest in the lawyer's role".[79] There is no assumption however that within this contract there was a fair balance between the parties. For the 45 years or so after the 1930s, when professionalism crystallised in its traditional form, the balance to the two sides of the equation remained constant.

---

[75] *ibid.*

[76] M. Burrage, "From a gentlemen's to a public profession: status and politics in the history of English solicitors" (1996) 3(1/2) *International Journal of the Legal Profession* 45–80, at p.46. In the twentieth century, solicitors have not generally been tempted by the new market openings provided by the welfare state.

[77] *ibid.* at p.48.

[78] A. Paterson, "Professionalism and the legal services market" (1996) 3(1/2) *International Journal of the Legal Profession* 137–168, at p.137.

[79] *ibid.*, at pp.140–141.

It may have been, however, that the profession was receiving a greater advantage than the public, and what has happened over the last decade has been renegotiation to strengthen the clients' side of the bargain. It is this "renegotiation of the concordat" that was seen by some in the profession as interfering with the autonomy of the profession.[80]

From where did the impetus come to renegotiate the contract? Some attribute the change to Thatcherite ideology, but Paterson says it is much more complex. Deregulation was also occurring in other common law countries,[81] some of which was introduced by socialist governments. Change was also occurring in European countries, part of the impetus for which was Articles 85 and 86 of the European Treaty, with its thrust towards competition in the supply of services. Indeed, legal professions world-wide "have been swept up in broader movement of deregulation" where professions were no longer seen as distinct from business, and no longer immune from competition.[82]

The move to deregulation was driven by a number of factors, including freedom of trade ideas which were global. Legal markets and legal ideas became globalised, with ever increasing commercial pressures. These changes were not entirely unwelcome, and many within the profession favoured increased competition. There has also been an increase in the strength of consumer movements, and more demanding and sophisticated clients. The state and the judiciary also took the initiative to examine the extent to which restrictive practices in legal services were in the public interest.[83] The changes which have occurred in the past two decades are therefore interpreted as a renegotiation of the contract, and a readjustment of the balance between the self-interest of the lawyers, and the consumer and public interest. This has involved a shift away from the acceptance of regulation by the profession itself, towards a view that the state and the market could regulate the profession more effectively.[84]

---

[80] ibid., at pp.140–141.

[81] ibid., at pp.146–147.

[82] C. Parker, "Lawyer Deregulation via Business Deregulation: An Opportunity and An Hypothesis" (1998) Paper presented at the Meeting of the Working Group on the Comparative Study of Legal Professions, Onati.

[83] A. Paterson, "Professionalism and the legal services market" (1996) 3(1/2) International Journal of the Legal Profession 137–168, at p.148.

[84] M. Burrage, "From a gentlemen's to a public profession: status and politics in the history of English solicitors" (1996) 3(1/2) International Journal of the Legal Profession 45–80, at p.50.

Regulation, consumer choice and the rule of law

Given the moves to deregulate the legal services market, the justifications for the regulation of the legal profession need to be examined. The word "regulation" can simply mean governing according to rules, but in economic theory, regulation describes the mechanisms used by the state to control the free market.[85] The legal system has been described as "a service industry working to serve the people, particularly the consumer of legal services".[86] As such, the work of the legal profession may be said to be an economic activity, the goal of which is the provision of legal services to consumers who choose them. Many western economists argue that the free market is the most efficient method of allocating goods and providing services to consumers, because it is based on consumer choice, and because economic self-interest ensures efficiency in the allocation of economic goods and services.[87] Moreover, it is argued that interference with the market, in particular state regulation, reduces competition, and hence economic growth.[88] Consequently, the market and competition are not only the most efficient, but also the most desirable way of conducting economic activity, and regulation is not only unnecessary, but in many cases, harmful.

There is a number of arguments against this proposition. At a philosophical level, Gerwirth[89] casts doubt on the classical free market system model as sufficient as a criterion of economic justice. He doubts whether the freedom of choice guaranteed by the market can be upheld, given the complexities of the productive process, and the difficulties of discovering whether an individual's abilities to take part in the productive process are derived from their own individual efforts, or "from a complex prior matrix of inheritance and social nurture, including education".[90] In other words, we are not all coming to the free market as equal players, and this inequality is not necessarily the outcome of our own action or inaction. The free market model does not acknowledge the inequalities which exist in society, except in so far as there seems to be a belief that inequality

---

[85] T. Daintith, "A Regulatory Space Agency" (1989) 9 *Oxford Journal of Legal Studies* 534.

[86] Austin Mitchell M.P., H.C. Vol. 170, col. 1521, April 18,1990.

[87] See generally, A. Ogus, *Regulation: Legal Form and Economic Theory* (1994). [Oxford: Clarendon Press].

[88] F. Hayek, *The Road to Serfdom* (1944) [London: Routledge].

[89] A. Gerwirth, "Economic Justice: Concepts and Criteria" in *Economic Justice and Private Rights* (K. Kiopnis and D.T. Meyers eds., 1985) [Rowman and Allanfield: Ottawa, N. J.].

[90] *ibid.*, at p.23.

may be a fair price to pay for the freedom to choose. Nor is there any acknowledgment that some individuals may require protection from unfettered market forces.

This view of markets is grounded in Gerwirth's view of human rights, which holds that all human beings have the equal and universal right to freedom and well-being.[91] The right to freedom includes the right to control one's own actions through choice, but choice may be hindered because of domination by others. One of the functions of government is to promote choice, and this may involve regulatory strategies which control the market in order to overcome inequalities to bring about effective rights to freedom and well-being. This argument is developed by Lewis,[92] who recognises that markets can be desirable because they enable choice, but that modern capitalism has created markets which stifle choice and competition.[93] It thus becomes necessary for the state to intervene to ensure that markets are really ensuring choice. Regulation is the means of doing this, and as such, rather than stifling choice, it enhances it.

This is not to argue that there is no place for the market system. The system can and does provide a large range of consumer goods and services abundantly and efficiently. To justify interference in the market, there is a need to show that civil law remedies, and a lack of regulation are inadequate in some way.[94] There are some services which cannot be left to the unregulated market system, and legal services come into that category for a number of reasons. It can be argued that legal services fail to satisfy the necessary requirements of a competitive market. If one of the arguments for the market is freedom of choice, then information is needed in order to exercise that choice in a meaningful way. As far as legal services are concerned there is an asymmetry of information. The nature of the product is such that individual, private clients may have difficulty in finding the product which most suits them. They have little information about the services, and inadequate mechanisms for checking the quality of those services.

This asymmetry of information is true of private clients, who are the focus of this book. Private clients vary in their sophistication and experience of legal issues. Some will only use a lawyer a few times in

---

[91] A. Gerwirth, *Reason and Morality* (1978) [Chicago: University of Chicago Press].

[92] N. D. Lewis, *Choice and the Legal Order* (1996) [London: Butterworths]. See also D. Beyleveld and R. Brownsword, *Law as a Moral Judgment* (1986) [London: Sweet and Maxwell].

[93] N. D. Lewis, *Choice and the Legal Order* (1996), at p.113 [London: Butterworths].

[94] A. Ogus, *Regulation: Legal Form and Economic Theory* (1994), at p.217 [Oxford: Clarendon Press].

their lifetime, perhaps to purchase a house or write a will, or because of divorce or criminal proceedings. They require legal services for a particular event. Corporate clients have a different relationship with their lawyers. They are "repeat players", and are better placed to safeguard their own interests than the private client. For the private client, this asymmetry of information is such that legal services do not take place in the free market with open competition. Consumers have little control over the work which is done for them, or the price charged for it. Lawyers, as other professionals, lay claim to special knowledge or experience, and they are consulted because of this very attribute by people who, on the whole, cannot make informed judgments about their skill, ability or integrity. This is not an equal relationship. Regulation is therefore needed because the relationship is one that inherently involves an asymmetry of information, and because the lawyer is "by definition in a superior position to evaluate the quality of and need for legal services".[95]

A second justification for regulation arises from the fact that, in the ordinary market for goods and services, suppliers compete with each other to attract customers by both price and quality. Other things being equal, customers usually seek the highest possible quality at the lowest possible price. Where legal services are concerned, the market is not adequate for maintaining high standards, because it can be difficult to communicate to consumers the quality of the product. Often, consumers can only compare the services on the basis of price, and this could have the effect of lowering standards, as producers attempt to cut costs in order to attract clients. This is especially detrimental in situations where inferior quality may have adverse effects on third parties, which is often the case with legal services. There are dangers to consumers of unethical or incompetent practice. For example, consumers could not only lose money, but also their liberty or their home and other property rights.

There is another aspect to the argument concerning market failure. The provision of legal services is not a free market because the legal profession has been granted certain privileges and monopolies. The market is thus regulated on the supply side. A consumer does not have the freedom to choose where to obtain legal services, but must, in many cases, seek them from a limited supply source. In return for the protected market, the profession is expected to subject itself to some form of regulation. In most cases this means that the legal profession is expected to observe and enforce, at its own expense,

---

[95] *Ordinary Justice. Legal Services and the courts in England and Wales: a consumer view* (1989), Chapter 7 ("Complaints about lawyers). National Consumer Council: London.

basic standards of conduct and consumer protection. Professions are also regulated by codes of ethics, the purpose of which is to adjust the balance of power in order to protect clients. These ethical codes and disciplinary mechanisms also work for the benefit of the profession as a whole, by protecting the profession from those who are not prepared to adhere to certain standards.

Regulation can occur for reasons other than market failure and the inadequacy of the market in protecting the interests of consumers. It can be necessary because of the social and political concerns of the wider society. A further justification for the regulation of the legal profession is the significant role that lawyers have in political, economic and social life. Lawyers do not just have duties in safeguarding the interests of their clients. They are perceived as the guardians of the state and society,[96] as gatekeepers to legal institutions and facilitators of a wide range of personal and economic transactions.[97] They have a role in mediating the exercise of state power, among individuals or organisations, or between citizens and the state.[98]

They are also officers of the court, and have duties not to mislead the court, and to uphold standards of justice. The legal system and the legal profession cannot be viewed solely as an economic activity, and "the interests of the community in the administration of justice, as well as the interests of the accused or of the litigants, have to be considered in terms of justice as well as cost".[99] The duties to the court and the demands of justice mean that the work of the legal profession "transcend[s] the mere economic activity of giving a service in return for a price".[1]

There is thus a constitutional concern with the way the legal profession performs its work, because aspects of this work are directly connected to the rule of law.[2] The rule of law can be seen as an

---

[96] D. Sugarman, "Historical Reflections on the Intersection between Law, Lawyers and Accountants in England" in *Professional Competition and Professional Power: Lawyers, Accountants and the Social Construction of Reality* (Y. Dezalay and D. Sugarman eds., 1995), at p.234 [London: Routledge].

[97] J. McCahery and S. Picciotto "Creative Lawyering and the dynamics of business regulation" in *Professional Competition and Professional Power: Lawyers, Accountants and the Social Construction of Reality* (Y. Dezalay and D. Sugarman eds., 1995), at p.240 [London: Routledge].

[98] R. Abel, "Lawyers in the Civil World" in *Lawyers in Society: the civil world* (R. Abel and P. Lewis eds., 1988), at p.4 [University of California Press, Los Angeles].

[99] *The Quality of Justice: the Bar's response* General Council of the Bar, at p.44.

[1] *ibid.*, at p.57.

[2] For an analysis of the rule of law see I. Harden and N. Lewis, *The Noble Lie* (1986) [London: Hutchinson]; P. Craig, *Public Law and Democracy in the UK and the USA* (1990) [Oxford: Clarendon Press]; M. Loughlin, *Public Law and Political Theory* (1992) [Oxford: OUP]; J. Jowell, "The Rule of Law Today" in *The Changing Constitution* (J. Jowell and

overriding principle of legality which forms our central constitutional principle, or it can be a legitimating feature of the exercise of public power. Whichever view one takes, one of its principal tenets is equality before the law. For the rule of law to be respected, the legal process must be accessible, costs must be affordable, and there must be access to the means of seeking legal redress. Lawyers provide the medium through which individuals gain such access, and therefore the way they carry out this skilled, facilitating function is a constitutional concern, and cannot be left entirely to the operation of the market.

For the rule of law to be respected, there must be public confidence in the legal system. Indeed, it has been observed that such confidence is "a cornerstone of a civilised society".[3] For there to be confidence in the legal system, there must be confidence that those operating the system are doing so competently, and that they can be called to account if they do not. Therefore, how lawyers behave is a concern of the state. It follows from this that how they conduct themselves in their grievance resolution function is also a concern of the state.

Regulation and self-regulation

As we have seen, the justifications for regulation are that it is necessary in the public interest, when there is market failure because of asymmetry of information, and the private law is inadequate or too costly to correct that failure.[4] Some form of regulation of the legal profession is therefore necessary in order to protect the interests of consumers. There are various mechanisms for regulation, but, of all the features traditionally associated with the concept of a profession, one of them, self-regulation, is seen as the hallmark. Other forms of regulation include direct regulation by the government, through a government department, or perhaps regulation by an agency, as is the case with the privatised utilities. There could also be overlapping forms of regulation. What is important is that the regulatory mechanisms address the source of the market failure, and avoid "regulatory failure".[5] Self-regulation is a very important regulatory

D. Oliver eds., 1994) [Oxford: Clarendon Press].

[3] A. Abraham, Legal Services Ombudsman, *New Law Journal* October 24, 1997.

[4] See A. Ogus, "Rethinking Self-Regulation" (1995) 15(1) *Oxford Journal of Legal Studies* 97–109

[5] R. Bowles, "The Public Interest and the Regulation of Professions" in *Profession, business or trade: Do the professions have a future?* (Proceedings from the Law Society Annual Research Conference, 1994), at p.58 [London: The Law Society].

mechanism for a wide range of activities, and it "remains as the principal controlling device for ... professional occupations".[6] In this section, it is proposed to examine the essential features of a system of self-regulation, and why it is perceived to be such an important aspect of professionalism.

Like the word profession, self-regulation has many different meanings. It has been described as a mechanism whereby the government "delegates public policy tasks to private actors in an institutionalised form",[7] and it therefore constitutes the privatisation of public policy.[8] At its broadest, it refers to regulatory mechanisms which are not governmental in nature, that is, they are not bureaucratic arrangements conducted by a government department, but have some input from the practitioners working in the field. According to the National Consumer Council, the essential feature of self-regulation is that the rules governing behaviour in the market are "developed, administered and enforced by the people ... whose behaviour is to be governed".[9] The input from practitioners can take various forms, and the extent to which they control the rules can vary considerably.

Self-regulation may be a completely private arrangement, or the arrangments may have to be approved by a public body. A completely private arrangement usually has a contractual basis, and is commonly used for sporting bodies. Sometimes self-regulation is a mixed arrangement, which has government backing and a statutory framework. It is this latter form which is used for the regulation of the professions. Self-regulatory mechanisms can apply to all the suppliers in a particular industry, or be limited to certain groups of suppliers. As to the enforceability of the arrangements, they can be formally binding, or consist of codes of practice, or they can be purely voluntary. The legal profession acts within a statutory framework, from where it derives its powers to make regulations for the profession as a whole, and impose disciplinary sanctions on its members.

In most contexts, where some form of regulation is necessary, self-regulation is perceived to be a better method than public regulation for a number of reasons, broadly concerned with cost and

---

[6] A Ogus, "Rethinking Self-Regulation" (1995) 15(1) *Oxford Journal of Legal Studies* 97–109, at p. 97

[7] P. Birkinshaw, I. Harden and N. Lewis, *Government by Moonlight* (1990), at p.190 [London: Unwin Hyman].

[8] G. Teubner, "Polycorporatism in Germany" (1993) 2 *Brigham Young University Law Review* 553

[9] *Self-Regulation* National Consumer Council, (1986), at p.1.

effectiveness. For regulation to be effective, resources are needed, and there has to be some measure of support for the regulatory strategy. One way of regulating is by command, or "imperium", which involves government passing legislation requiring or forbidding certain forms of activity. Public bodies can then be charged with implementing these policies, through delegated powers. This process requires government resources. In order to enact the legislation, a considerable amount of civil service and Parliamentary time is needed, and the process could take months if not years. In addition, the public body charged with regulation will have to rely on the industry being regulated for expertise and technical knowledge. The information costs become very expensive, and, unless completely funded by a levy on the industry, the public body will be a cost to the taxpayer.

Self-regulation developed as a way of overcoming the problems of implementation and legitimation associated with state intervention.[10] Because the industry concerned has the relevant expertise and technical knowledge of practice, and also of any innovatory possibilities, information costs for the formulation of standards and interpretation is lower. There is a reduction in monitoring and enforcement costs, and costs are borne by the practitioners. As the self-regulatory authority's processes and rules are less formalised, the cost of amending the standards is reduced.[11] It can be more effective than government regulation, because it aims to induce rather than command industries to achieve higher standards. Coercion is not always the best means of changing behaviour, and it is sometimes preferable to use a carrot rather than a stick. This is not the place to discuss the effectiveness, or otherwise, of legal norms. Teubner however concluded that the "greater the degree of knowledge, the greater the severity and probability of sanctions, and the lower the degree of competing normative orientation and of the positive sanctioning of the deviance, then the greater is the degree to which a law is followed".[12] In self-regulatory regimes, competing norms and sanctioning of the deviant conduct are unlikely, because the regime has been devised by bargaining with the interest group concerned.

Self-regulation therefore presents an attractive alternative to government regulation. It is cheaper for the state, as private

---

[10] Streek and Schmitter, "Community, Market, State—and Association? The Prospective Contribution of Interest Governance to Social order" in *Private Interest Government: Beyond Market and State* (Streek and Schmitter eds., 1985), pp.22–25. [London: Sage].

[11] A. Ogus, *Regulation: Legal Form and Economic Theory* (1994), at p.107 [Oxford: Clarendon Press].

[12] G. Teubner, "Regulatory Law: Chronicle of a Death Foretold" (1992) 1 *Social and Legal Studies* 451–475, at p. 452.

organisations bear the costs of the activity regulated rather than the taxpayer. Conflict is reduced, because the regulatory framework is negotiated with, and agreed by, those who are to be regulated. It is quicker, both in setting up and making changes which are necessary, and therefore it is more flexible, and can respond to changing circumstances. It uses the expertise of those involved in the activity to be regulated, and the standards may be set higher than would be possible in a statutory scheme. From the point of view of the industry concerned, self-regulation can protect against disreputable practitioners. This is particularly important for the professions, as it contributes to an increase in their status.

Despite these advantages, self-regulation is not without its critics. Both lawyers and economists have been vociferous in their criticisms, claiming that it is a form of "corporatism", the acquisition of power by groups which are not accountable through conventional constitutional channels.[13] There may also be a lack of democratic legitimacy in relation to the members of association, and to third parties if the rules affect them too. It has also been claimed that self-regulation involves a breach of the doctrine of the separation of powers, if, as is often the case, the self-regulatory authority's functions cover policy formulation, the interpretation of rules, adjudication and enforcement.

A further criticism relates to the anti-competitive nature of self-regulatory regimes, some of which impose barriers to entry to the system. Restrictive practices distort competition, ensure that exorbitant profits are generated for practitioners, and result in consequent high costs for consumers.[14] Schemes may also be established without any input from those outside the industry, particularly consumers, and consumers may fail to perceive the scheme as sufficiently independent from the industry. It may not be effective because consumers may not know it exists, and there may be a limited range of sanctions available for those who infringe the rules. Where schemes do not cover the entire industry their value is particularly doubtful, as it is those who are not members who tend to be the most problematic.[15]

The National Consumer Council is not opposed to self-regulation, but has indicated the characteristics self-regulatory schemes should

---

[13] See, for example, N. Lewis "Corporatism and Accountability: The Democratic Dilemma" in *Corporatism and Accountability: Organised Interests in British Public Life* (C. Crouch and R. Dore eds., 1990).

[14] A. Ogus, *Regulation: Legal Form and Economic Theory* (1994), at p.108 [Oxford: Clarendon Press].

[15] C. Graham, "Self-Regulation" in *Administrative Law and Government Action* (G. Richardson and H. Genn eds., 1994), at pp.194–195 [Oxford: Clarendon Press].

have in order to be effective and accountable. These address some of the criticisms of this form of regulation. Schemes must be able to command public confidence, and there must be strong external involvement in their design and operation. As far as practicable, the operation and control of schemes should be separate from the institutions of the industries concerned, and consumers and other outsiders should be fully represented on the governing bodies of schemes. There should be clear statements of principles and standards, and there should normally be a code of practice. Where there is a breach of the code, there must be clear, accessible and well-publicised complaints procedures, and the sanctions must be adequate and meaningful. Schemes must be monitored and updated in the light of changing expectations and circumstances, and there must be some public accountability, such as an annual report. It is preferable for a scheme to be organised within a basic statutory framework.[16]

Despite the criticisms of self-regulation, its many advantages will ensure its continuation and, certainly for the professions, it remains a very important aspect of the professional culture. The ability to make regulations and impose disciplinary sanctions for breach of the professional code is considered to be fundamental to professionalism. Self-regulation is part of the bargain the professions have made with the state. Some mechanisms are needed to prevent abuse of the monopolies granted to the professions, and the professions have insisted that they, not the state, must possess these mechanisms.[17] Indeed, it has been argued that the power to engage in self-regulation is one of the goals that motivates an occupation to seek professional status, and that the efficacy of self-regulation is one of the measures by which outsiders judge whether a profession deserves that status.[18] A key argument for self-regulation by the professions is that it maintains public confidence in the services provided, as the profession has a collective interest in protecting its reputation. It has an interest in disciplining those of its members who do shoddy work, or charge excessive fees, and will take appropriate action in these circumstances.

Professional regulation

Professional regulation in Britain conforms to a standard pattern, whereby a professional body, usually dominated by representatives of

---

[16] National Consumer Council, *Self-Regulation* (1986), p.15.
[17] R. Abel, *The Legal Profession in England and Wales* (1988), at p.29 [Oxford: Blackwell].
[18] *ibid.*, at p.248

the occupation, is empowered by legislation to establish a register of practitioners, and to lay down quality standards for practice.[19] The professions therefore act within a statutory framework, with the relevant regulatory bodies deriving their power from the state. Although self-regulation is seen as fundamental to the professions, regulation is actually a mixture of statutory and self-regulation, and self-regulation only exists with government backing, and within a statutory framework.

Although there can be no doubt that self-regulation will continue to play an important part in the regulatory framework, for the legal profession there is a growing consensus that, in its present form, self-regulation is no longer acceptable in terms of consumer protection. This is partly a result of the increased competition within the legal profession, and the rise of the consumer movement. Self-regulation is criticised because the rules of conduct are drafted in vague and ambiguous terms, and are not so much to do with consumer and society protection, but rather aspects of market control[20] or the need to present an image of gentility.[21] Certainly, in the case of solicitors, increasing self-regulation did not immediately result in a tougher regime for professional discipline and conduct.[22] There is also concern about the lack of independence, as, traditionally, the rules of conduct and the licence to practice are controlled by bodies drawn exclusively or predominantly from the profession.[23]

The role of the legal profession's governing bodies is also being called into question, because of the conflicting objectives in both promoting and regulating the profession. There are doubts as to whether one body can effectively both protect the public and serve the profession at the same time, and whether it can advocate the interests of the profession, as well as carrying out the necessary disciplinary functions. The solicitors' profession itself has doubts about whether the two roles can be reconciled. Many believe that, so long as the Law Society assumes a regulatory position, it is unlikely that it can strengthen its representative role.[24] Some feel that unless the Society can reconcile these conflicting roles it is likely to lose its regulatory status, and many are urging that the regulatory and interest

---

[19] ibid., at p.220

[20] ibid., at p.30

[21] D. Sugarman, "Bourgeois collectivism, professional power and the boundaries of the State. The private and the public life of the Law Society, 1825 to 1914" (1996) 3(1/2) International Journal of the Legal Profession 81–135.

[22] ibid., at p.106.

[23] A. Ogus, Regulation: Legal Form and Economic Theory (1994), at p.107 [Oxford: Clarendon Press].

[24] Editorial, "A New Law Society" (1998) New Law Journal February 20.

group functions be separated. Within the profession, many are disenchanted with self-regulation, with some solicitors seeing it as "cripplingly expensive, over-complicated", and hampering competition, yet failing to provide the protection afforded by the traditional professional control of the market.[25] Self -regulation is not protecting solicitors as it did in the past, but is seen as increasingly burdensome, because of the rising costs of practising certificates and indemnity fees. The Law Society no longer sees itself as being concerned with the protection of particular monopolies and privileges, but wants to reinforce "a change in the culture of the profession... which emphasises client care, promotes professional excellence, and does not regard the following of sound business practice as somehow alien to the values of a profession".[26]

Attempts by the state to intervene in the regulatory framework of professions are often resisted on the grounds that this is a challenge to self-regulation, and an attack on the independence and autonomy of the profession. The legal profession has always defended its independent status, linking it to the notion of public protection, as the profession plays an essential role in protecting the rights of citizens. However, state intervention and professional autonomy are not necessarily opposed processes, and therefore more state intervention does not mean that there will be less autonomy.[27] Although lawyers are concerned to remain independent of the state, it is the state which granted their privileges in the first place, and changes to the regulatory framework do not necessarily attack the autonomy of the profession. Such autonomy can only exist through the articulation of the state. The changes which are taking place can be interpreted as part of the renegotiation of the bargain between the profession and the state, and a shift in the balance of the regulatory mechanisms, which could involve a readjustment between autonomy and state control.

---

[25] C. Bramall, "Regulation: An Unnecessary Burden or a Professional Necessity?" in *Profession, business or trade: Do the professions have a future?* (Proceedings from the Law Society Annual Research Conference, 1994), at p.54 [London: The Law Society].

[26] J. Hayes, Secretary-General of the Law Society, "Protecting the Public and Serving the Profession" (Paper presented to the *Legal Professions in Transition* Conference, 1994). Centre for Law and Business, Centre for Social Ethics and Policy, The University of Manchester.

[27] T. Johnson, "The State and the professions" in *Social Class and the Division of Labour* (A. Giddens and G. Mackenzie eds., 1982) [Cambridge: Cambridge University Press].

Conclusion

The nature of the legal profession, and professionalism is changing. Demographic change has produced a less homogeneous profession. The nature of the market for legal services is becoming more varied, and clients are becoming more diverse. Added to this is the shift away from an acceptance of deference to professionals, and a more consumer-orientated society. The demand, from the Government and consumers, is for high quality and affordable legal services and more consumer choice. There is also a demand for effective mechanisms of redress for consumers when there are complaints.

All this is impacting on the governance of the profession. Some have argued that these changes indicate the end of the legal profession, but others have argued that they represent a change, or renegotiation, of the basis on which professionals perform their function. The changes therefore represent a readjustment of the balance between the interests of the legal profession and the consumer and public interest. It is no longer appropriate for the legal profession to resist change by clinging to an outdated model of professionalism and self-regulation.

The legal profession has always been subject to a wide range of regulatory mechanisms. Despite the changes to the regulatory framework introduced by the Courts and Legal Services Act, much regulation still takes the form of self-regulation. What the Act did do was to provide for more competition, and closer scrutiny of the regulatory regime. It established the Legal Services Ombudsman[28] to oversee the complaint-handling functions of the profession. The Act did not abolish self-regulation, but preserved it "with a more powerful watchdog".[29]

The various regulatory mechanisms should be achieving the objective of providing a regulatory framework for the legal profession, which monitors the quality of legal services and ensures that there are adequate redress mechanisms when that quality is called into question. The question is whether the present system does achieve an appropriate balance between self-regulation and external regulation. Subsequent chapters will evaluate these regulatory mechanisms, in order to examine the extent to which they do operate in the interests of consumers, and whether, taken together, they provide adequate protection for the consumers of legal services.

---

[28] This is discussed in Chapter 6.

[29] J. Hayes, Secretary-General of the Law Society, "Protecting the Public and Serving the Profession" (Paper presented to the *Legal Professions in Transition* Conference, 1994), at p.6 [Centre for Law and Business, Centre for Social Ethics and Policy, The University of Manchester].

Chapter 2

Private Law Remedies

Although the legal profession is governed by a mixture of self-regulation and statutory controls, private law remedies also provide a mechanism for regulating the profession and protecting the interests of consumers. Individual members of the legal profession are subject to the general private law of tort and contract, when performing their professional duties. Breach of contract, or the negligent performance of their duties, will expose individual members of the profession to action in the courts. This chapter will describe the liability of solicitors and barristers in both contract and tort, and evaluate the effectiveness for the consumer of private law redress.

The law of contract

A contract is an agreement enforceable by law. For there to be a valid contract there must be an agreement between the parties as to its nature. The terms of the agreement need not be written, and oral contracts are perfectly valid. It must be possible, however, to ascertain the terms of the agreement, and, except in the case of fairly simple contracts, the terms are often committed to writing. There is usually an express agreement between the parties to the contract, but contractual obligations can be implied from the conduct of the parties. Even where there is an express contract, some of the terms within the contract can be implied.

The legal duties of the contract are imposed by the terms of the contract itself (and by any implied terms) and they are imposed only on the parties to the contract. This means that only the parties to the contract can sue and be sued on the contract, a doctrine known as "privity of contract". The purpose of the law of contract is to protect economic interests, and the essence of contractual liability is that any loss suffered in reliance on the promise of another ought to be compensated. The basis of the law of contract is the idea of a bargain, or an exchange of promises. Contract law will not enforce gratuitous promises, because there has to be an element of reciprocity, or "consideration" for the promise. Without this consideration, promises are generally unenforceable.[1] In contracts for professional services the consideration will normally be the promise to perform those services in exchange for fees.

Contractual liability and solicitors

Solicitors are in a contractual relationship with their clients, the contract being one of professional services, in return for fees. Liability for breach of contract can arise if the act or omission comes within the scope of the agreement under which the client instructs the solicitor. The duties that the solicitor owes to the client will depend upon the particular terms of the contract. There are, however, a number of terms which are implied into the contract, an important one for consumers being the implied duty to protect the clients' interests. This duty will apply irrespective of the express terms of the contract. So, for example, where a solicitor was instructed to discharge a debt on behalf of a client, he was held liable for failure to disclose to the client that he knew that the debt was probably unenforceable.[2] This was despite the fact that there was no express term in the contract to investigate whether or not the debt was enforceable. There is also a duty to consult the client on all questions of doubt which do not fall within the express or implied discretion which is left to the solicitor.[3]

The implied duty to protect clients' interests means that a solicitor must not act for a client where there may be a conflict of interest, as the solicitor would not be able to give advice with only the client's interest in mind. Conflicts of interests can occur where the solicitor has a personal interest which might be opposed to that of the client. In such cases, the solicitor must refuse to act. More commonly, problems occur where a solicitor is acting for two clients, between whom there may be a conflict of interest. In such cases, if there is an actual, rather than a potential, conflict, a solicitor must not act for both clients. For example, there would be an actual conflict if a

---

[1] Gratuitous promises must be by deed, in order to be enforceable.
[2] *Spector v. Ageda* [1973] Ch. 30.
[3] *Groom v. Crocker* [1939] 1 K.B. 194.

solicitor were acting for both clients in litigation. The solicitor would have to ensure that at least one of the parties was independently represented. If the solicitor has obtained knowledge of both sides of the case, the appropriate course of action might be for both clients to engage new solicitors.

Conflicts of interest often arise in conveyancing matters, where the solicitor is acting for both the vendor and the purchaser. The Law Society guidance[4] is clear that one of the clients should be independently represented if a conflict of interest is likely to arise. If solicitors do act for both parties in conveyancing matters, they risk being liable to one of the clients. Conflicts of interests can also occur where solicitors act for both borrowers and lenders in mortgage transactions. Traditionally, solicitors have acted for both of these parties in domestic conveyancing matters. This was not considered to be problematic, as the duties of the solicitor to the lender (the building society or bank) were restricted to the matters to do with the title to the property. Not only was there no conflict, but the interests of both parties coincided, it being in the interests of both borrower and lender that there were no defects in the title to the property.

Some recent cases have cast doubt on the view that there was no potential conflict of interest, and have re-examined the scope of solicitors' duties to lenders in such situations. In one case,[5] the Court of Appeal held that a solicitor who discovers facts in the course of investigating a title that a reasonably competent solicitor would realise might have a bearing on the valuation, or on another aspect of the lending decision, is under an implied duty to report such facts to the lender. This may occur where the solicitor knows that the vendor has bought the property at a much lower price immediately before re-selling it to the borrower. Such situations can arise in cases of mortgage fraud, where borrowers are attempting to obtain funds, which are in excess of the real value of the property. In a later case[6] the Court of Appeal was unwilling to accept extensive implied duties being owed to lenders. The case confirmed that solicitors are not required to investigate beyond checking the title, unless specifically instructed. However, if the solicitor does obtain information, which casts doubt on the valuation, this must be disclosed to the lender.

---

[4] Practice Rule 6 of *The Law Society's Guide to Professional Conduct* sets out the circumstances in which a solicitor may act for more than one party in conveyancing and mortgage transactions, so that potential conflicts of interest may be avoided.

[5] *Mortgage Express Ltd v. Bowerman* [1996] 2 All E.R. 836.

[6] *National Home Loans Corporation plc v. Giffen Couch and Archer* (1997) 94(2) L.S.G. 24; (1997) S.J.L.B. 29 Q.B.D.

There is also no general implied duty on solicitors to disclose information about the credit-worthiness of their borrower clients. Additional duties in relation to valuations and credit-worthiness have gone beyond normal practice. This has caused problems where solicitors have not been able to check that certain assumptions in valuation reports were correct. Where there have been problems, and lenders have been unable to recoup losses, solicitors have been liable in damages.[7] There is also a potential conflict of interest, in cases where lenders expect solicitors to investigate the financial circumstances of borrowers. Some believe that this practice is an attempt by lenders and valuers to shift responsibility for assumptions made in connection with the property onto solicitors.[8]

As a result, the Law Society has issued an amendment to the practice rule, which deals with situations where a solicitor acts for both the lender and borrower.[9] In future solicitors will only be able to act for both parties where the solicitors' duties are limited to matters of title, as set out in the rule. The new rule was due to come into effect on April 1, 1999 but has now been deferred.[10] The Law Society hopes that joint representation of borrower and lender will continue, as it is beneficial to lenders and the profession. Separate representation would increase the costs of conveyancing, and therefore it is in the interests of consumers that joint representation continues to be the normal practice in domestic conveyancing.[11]

An important term in contracts for professional services is that implied by section 13 of the Supply of Goods and Services Act 1982. This section implies into contracts for services the term that "the supplier will carry out the service with reasonable care and skill". This provision codifies the common law position, where the standard has been defined as "what the reasonably competent practitioner would do having regard to the standards normally adopted in his profession".[12] In contracts for professional services, there will often be no liability for failure to achieve a specified result, provided that reasonable care was taken in the attempt to do so. Just as there is no implied term that a doctor will cure a patient, only that he or she will

---

[7] In fact, it is the Solicitors Indemnity Fund which has made the necessary payments. The role of the Fund will be dealt with later in the chapter.

[8] See K. Byass, "On Both Sides" *The Law Society Gazette*, October 21, 1998, at p.22.

[9] Practice Rule 6(3).

[10] It is deferred until June 1999, to give lenders more time to change their procedures and systems to comply with the rule. It is likely, however, that there will be a further delay to September 1, 1999. Additional changes to the rule are also likely (see *Law Society Gazette*, March 3, 1999, at 38).

[11] See *The Law Society Gazette*, October 28, 1998, at p.5.

[12] *Midland Bank Trust Co Ltd v. Hett, Stubbs & Kemp* [1979] Ch. 384 at 403, *per* Oliver J.

exercise reasonable care and skill to do so, similarly there is no implied term that a solicitor will win a case. There will, therefore, be no liability for breach of contract if the case is lost, provided that the solicitor exercised reasonable care and skill in dealing with the case. In order to discharge their duties to clients, solicitors must explain the likely outcome, as far as possible, of litigation, and discuss the risks involved.

Contractual liability and barristers

There is no contractual relationship between a barrister and the lay client. Therefore, this type of liability is of no assistance to the consumer of legal services. Barristers cannot sue for their fees, nor can they be sued for breach of contract, even if they take their fees, but fail to carry out the work. Although it is the solicitor who instructs the barrister, this is traditionally not on the basis of any contractual liability, and fees are paid as a matter of honour.[13] The Courts and Legal Services Act 1990 abolished any common law rule which prevents a barrister from entering into a contract for the provision of services as a barrister, but allows the Bar Council to make rules prohibiting or restricting barristers from entering into contracts.[14]

The law of negligence

Some understanding of the law of negligence is required in order to assess whether a solicitor is liable for breach of the implied term to perform the contract of services with reasonable care and skill. This is because evidence will be required that the solicitor has not met the required standard, that is, acted negligently. Negligence is part of the law of tort, and the purpose of tortious liability is to provide a remedy to those who have been harmed by the conduct of others. This is usually by means of monetary compensation for the harm caused, although other remedies, such as injunctions, are also available. Unlike contract, liability in tort does not depend on an agreement between the parties. Tort covers a range of civil wrongs, including trespass and

---

[13] From a practical point of view, solicitors pay because otherwise they would have their credit withdrawn. They would then have to pay the barrister's fee before he or she accepted instructions.
[14] s. 61.

defamation, but from the point of view of professional liability, the most important area of tort is negligence.

Essentially, liability for negligence occurs where there is a duty of care, a breach of that duty, and damage resulting from the breach. Before 1932 there was no generalised duty of care in negligence, and it was confined to particular situations, for example, road accidents. The modern law of negligence originated in the case of *Donoghue v. Stevenson*,[15] where a generalised duty of care was formulated, which was to apply to those who were not in a contractual relationship. The case concerned a manufacturer of ginger beer, one bottle of which was alleged to contain a decomposed snail. The unfortunate consumer of the product sued the manufacturer, and the case decided that there was a cause of action, despite the absence of a contractual relationship between the parties.

The general test for establishing whether a duty of care will be imposed is set out in the judgment of Lord Atkin. He said that a person must "take reasonable care" to avoid acts or omissions which that person could "reasonably foresee" would be likely to injure his or her "neighbour". This is the famous "neighbour" principle. Lord Atkin went on to describe "neighbours" as persons who are so closely and directly affected by one's act that one ought reasonably to have them in contemplation as being so affected when one is directing one's mind to the acts or omissions in question. The duty of care, therefore, is owed to someone who ought reasonably to be in the contemplation of the defendant. Such a duty is owed by manufacturers to the ultimate consumers of manufactured products.

Later developments in the law of negligence extended liability far beyond manufacturing defects. Negligence liability can now exist in relation to building defects, medical treatment, and professional services. It can be imposed for statements, and for omissions as well as actions. The relevant test for establishing the duty of care is now to be found in the case of *Caparo Industries plc v. Dickman*.[16] A tri-partite test was established in that case.[17] The duty of care will be said to exist where there is a sufficient relationship of proximity between the parties, where the damage can be foreseen, and where it is fair, just and reasonable to impose such a duty.

Once it has been established that a duty of care is owed, the plaintiff will have to demonstrate that there has been a breach of the duty. This will be proved by showing that, in all the circumstances,

---

[15] [1932] A.C. 562.
[16] [1990] 1 All E.R. 568.
[17] See J. Murphy, "Expectation Losses, Negligent Omissions and the Tortious Duty of Care" (1996) 55(1) *Cambridge Law Journal* 43–55.

the defendant has failed to take reasonable care to avoid the damage or injury complained about. It is a reasonableness test, and this depends upon a number of variables, including the nature of the risk, the extent of the risk, and the cost, in physical or economic terms, of taking precautions. There has to be evidence of fault on the part of the defendant, on the basis of an objective standard. In order to avoid liability, a solicitor will have to show that he or she acted reasonably, according to the standard in the profession. This is, of course, a higher degree of reasonableness than that expected of the ordinary reasonable person.

Finally, if there is to be liability, it must be shown that damage has resulted from the breach of the duty of care. Damage includes personal injury or material loss to property. In addition, economic loss as a result of such harm can be recovered. For example, loss of earnings would be a financial loss resulting from the inability to work as a result of an accident. In certain circumstances, pure economic loss, that is financial loss, which is not the result of physical damage or injury, can also be recovered. The damage must be foreseeable, and must not be too remote.

Professional negligence

Where consumers are the clients of solicitors, there is no problem in establishing that a duty of care is owed. This is implied by the contract for services. The problems arise in establishing that there was a breach of that duty. Although particular professions may have special duties of care attached to them, there are general rules of professional liability.[18] Professionals hold themselves out as being experts by virtue of their training and experience. The duty of care placed on them is to be as skilful and careful as the average member of that profession. The standard is thus that of an ordinary competent professional in that particular profession, and a reasonable degree of skill in the performance of his or her duties is required. If the professional holds himself or herself out as possessing a higher degree of skill, he or she will be held to that higher duty.

Many of the decided cases in the area of professional negligence concern medical matters. In the leading case,[19] the test for the appropriate standard of care was described as follows:

---

[18] See K. M. Stanton, "Is there a general theory of professional negligence liability in tort?" (1994) 10(4) *Professional Negligence* 110–113.

[19] *Bolam v. Friern Hospital Management Committee* [1957] 2 All E.R. 118 at 121.

"The test is the standard of the ordinary skilled man exercising and professing to have that special skill. A man need not possess the highest expert skill ... it is sufficient if he exercises the ordinary skill of a competent man exercising that particular art."

This case indicates that doctors will not be held liable for negligence if they have acted in accordance with a practice which is accepted as proper by a responsible body of medical opinion. This will be so, even if there is a body of opinion which takes a contrary view. This standard of care applies to all other professions, where professionals are required to exercise the ordinary skill of their speciality.

Consumers who wish to sue their solicitors may find it difficult to show that there has been a failure to adhere to the standard. There is clearly room for disagreement about what is accepted practice, and different opinions about matters which depend upon professional judgment. Professionals will not be held liable for "errors of judgment". Provided that a solicitor can show that he or she acted reasonably according to the accepted standard in the profession, there will be no liability. What is an accepted standard may be difficult for a consumer to prove. In one case,[20] it was held that the fact that a solicitor had breached the Law Society's *Guide to Professional Conduct* did not necessarily prove negligence.

In many cases, solicitors do not, nor can they, guarantee to achieve a specified result. This is clearly the case in litigation. Solicitors must, however, explain the likely outcome of a particular course of action to clients. Clients must be made aware of the risks involved. The more inexperienced the client, the more explanation and advice may be needed to meet the standard of reasonable care. Solicitors have a duty to understand the law, and their own particular specialisms, but there will be no liability in negligence if the solicitor gives incorrect advice on a point of law which is disputed.[21] Similarly, there will be no liability if the advice, which is given, becomes incorrect because of a subsequent judicial decision.[22] When deciding the extent of liability, in cases where knowledge of the law is at issue, the standard used is that of accepted professional practice. Solicitors are not required "to know the contents of every statute of the realm,"[23] but there are some which would be standard knowledge. The courts usually make a distinction between incorrect advice on a legal problem, and a failure

---

[20] *Johnson v. Bingley* [1997] P.N.L.R. 392.
[21] *Godefroy v. Dalton* (1830) 6 Bing. 460.
[22] *Simmons v. Pennington & Son* [1955] 1 All E.R. 240.
[23] *Fletcher & Son v. Jubb, Booth and Heliwell* [1920] 1 K.B. 275 at 281.

to adopt the correct procedure. In the latter case, there is more likely to be a finding of professional negligence, although every case is decided on its merits.

Where an area of law is in dispute, it is normally reasonable for a solicitor to rely on the advice of counsel. However, this will not excuse a solicitor who has failed to put all the relevant facts to counsel. Solicitors can generally discharge the duty of care by relying on the advice of properly instructed counsel. But this alone will not give them immunity from liability. Solicitors are still expected to apply their professional skill, and will be liable where they should have appreciated that the advice was incorrect. Solicitors are "highly trained and ... expected to be experienced in [their] particular legal fields". They are not therefore entitled "to rely blindly and with no mind of [their] own on counsel's views".[24] Solicitors will, however, be justified in relying on counsel's advice where it embodies a careful and sensible assessment of the legal and factual situation.[25] It is difficult for a consumer to predict where a court would draw the line, as this, of course, is a matter of judgment.

Concurrent liability

There is some overlap between tort and contract when assessing the liability of solicitors, because the standard of care will be decided according to the principles of negligence. However, contractual remedies are of fundamental importance for consumers, because of the implied term in contracts for services that the contract will be performed with reasonable care and skill. Despite the developments in the area of professional negligence, and although the same fault can result in liability for both contract and tort, decided cases indicate that liability for failure to exercise reasonable care and skill arises out of contract.[26] Negligence in the conduct of a client's affairs is therefore an action for a breach of contract.[27]

Although the basis for liability, for the client of the solicitor, is the contract for services, the solicitor can be liable in both contract and tort. This was established in the case of *Nocton v. Lord Ashburton*,[28] when the House of Lords said that:

[24] *Davy-Chiesman v. Davy-Chiesman* [1984] 1 All E.R. 321, C.A.
[25] *Ward v. Chief Constable of Avon and Somerset, Daily Telegraph*, September 18, 1987. C.A.
[26] *Groom v. Crocker* [1939] 1 K.B. 194.
[27] *Heywood v. Wellers* [1976] Q.B. 446.
[28] [1914] A.C. 932 at 956.

" . . . the solicitor contracts with his client to be skilful and careful. For failure to perform his obligation he can be made liable in contract or even in tort, for negligence in breach of a duty imposed on him."

It is more advantageous, however, for the consumer to sue under the contract rather than tort. One reason for this is the range of remedies available for breach of contract, which is far more extensive than for the tort of negligence. The remedy for negligence is damages, but in contract the remedies could include specific performance of the contract, as well as rescission of the contract and rectification. There can also be remedies for economic loss,[29] and breach of contract may affect rights in relation to the payment of fees. This can be an important remedy where large fees are involved. In addition, a contract may impose a higher duty of care than that demanded by the implied terms of the contract.

The existence of a contract does not preclude an action in tort,[30] but, given the advantages of suing under the contract, why would a consumer choose a tortious remedy? One reason may be where a pre-contractual statement is not incorporated into the terms of the contract. Such a statement has been held to be a negligent misrepresentation, which survived after the contract came into existence.[31] There was therefore a remedy in tort for negligent misrepresentation.

A remedy in negligence may also be useful where action under the contract is statute-barred. Actions for simple breach of contract have to be brought within six years of the date on which the cause of action accrued.[32] In some cases where there is a breach of contract, the breach does not manifest itself until some time after this, and there is thus no opportunity to sue. In the tort of negligence, the statutory limit is still six years,[33] but the time begins to run from the occurrence of the damage. An action in negligence may be useful, therefore, where the damage does not occur until some time after the breach of contract.

An illustration of this is found in the case of *Midland Bank Trust Co Ltd v. Hett, Stubbs & Kemp*,[34] where a solicitor failed to register an option to purchase land, until it was too late to do so. The failure

---

[29] In certain circumstances, remedies for economic loss in tort are available. This is discussed later in the chapter.
[30] *Esso Petroleum Co Ltd v. Mardon* [1976] Q.B. 801; *Batty v. Metropolitan Property Realisation Ltd* [1978] Q.B. 554.
[31] *Esso Petroleum Co Ltd v. Mardon* [1976] QB 801.
[32] Limitation Act 1980, s. 5.
[33] Except in the case of personal injury, when it is three years.
[34] [1979] Ch. 384.

only became apparent over six years later, when a third party acquired an interest in the land. Therefore, action for breach of contract was statute-barred. Liability in tort accrues from the date of the damage, and it was argued that this occurred when the third party acquired the interest in the land. The court decided that it was possible to bring an action in tort, but also decided that the action for breach of contract was not statute-barred. This was because the duty under the contract was held to be a continuing one and therefore the breach was the non-performance to register before the third party acquired an interest.

However, consumers may find that attempts to bring a case within the limitation period, by using tort, may not prove to be as successful in future. In *Bell v. Peter Browne & Co*,[35] the plaintiff agreed to transfer the matrimonial home to his former wife, as part of the settlement after divorce. In return, he was to receive one-sixth of the gross proceeds of the sale of the house when it was sold. The transfer took place in 1978, but the defendant solicitors failed to execute a mortgage or trust deed to protect the plaintiff's interest in the proceeds of sale. The wife sold the house in 1986, and spent the proceeds of sale, without accounting to the plaintiff for his one-sixth share.

The plaintiff claimed against his solicitors for professional negligence. The solicitors claimed that the action was statute-barred. The Court of Appeal held that the failure to prepare a declaration of trust, or to register the plaintiff's interest in the property at the time of the transfer of the property, was a breach of contract. The Court decided that the limitation period ran from September 1978, and had therefore expired by August 1987, which was when the writ was served. This was despite the fact that the breach of contract could have been remedied (by lodging a caution on the land charges register) at any time before the wife sold the house. The *Midland Bank Trust*[36] case was distinguished on the basis that in that case there had been a continuing contractual obligation on the part of the solicitor to register the option to purchase. The Court was not prepared to accept a continuing obligation to perform the contract in this case, because this would frustrate the purpose of the Limitation Act, as remediable breaches of contract might never become statute-barred.

The plaintiff also sued in tort, where the cause of action begins to accrue when the damage is suffered.[37] However, the Court held that

---

[35] [1990] 3 W.L.R. 510 C. A.
[36] [1979] Ch. 384.
[37] Limitation Act 1980, s. 2.

the damage occurred when the house was transferred to the wife without any formal protection of the plaintiff's interests. Even though the damage could have been remedied at any time before the wife sold the house, the Court decided that the negligence action was also statute-barred. This was despite the fact that the actual loss remained nominal until the property was sold. This decision closes up a useful avenue of redress for consumers.

Another case[38] where the plaintiff tried to use tort to bring the action failed for similar reasons. In this case, the client put the solicitor in funds to purchase the freehold of property, which the client held on a long lease. Nine years later, the client discovered that the solicitor had not purchased the freehold. By this time, the price of the freehold was over 10 times the original price. The contract claim was statute-barred. The plaintiffs argued that the tort action should run from the time the omission was discovered because it was only at that time that the loss could be quantified. The Court of Appeal decided that the claim in tort was similarly barred. The loss arose when the damage was suffered. This was when the solicitor failed to purchase the freehold. Any damage could easily have been quantified before the breach was discovered.

Despite the existence of concurrent liability in contract and tort, it would seem that there is little advantage in clients pursuing a remedy in tort if the damage is said to occur at the time of the breach of contract. This nullifies the effect of the *Midland Bank* case, except in those rare circumstances where the courts decide that there is a continuing duty towards the client.

The Latent Damage Act 1986 may also prove to be of little help where clients are suing solicitors. This act[39] changed the law on limitation periods, to deal with the situation where damage caused by negligence is latent, that is, not discoverable when it occurs. The Act has been held to apply only to negligence claims in tort, rather than contract.[40] If the courts reject the contention that there is concurrent liability in contract and tort,[41] this act will be of no use to consumers where there is a contract for services between the parties.[42]

---

[38] *Lee v Thompson* [1989] 40 E. G. 89. C. A.

[39] See K. Puttick, "Latent Damage Act" (1986) *New Law Journal* 866; M. Rutherford, "The Latent Damage Act 1986" (1986) 83(32) *Law Society Gazette* 2620–2622; W. Hanbury, "Latent Damage: some recent developments" (1988) 85(40) *Law Society Gazette* 37–38.

[40] *Iron Trades Mutual Insurance Co. v. Buckenham* [1990] 1 All E.R. 808.

[41] The Court of Appeal noted in the case of *Lee v. Thompson* ([1989] 40 E.G. 89) that *Groom v. Crocker* ([1939] 1 K.B. 194), which had decided that a client's claim against his or her solicitor lay in contract only, had never been overruled.

[42] H. Evans, "Negligent omissions by solicitors and limitation" (1991) *Professional Negligence* 50–53, at p. 53.

The Latent Damage Act provides that the limitation period of six years continues to run from the date of the damage, as before, but provides an alternative limitation period for latent defects. Where there are latent defects, the limitation period is three years from the discovery, or reasonable discoverability, of the defect, if this expires after the six-year limitation period. Actions are subject to a "long-stop" provision, which bars any action at the end of a 15-year period from the date of the act or omission of the defendant. Even if the Act can be applied to clients of solicitors, it will be of no benefit if the action was statute-barred before the Act came into force.[43] The fifteen-year "long-stop" provision will also ensure that there is no remedy for consumers where the act or omission causing the damage occurred before this.

Economic loss

One of the advantages of contractual liability is that, under a contract, damages can be obtained for economic loss. Pure economic loss is financial loss, which is not a result of physical damage or injury. The purpose of damages for breach of contract is to put the plaintiff in the position he or she would have been in if the contract had been performed properly. Provided that the damage is not too remote, plaintiffs can recover for loss of profits and other economic losses. For example, in a case where a client lost the purchase of a house, through the negligence of the solicitor,[44] the damages were the difference between the market price at the time of the abortive purchase, and the (greatly inflated) market price when the client successfully purchased the property.

The position is different in tort. The law of negligence was developed to provide compensation for injury to persons and damage to property, and for financial loss arising from such damage. At one time, pure economic loss was not considered the kind of loss which could be compensated through the tort of negligence. This had obvious advantages for those professions, including the legal profession, where the negligent performance of duties was only likely to result in financial loss, rather than physical damage or personal injury. As such loss could only be recovered in contract, this limited the opportunity for non-contracting parties to sue solicitors.

---

[43] The Act came into force on September 18, 1986. It was of no use in the *Bell v. Browne* case, as the action became statute-barred before this.
[44] *Simpson v. Grove Tompkins & Co* (1982) 126 *Solicitors Journal* 347.

However, in the case of *Hedley Byrne & Co Ltd v. Heller & Partners Ltd*[45] it was decided that some limited liability might arise in negligence, for economic loss, as a result of negligent advice. This would arise where there was a "special relationship" between the parties. Despite the absence of a contract, there could be a duty of care where the plaintiff relied upon the defendant's skill and judgment; the defendant knew, or ought reasonably to have known that the plaintiff was relying on him or her; and it was reasonable in the circumstances for the plaintiff to rely on the defendant. This case had obvious consequences for those professions giving advice, as for the first time they could be made liable for that advice to those who were not their clients.

In the 1970s and 1980s, recovery for economic loss was expanded to include structural defects (*Dutton v. Bognor Regis U.D.C*;[46] *Anns v. Merton London B.C*[47]), and loss of profits (*Junior Books Ltd v. Veitchi Co*[48]). Foreseeability of damage was regarded as a sufficient criterion for the existence of a duty of care. However, the courts then began to restrict liability for pure economic loss.[49] In *Murphy v. Brentwood D.C.*,[50] the House of Lords decided that a local authority is not liable for negligent application of the building regulations, where the resulting defects are discovered before physical injury occurs. The loss suffered was purely economic, and therefore not recoverable, and the previous decisions in *Dutton* and *Anns* were overruled. Recovery for economic loss in tort was restricted to cases involving negligent mis-statements,[51] or the kind of proximity found in the *Junior Books* case.[52]

In the case of *Caparo Industries plc v Dickman*,[53] the House of Lords restated the extent of the duty for negligent mis-statements in more limited terms. There was no duty of care owed to the public at large who might rely on the auditor's accounts in deciding whether to purchase shares, or to existing shareholders. There will only be a duty of care where there is a sufficient relationship of proximity between the parties, where the damage can be foreseen, and where it is just and reasonable to impose such a duty. Nevertheless, if there is a

---

[45] [1964] A.C. 465.
[46] [1972] 1 Q.B. 373 C.A.
[47] [1978] A.C. 728 H.L.
[48] [1983] A.C. 520.
[49] S. Fennel, "The solicitors profession since 1984: duties to third parties" (1994) 10(4) *Professional Negligence* 142–146.
[50] [1991] 1 A.C. 398.
[51] *Hedley Byrne & Co Ltd v. Heller and Partners Ltd* [1964] A.C. 465.
[52] See J. Cooke, "Economic Loss in Negligence: The Corpse Twitches" (1995) 29(3) *The Law Teacher* 367–375.
[53] [1990] 1 All E.R. 568.

special relationship, a duty of care will be, and has been, imposed on members of the legal profession, for negligent advice resulting in pure economic loss.

Liability to third parties

The basis of the liability to the client in professional services is the contract which the client has with the solicitor. Because of the rule relating to privity of contract, the only remedy a non-client has against a solicitor is in negligence. Negligence liability is not restricted to the parties to the contract, and duties may be imposed for negligence where services are given gratuitously. The expansion of liability in negligence has resulted in civil liability for the professions being "revolutionised in recent years".[54] The extent of the duty of care to non-clients, where there is no physical harm or damage, is a developing area of law. There are two main issues to be addressed, when examining a solicitor's liability to third parties: that of conflicts of interests between clients and third parties, and that of liability for economic loss.

The general rule is that, under normal circumstances, solicitors must do all that they properly can for their clients. There is therefore no general duty towards those who are not clients. The courts are cautious about imposing on professionals a duty of care to third parties affected by services to their clients because these duties may conflict. Solicitors cannot be the guardians of third-party interests in such cases because what is done for the client may be hostile and injurious their interests.[55] There is no general duty of care to the opposing side in litigation, unless the solicitor expressly undertakes a specific responsibility. In one case,[56] the judge said that he approached the question of imposing a third-party duty on a solicitor with "great circumspection".

Public policy generally requires that solicitors be protected from claims by their clients' opponents. To do otherwise may prevent solicitors acting in the best interests of their clients. There are situations, however, where solicitors will be found to owe duties to third parties despite the fact that the third party is in conflict with the

---

[54] A. M. Dugdale and K. M. Stanton, *Professional Negligence* (2nd ed., 1989), p.63 [Butterworths: London].
[55] *Ross v. Caunters* [1980] Ch 297.
[56] *Al-Kandari v. J. R. Brown & Co* [1987] 2 W.L.R. 469.

client. In one case,[57] concerning a dispute about the custody of children, the solicitor of the plaintiff's husband gave an undertaking to retain the husband's passport, to prevent his removing the children abroad. By deception, the husband managed to obtain his passport. He kidnapped his children, took them abroad, and they were never seen again by the plaintiff. She claimed damages against his solicitors in negligence for the loss of her children, anxiety and distress, and the costs incurred in attempting to recover the children. The Court of Appeal[58] decided that by voluntarily agreeing to hold the passport, the solicitors owed the plaintiff a duty of care. They were in breach of the duty, and the damage suffered by her was a natural and probable consequence of that breach. The Court rejected the view that to impose this duty would create a conflict of interest with their client. Although undertakings to third parties could involve a conflict, it was often to the client's benefit. In this case, the undertaking had allowed the client access to his children.

Many of the problems in imposing on solicitors duties of care towards third parties is that this would allow claims for pure economic loss. Other professions have however been held to be liable to third parties for economic loss in particular situations. One case concerned whether a surveyor, instructed by a lender to value a house, owed the prospective purchaser a duty in tort to carry out the valuation with reasonable care and skill. The court decided that a surveyor did owe such a duty of care to both the lender and the purchaser. The court was influenced by the fact that both parties would rely on the valuation, and the intending purchaser would be paying for the valuation. The duty is limited to the purchaser, and not to subsequent ones. The court was clearly adopting a consumer protection approach, being influenced by the fact that those affected were "people buying at the bottom end of the market," many of whom would be "young first-time buyers" who were "likely to be under considerable financial pressure".[59] In the case of *Henderson v Merrett Syndicates Ltd*,[60] the House of Lords decided that members of a Lloyd's syndicate owed a duty of care to the relevant names of the syndicate. There is no reason in principle, therefore, why solicitors should not be held liable for economic loss in relation to third parties.

---

[57] *Al-Kandari v. J. R. Brown & Co.* [1988] 2 W.L.R. 671.
[58] For a discussion of the first instance decision see B. Markesinis, "Fixing acceptable boundaries to the liability of solicitors" (1987) 103 *Law Quarterly Review* 346–353.
[59] *Smith v. Bush* [1989] 2 All E.R. 514 at 531.
[60] [1994] 3 All E.R. 506.

Beneficiaries of wills

One area of particular concern for non-client consumers is in relation to wills and the administration of estates. Problems can arise where the negligence of a solicitor has resulted in an invalid will. The client is the testator, but it is usually after the death of the testator that the problems with the will become apparent. The testator obviously cannot sue once deceased. Those who have suffered a detriment are the disappointed beneficiaries, but they are prevented by the privity rule from suing for breach of contract. Despite the privity rule, it was decided, in the case of *Ross v. Caunters*[61] that there could be a duty of care to intended beneficiaries, even though they were not parties to the contract. In this case, a will was witnessed by the spouse of a beneficiary, the result of which was that the beneficiary was not entitled to the legacy. The beneficiary claimed that the solicitor had been negligent in not ensuring that the witnesses were neither beneficiaries nor spouses of beneficiaries. The solicitor argued that there was no duty of care to the beneficiary, only to the client under the contract. The court was clear that the existence of a contractual duty to the client did not preclude the existence of a non-contractual duty to others. It was decided that the plaintiff could recover damages for pure economic loss, because of the close degree of proximity in the relationship between solicitors and intended beneficiaries. Another important factor in the case was that there was no conflict of interest between the beneficiary and client. This decision was "widely acclaimed ... throughout the common-law world,"[62] and it gave consumers a remedy where none existed before.[63]

The scope of the solicitor's duty to third parties in executing wills was extended in the case of *White v. Jones*.[64] This case arose because a family quarrel caused the testator to cut his daughters out of his will. Some three months later, he became reconciled to them, and he therefore sent a letter to his solicitors asking them to draw up a new will. It was some two months after receiving instructions before the solicitors prepared the new will, by which time the testator had died. The disappointed beneficiaries sued the solicitor on the basis that the

---

[61] [1980] Ch. 297.

[62] J. C. Brady, "Solicitors' Duty of Care in the Drafting of Wills" (1995) 56(3/4) *Northern Ireland Law Quarterly* 434–442, at p. 436.

[63] For a fuller discussion of the implications of this case see J. Murphy, "Expectation losses, negligent omissions and the tortious duty of care" (1996) 55(1) *Cambridge Law Journal* 43–55; S. Whittaker, "Privity of contract and the tort of negligence: future directions" (1996) 16(2) *Oxford Journal of Legal Studies* 191–230.

[64] [1995] 1 All E.R. 691.

failure to draw up the will had resulted in the loss of their legacies. This case differed from *Ross v. Caunters*,[65] as there the will had been drawn up, but the solicitor had failed to ensure that it was properly witnessed. In *White v. Jones* the solicitor had omitted to do anything. The case was decided by the House of Lords. It established that where solicitors accept instructions to draw up a will, they may owe a beneficiary a duty of care if they negligently perform or omit to carry out the instructions of the testator. The case was decided by a majority of three to two. The decision was based[66] on the fact that there would be no remedy for the loss caused by the solicitor's negligence unless the intended beneficiary could claim. There would thus be a lacuna in the law. It was felt that the assumption of responsibility by the solicitor towards the client should be extended in law to an intended beneficiary who was reasonably foreseeably deprived of the intended legacy as a result of the solicitor's negligence. This would occur when neither the testator nor the estate had a remedy against the solicitor. It was felt that the principle of assumption of responsibility should be extended to a solicitor who accepted instructions to draw up a will. The solicitor should be held to be in a special relationship with those intended to benefit under it. This was a development of the law of negligence, using an incremental approach.[67]

The two dissenting judges[68] were concerned that the principle of privity of contract should not be infringed. The contractual duty of the solicitor to the testator was to secure that his testamentary intention was put into effective legal form promptly. To allow the plaintiffs' claim that the same duty was owed to them in tort, would have the result of circumventing the rule against privity of contract. The beneficiaries would be thus given the benefit of a contract to which they were not a party. The dissenting judges distinguished the case from *Henderson v. Merrett*,[69] as the solicitor in the present case was not handling the plaintiff's affairs. There was, therefore, no relationship between the plaintiffs and the solicitor, nor did the solicitor do or say anything upon which the plaintiffs acted to their prejudice. The dissenting judges could find no precedent for such liability, and did not feel that it would be appropriate to extend the law of negligence in this case on an incremental basis.[70] There was

---

[65] [1980] Ch. 297.
[66] See the judgments of Lord Goff and Lord Nolan.
[67] See the judgment of Lord Browne-Wilkinson.
[68] Lord Keith and Lord Mustill.
[69] [1994] 3 All E.R. 506.
[70] See, in particular, Lord Keith's judgment.

also concern that the courts should not be acting "as second-line disciplinary tribunals imposing punishment in the shape of damages".[71]

It is true that *White v Jones* is not easy to accommodate with the English law of obligations. The law of contract is concerned with financial loss, and loss of expectations. In this case there was not a loss but a failure to obtain a benefit. There was no act by the solicitor, but a failure to act. There is no tortious liability for an omission, unless a person is under a duty. However, despite these objections, the majority of the House of Lords were convinced that there should be a cause of action. If there was no duty in this case, the only person able to make a valid claim (the deceased testator) has suffered no loss, and the only person who has suffered a loss (the disappointed beneficiary) has no valid claim.

Lord Goff was clear that "as a matter of justice" a duty of care must be owed. This was a policy decision based on public protection reasons, particularly for those members of the public who have limited means. He was also influenced by the fact that society places great importance on the individual's right to leave assets to whom he or she pleases. It was people of modest means instructing small firms of solicitors in respect of, often relatively modest, legacies, who were statistically most likely to suffer from mistakes[72] of the kind made by the defendants. There was therefore a consumer protection element in finding a practical solution.[73] Also influential in the decision was the consideration of the role played by solicitors in society. The public interest in preserving the reputation of the profession was also important. In other cases, the "privileged position of solicitors and the unique nature of their work" has justified "wider than normal liabilities".[74]

The decision in *White v. Jones* attracted much comment from academics and practitioners. There is no doubt that it has extended liability for negligent omissions, and the recovery of pure economic loss in non-contractual cases, but the basis of the decision is not clear.[75] The facts of the case do not fall into the category of special relationship, or reliance in the *Hedley Byrne* sense. Liability for economic loss is based upon a voluntary assumption of responsibility by the defendant towards the plaintiff, and some reliance by the

---

[71] See Lord Mustill's judgment.

[72] This was claimed by Lord Goff, but the basis of this assertion is unclear.

[73] See C. Kessel, "Solicitors' professional negligence" (1995) 145 *New Law Journal* 499–500.

[74] S. Fennell, "Representations and statements by solicitors to third parties" (1992) *Professional Negligence* 25–28, at p.28.

[75] J. Murphy, "Expectation losses, negligent omissions and the tortious duty of care" (1996) 55(1) *Cambridge Law Journal* 43–55.

plaintiff. This reliance was thought to be shown by the plaintiff acting to his or her detriment. In *White v. Jones* it seems that the "reliance" can include the plaintiff expecting the defendant to exercise due care and skill.

The extension of liability for pure economic loss in negligence has been welcomed, on the grounds that it achieved a just result, and sets out a clearer concept and broader principle of professional liability.[76] The House of Lords is commended for moving away from the conservative position adopted in *Murphy* and for attempting to provide a more flexible approach to deal with problems created by economic loss.[77] After this case, liability is not restricted to advice and statements, but can be imposed when the special skills and expertise are relied upon by non-clients. It has been argued that the imposition of this duty on solicitors should be welcomed, not only by the fee-paying public, but also by the profession itself. This is because it is in the interests of the profession that those responsible for such negligence are held liable, as this reflects well on the profession as a whole.[78]

The decision has also attracted criticism. It has been argued[79] that the imposition of this liability will not be in the interests of consumers, and will deny legal services to the very consumers that the House of Lords wished to protect—those with limited means who want low-cost wills. It is suggested that, if solicitors cannot allow any delay in drafting wills, they may not be able to offer low-cost wills in the future.[80] Another criticism is that the law has developed pragmatically and untidily to do justice despite the rule of privity. While not objecting to the outcome of the case itself, it is argued that the courts should not be using the law of tort in this way, but should be developing exceptions to the privity rule, within the framework of contract law.[81]

The imposition of a duty of care in these circumstances fills the gap left by the absence of an effective remedy in contract on the part of the estate of the testator. It has given an additional remedy to

---

[76] C. Kessel, "Solicitors' professional negligence" (1995) 145 *New Law Journal* 499–500, at p.500.

[77] J. Cooke, "Economic Loss in Negligence: The Corpse Twitches" (1995) 29(3) *The Law Teacher* 367–375.

[78] N. Collins, "*White v Jones*: a new approach to solicitors' negligence" (1995) 11(3) *Professional Negligence* 97–98, at p.98.

[79] R. M. Abbey, "Solicitors, negligence and public policy" (1993) 137(33) *Solicitors Journal* 859.

[80] It is difficult to understand why simple, low-cost wills cannot be drafted efficiently.

[81] S. Whittaker, "Privity of contract and the tort of negligence: future directions" (1996) 16(2) *Oxford Journal of Legal Studies* 191–230.

consumers in actions against solicitors. It has endorsed the decision in *Ross v. Caunters*, despite the harsher climate for pure economic loss imposed by *Caparo*.[82] It has been applied in subsequent cases. In one,[83] solicitors failed to sever a joint tenancy, which rendered a gift in a will ineffective. The question to be decided was whether the solicitor's responsibility extended beyond the intended beneficiary in connection with the preparation of the will, to include intended beneficiaries in connection with the failure to serve a notice of severance which rendered the will ineffective. The Court of Appeal decided that the assumption of responsibility towards the client extended to the intended beneficiary, who suffered a loss of expectation. The service of a notice of severance was part of the will making process, and the plaintiff was to be treated as an intended beneficiary.

The courts seem anxious to protect consumers in these situations. However, it may be that the liability to beneficiaries is an isolated example of the duty of care being owed to non-clients, and that it should be seen as a last resort when contract remedies are not suitable.[84] Solicitors will not usually be liable to third parties, for failing to draw up documents in correct form, where the client is still alive. A duty of care will only be owed to third parties in *inter vivos* transactions where the solicitor's negligence renders it impossible for the client to put matters right.[85]

The extent of the duty to beneficiaries also has its limits. In one case[86] the client was a beneficiary of her brother's estate. She made a will leaving her residuary estate to a number of charities. She died without executing a deed of variation of her brother's will, under the Inheritance Tax Act 1984, which would have mitigated the tax liability on the estate. The executors of her will advised neither her nor the charities of the possibility of tax mitigation, and the charities sued the executors alleging negligence, their loss being the tax liability which could have been mitigated. The court refused to allow the claim on the basis that the executors had carried out their duties properly and were under no obligation to advise the charities. It appears from this case that there is no duty to provide fiscal advice to beneficiaries. In any case, if such advice is given to testators, there is

---

[82] S. Baughen, "The will that never was: *Ross v. Caunters* extended" (1992) 8(3) *Professional Negligence* 99–102.

[83] *Carr-Glynn v. Frearsons* [1998] 4 All E.R. 225.

[84] S. Fennel, "The solicitors profession since 1984: duties to third parties" (1994) 10(4) *Professional Negligence* 142–146, at p.142.

[85] *Hemmens v. Wilson Browne, The Times,* June 30, 1993.

[86] *Cancer Research Campaign v. Ernest Brown & Co.* [1997] P.N.L.R. 592; [1997] S.T.C. 1425.

no guarantee that they would organise their fiscal affairs to ensure that their estates suffered minimal tax liability.[87]

Exclusion of liability for negligence and breach of contract

The general position is that it is possible to exclude liability for negligence, but the common law and statute has placed a number of restrictions on this. The Solicitors Act 1974[88] makes void any provision in a contentious business agreement that a solicitor shall not be liable for negligence, or that he or she shall be relieved from any responsibility to which he or she would otherwise be subject as a solicitor. Other professionals, for example, auditors, and officers of companies, have similar restrictions on exclusion of liability in a business context.

Under the Unfair Contract Terms Act 1977,[89] it is not possible for any party to exclude or restrict liability for death or personal injury in negligence. In negligence cases not involving death or personal injury, there is a reasonableness test, which means that any exclusion of liability will only be allowed if it is reasonable.[90] It seems unlikely that the courts would be sympathetic to such disclaimers in professional contracts in relation to consumers. For example, in a case involving the liability of valuers,[91] the court said that it would not be fair and reasonable for valuers to impose on purchasers of residential property the risk of loss arising as a result of the incompetence or carelessness on the part of the valuers. There is similar provision in the Act for exclusion of liability for breach of contract. Section 3 of the Act provides that this has to be reasonable.

Barristers' immunity from negligence

As we have seen, there is no contractual relationship between a barrister and the client. At one time, the absence of a contract was used to argue that there was complete immunity for all the work

[87] J. Murphy, "Probate solicitors, disappointed beneficiaries and the tortious duty to advise on tax avoidance" (1998) 14(2) *Professional Negligence* 107–114.
[88] s. 60(5).
[89] s. 2(1).
[90] s. 2(2).
[91] *Smith v. Bush* [1989] 2 All E.R. 514.

which a barrister performed, and that therefore barristers were also immune from negligence claims. There was an opportunity to test the validity of this view in 1967, when a client, convicted of causing grievous bodily harm, attempted to sue his barrister, on the basis that the conduct of the case had been negligent. The case, *Rondel v. Worsley*,[92] went to the House of Lords on the issue of whether there was any cause of action. The House of Lords said that there was no cause of action, holding that barristers were wholly immune from being sued in negligence by a client in respect of the conduct and management of a case in court, and the preliminary work connected with it.

What was important about this case was that it established that that the basis of the immunity was public policy, rather than the relationship of the barrister to the client. The idea that the immunity was based on the absence of contract was dismissed. The earlier case of *Hedley Byrne v. Heller*[93] had established that there was no need for there to be a contract before a case for negligent advice could be brought. A duty of care was owed to all those relying on the skill and judgment of those giving advice, provided that there was an assumption of responsibility by the professional person. The immunity of barristers was therefore not based on the absence of a contract between the barrister and client, but on public policy. As such it is an exception to the general rule of professional liability.

Three public policy justifications for the immunity are given in the judgment. The first of these is that the administration of justice requires that barristers should be able to carry out their duties to the court fearlessly and independently. The second justification is that actions for negligence against barristers would make the retrying of the original action inevitable, and thus prolong litigation, which was contrary to the public interest. A final justification is that barristers are obliged to accept any client, however difficult, who seeks their services.

Once it was established that immunity was not based on the absence of contract, its scope and extent was brought into question. Public policy justifications do not necessarily apply to matters unconnected with cases in court, so the case left some uncertainty as to whether the immunity would still extend to these matters. If barristers failed to exercise the ordinary skill and care that could reasonably be expected of them, should they be in a better position than any other professional person?

---

[92] [1969] 1 A.C. 191.
[93] [1963] 2 All E.R. 575.

The case of *Rondel v. Worsley* did not establish the limits of the immunity, and it was not until the case of *Saif Ali v. Sydney Mitchell and Co*,[94] that the extent of the immunity was reconsidered. In this case, the plaintiff was injured in a motor accident. Because of the alleged negligence of his barrister and solicitor, by the time those responsible were sued, the action was statute-barred, because it was out of time. The plaintiff sued his solicitor on the grounds of negligence, and the solicitor joined the barrister to the action. The case went to the House of Lords on the question of the extent of the barrister's immunity. The House of Lords made it clear that in principle there was a duty to take reasonable care. The basis of barristers' immunity from actions in negligence was public policy. These policy reasons also applied to pre-trial work, as well as matters in court. In the interests of justice, however, the immunity should not be given any wider application than was absolutely necessary. If the work was intimately connected with the conduct of the case in court, then it would be covered by the immunity. This was a factual matter to be decided in each case. On the facts of the present case, it did not come within the immunity. The negligence related to the conduct of civil proceedings outside court. Because of the negligence of the barrister, the client lost the opportunity of bringing an unanswerable claim. There was no public policy reason for preventing legal redress against the legal advisers in such a case.

This case settled the position that barristers could be sued for negligent advisory work, but not for work which is intimately connected with the conduct of a case in court. Barristers, like solicitors, can be sued for giving negligent advice on the drafting of wills or deeds, or for advice which results in the wrong party being sued. The House of Lords wished to draw a distinction between the "hurly-burly of the trial" process, and work which took place in the "relative tranquillity of the barristers' chambers".[95] In the latter case, barristers were no different from other professionals. However, given that most barristers' work is advocacy, a large part of their work will be protected by the immunity. Negligence claims against barristers used by be a very rare occurrence,[96] but the trend is for such claims to become more frequent.

---

[94] [1980] A.C. 198.
[95] *Per* Lord Diplock.
[96] National Consumer Council, *Ordinary Justice* (1989), p.220 [London: HMSO].

Justifications for the immunity

In the case of *Rondel v. Worsley* three justifications for the immunity were given. One of these was the "cab-rank" principle, which means that barristers cannot choose their clients, but have to accept anyone, provided they are not engaged elsewhere, and the client is prepared to pay the fee requested. Barristers would be unable to refuse clients who are litigious, and who may commence vexatious proceedings if dissatisfied with the outcome of a case. This argument is unconvincing. In the *Saif Ali* case it was conceded that, under modern conditions, a very large part of the "cab-rank" principle had disappeared with the abolition of the dock brief. Solicitors provided the necessary filter for clients.

Another justification was that the administration of justice required that barristers should be able to carry out their duties to the court fearlessly and independently. Barristers have duties to their clients to raise every issue to advance their case. But they also have a duty to the court, which transcends the duty to the client, and which may conflict with the client's wishes. If a case is lost, clients may seek legal redress. This redress would involve suing the barrister for negligence, and thus the efficient administration of justice may be hampered if barristers have to consider the possibility of negligence claims. It must be rare for there to be a conflict between the advocate's duty to the court and the duty to the client. Where there is a conflict, the duty to the court will always prevail, and it can never be negligence to put this duty first. The claim that immunity promotes values of fearlessly pursuing a case is unconvincing, and it is difficult to understand "how these values are promoted by immunity from incompetence".[97]

Judges have remarked how fearsome it is "for a barrister to have an action brought against him," and "to have his reputation besmirched by a charge of negligence". This may be true, but it is not a very convincing argument for immunity from negligence. All professions dislike negligence claims against them, and the Bar is probably better placed to resist unjust claims. There is an assumption that to abandon the immunity would result in the opening of the floodgates of litigation. This is unlikely. There are strong disincentives for consumers to sue lawyers, because of the cost, time and distress and inconvenience of pursuing civil actions. As for vexatious litigants and unwarranted claims, many other professionals have to suffer these, and

---

[97] R. Cranston, "Legal Ethics and Professional Responsibility" in *Legal Ethics and Professional Responsibility* (R. Cranston ed., 1995), at p.11 [Oxford: Clarendon].

there is no greater danger of a professional acting negligently with a difficult client than with any other client.

A more convincing argument for the immunity is the fact that if barristers could be sued in negligence it would really involve a re-hearing of the case, and would thus result in re-litigation. Any action for negligence would involve a retrial of the issues in order to show whether the negligence had caused the damage complained of. It is undesirable to have negligence claims used as an indirect method of appealing, and there is a public interest in the finality of verdicts. However, this has to be balanced against the public interest in ensuring the right result. There is no absolute virtue in having an end to litigation, and an un-remedied breach of a duty to take care cannot be acceptable. In any case, negligence claims in civil proceedings need not affect the outcome of the trial. It would not be re-litigation. The decision in the original trial would stand, but the injured party should be awarded damages for negligence.

One argument for the immunity is that negligence actions may permit defendants in criminal trials to re-open their convictions. This is not necessarily unreasonable, if they have been convicted as a result of their lawyers' negligence.[98] Indeed, negligence may be grounds for an appeal against conviction.[99] Successful criminal appeals based on the incompetence of counsel may be extremely rare,[1] but where they are brought, the court assesses the effect of counsel's incompetence on the trial and verdict. If the advocate's negligence can be used to overturn convictions on appeal, there is little justification for not allowing a defendant to sue in negligence.

In the *Saif Ali* case itself, Lord Diplock felt that it was unsatisfactory that the parties were not arguing for the abolition of the immunity. Such arguments may be justified in view of the developments in the law of negligence which had taken place during the 11 years since *Rondel v. Worsley*. He surmised that this was perhaps because the parties to the dispute were solicitors and barristers, and that it would not be in their interests to argue against the immunity. The court adopted a narrower view of the immunity in *Saif Ali* than in *Rondel v. Worsley*, on the basis that there was no justification for it outside of court work, when there was no such immunity for other professions.

---

[98] M. Zander, *Legal services for the community* (1978), p.135 [Temple Smith].

[99] See *R v. Irwin* [1987] 2 All E.R. 1085. In this case, the defendant appealed against conviction on the grounds that his barrister failed to consult him about a decision not to call two alibi witnesses. The Court of Appeal quashed the conviction on the ground that this failure to consult was a material irregularity, which made the conviction unsafe.

[1] *R v. Clinton (Dean)* [1993] 1 W.L.R. 1181 was one of these rare cases. In this case, counsel's conduct in not calling evidence to rebut the prosecution's case, on behalf of the defendant, rendered the conviction unsafe.

As the House of Lords had tended to extend the ambit of the duty of care in other negligence cases, it was felt that a blanket immunity could not survive in the "realistic atmosphere" of the late twentieth century.[2]

The justifications for the immunity have been described as "logically unsound and based on dubious, empirical assertions about the legal process".[3] There are no compelling reasons why barristers should be treated differently from other suppliers of services who hold themselves out as possessing particular skills and knowledge. Although there is a general immunity for all those taking part in trials, including witnesses, judges and jurors, this should not apply to advocates. There is some merit in providing protection for lay people, who act in good faith in the trial process, to be given protection from liability for negligence. Paid advocates with special skill and knowledge should be expected to exercise reasonable care.

The National Consumer Council believes that the immunity should be abolished. The arguments in favour of the immunity are not of sufficient force and gravity to "outweigh the hardship to consumers who may fall victim to an advocate's negligence".[4] Others[5] have called upon Parliament to abolish the immunity, on the grounds that it is outdated and based on flimsy public policy justifications. The rule serves little function, except to protect lawyers, and its operation leads to cynicism and distrust by consumers. Rather than justifying the immunity, public policy requires that advocates should be accountable for the shortcomings of their work.

It is perhaps worth noting that no other country in Europe has this immunity.[6] Moreover, the Government has been asked to justify the immunity by the European Commission of Human Rights. This request was made as part of its investigation into a case brought by a bank accountant, who was convicted of prejudicing a drug-trafficking investigation. He blamed his barrister for what he alleged was a miscarriage of justice. The concern is whether the immunity can be justified in the light of the right to a fair trial, under Article 6 of the European Convention on Human Rights.[7]

---

[2] See Lord Diplock's judgment in *Saif Ali v. Sydney Mitchell & Co.* [1980] A.C. 198, especially at pp. 223, 229–230.

[3] C. G. Veljanivski and C. J. Whelan, "Professional Negligence and the Quality of Legal Services—An economic perspective" [1983] *Modern Law Review* 700–718, at p.712.

[4] National Consumer Council, *Ordinary Justice* (1989), at p.223 [London: HMSO].

[5] K. Richards, "Advocates' immunity: justice delivered by the law" (1995) 5(5) *Consumer Policy Review* 161–167.

[6] J. A. Hayes and J. Poll, "Lawyers' immunity: the wider English and European framework" (1991) 7(4) *Professional Negligence* 184–187.

[7] See *Law Society Gazette*, November 18, 1998, p.5.

The extent of the immunity

Solicitor-advocates are also covered by the immunity. This extension
had been suggested in *Rondel v. Worsley*. Given that the immunity was
based on public policy, solicitors who acted as advocates in court
should be similarly protected, because the same public policy reasons
for the immunity would apply to them. The case of *Saif Ali*
confirmed that solicitors are in the same position as barristers in
relation to advocacy and pre-trial work. Statute has now confirmed
the same immunity applies to all advocates.[8] Unlike barristers,
solicitors are not protected if they fail to appear on the day of the
trial, because that would involve a breach of contract.

The immunity is "unique in the modern law of professional
services".[9] It covers the entire conduct of a case in court, including
the failure to put a defence to the court, or to call an important
witness. This is settled law. Where there is uncertainty is its extent in
relation to work which is so intimately connected with the conduct of
the case in court that it could be said to be a preliminary decision
affecting the way the cause is to be conducted when it comes to
trial.[10] The House of Lords, in the *Saif Ali case*, was unwilling to lay
down guidelines about the precise types of pre-trial work covered by
the immunity.[11] The case does not, therefore, give a catalogue of pre-
trial work which would fall within the immunity. Every case has to be
decided on its merits.

A failure to give notice of appeal at the proper time would be
actionable, as would a failure to arrange for key witnesses to appear at
a trial. The immunity does not cover the giving of advice on the
prospects of an appeal.[12] In the case of *Kelley v. Corston*, the judge said
that immunity constituted an exception to the fundamental principle,
that those who have suffered loss or damage as a result of the
negligence of their professional advisers, should normally be entitled to
their remedy.[13] On this basis, the trend now is to limit the
circumstances in which the immunity applies, and to restrict its

---

[8] Courts and Legal Services Act 1990, s. 62. This section does not give the immunity a
statutory basis. It simply extends the common law immunity from negligence enjoyed
by barristers to all advocates.
[9] C. Miller, "The advocate's duty to justice, where does it belong?" (1981) 97 *Law
Quarterly Review* 127, at p.137.
[10] *Saif Ali v. Sydney Mitchell and Co* [1980] A.C. 198.
[11] H. Harrop-Griffiths and J. Bennington, *Underwood and Holt's Professional Negligence*
(2nd ed., 1985), p.36 [London: Fourmat].
[12] *Atwell v. Michael Perry & Co* [1998] 4 All E.R. 65.
[13] [1997] 4 All E.R. 466 at 475, *per* Judge L.J.

application.[14] *Kelley v. Corston* concerned the status of the advice given by the advocate before the trial, in a matrimonial dispute. The advice culminated in a settlement which required approval of the court. It was held that the advocate was immune from suit in respect of the advice, because the settlement made at the door of the court was "inextricably linked" with the proceedings within the court.

This case narrows the scope of the immunity for pre-trial matters. It appears that the immunity will only apply where a judge has participated to such an extent that the issue can be regarded as a decision of the court. This aspect of the immunity only exists, therefore, to support the primary immunity, which applies to the conduct of a case in court. It restricts the ability of advocates to claim the immunity where a settlement is reached at the door of the court. This may lead to more claims being made against advocates, but it may also mean that more care will be taken in this area. As one commentator has noted, the most effective protection against successful claims is to ensure that the client has given properly informed consent to the settlement.[15]

The immunity applies where a negligence claim amounts to a collateral attack on the original court decision. Such a claim is seen as an abuse of the court process.[16] In one case,[17] after a defendant was refused leave to appeal against his conviction, he sued his solicitors alleging negligence in their advice to him and in the way they conducted the case. The Court of Appeal decided that it was an abuse of process to bring an action, which would involve challenging the correctness of the decision of the criminal court, in order to succeed. There was a similar result in a case[18] where a defendant, after serving his prison sentence, tried to claim in negligence against his solicitors. Although in this case, the motive was not to avoid his sentence of imprisonment, this was irrelevant, as he had had full opportunity to put his case at the trial. The rule about collateral claims will not apply where a conviction has been overturned, and the defendant then sues for the negligent conduct of the defence of his or her case in court.[19] There is no question in such a case of a successful negligence action being an affront to justice. It is in the interests of justice that a

---

[14] T. Dugdale, "Advocates' immunity under scrutiny" (1998) 14(2) *Professional Negligence* 75–82.
[15] *ibid.*
[16] *Hunter v. Chief Constable of the West Midlands Police* [1982] A.C. 529.
[17] *Somasundaram v. M. Julius Melchior & Co* [1988] 1 W.L.R. 1394.
[18] *Smith v. Linskills* [1996] 1 W.L.R. 763.
[19] *Acton v. Graham Pearce Co* [1997] 3 All E.R. 909.

plaintiff wrongly convicted as a result of negligence, who has succeeded on appeal, should have a remedy in damages.[20]

The extent of the immunity now seems to be limited to the conduct of cases in court, together with actions which are inextricably linked to this. In addition, negligence actions will not be allowed where they constitute collateral challenges to a final decision of a court. There are few actions in negligence against barristers, because of the immunity, even in its restricted form, and cases where barristers have been found liable for negligence are rare.[21]

Remedies

Where consumers do successfully sue their legal advisers, it is important that they obtain appropriate remedies. The most widely used remedy is damages. The most common types of solicitors' negligence cases involve failures to keep to time limits in litigation; failures to serve notices in time in business leases; and problems in conveyancing. In these cases, there is rarely a contest about liability. Difficulties occur over the amount of damages to be paid.[22] For example, in one case,[23] solicitors admitted negligence in the conduct of the plaintiff's divorce settlement. They disputed the quantum of damages. The court decided that that damages should be assessed on what the plaintiff's husband would have been ordered to pay on the application of the Matrimonial Causes Act 1973. This was most likely to be one-third of his income and capital, and this amount should be paid in damages.

The purpose of damages is to put the plaintiff in the same position as if no wrong had been done. Actual loss must be shown before compensation will be given, and the damage suffered must not be too remote. The damage must be reasonably foreseeable, and must result from the breach of contract, or breach of duty. Intervening acts may break the chain of causation. In one case,[24] a solicitor summarily terminated the contract with the plaintiff. The plaintiff therefore acted for herself in her claim for ancillary relief from her former husband. Because she remarried before claiming financial assistance, her claim

[20] T. Dugdale, "Advocates' immunity under scrutiny" (1998) 14(2) *Professional Negligence* 75–82.

[21] National Consumer Council, *Ordinary Justice* (1989), p.220 [London: HMSO].

[22] H. Evans, "Damages for solicitor's negligence: (1) the loss of litigation" (1991) *Professional Negligence* 201–205.

[23] *Dickinson v. Jones Alexander & Co* (1993) 2 F.L.R. 521.

[24] *Young v. Purdy* [1996] 2 F.L.R. 795 C.A.

was barred. She sought damages from her solicitor for wrongful termination of the retainer without notice. At first instance, the trial judge ruled that the wrongful termination had caused her to lose her right to claim financial provision, and therefore her solicitor was liable for that loss. On appeal, it was decided that the termination of the retainer was not a cause of her financial loss. It merely afforded the plaintiff the opportunity of acting negligently in her own cause. This could not have been reasonably foreseen by her solicitor. There had been a wrongful termination of the contract, but the loss was nominal, and she was awarded £2 in damages.

Usually, consumers claim damages for financial loss, but it is also possible to claim for personal injury,[25] distress, and pain and suffering. One woman obtained £3,000, for anxiety, worry and distress suffered over a number of years because there was the possibility of losing occupation of her home, as a result of her solicitor's negligence.[26] In another case[27] damages for mental distress, anxiety and vexation were awarded against a solicitor, as they were a direct and foreseeable consequence of the solicitor's handling of a divorce case.

The role of insurance

The most important aspect of remedies for consumers is that the defendant has the means to pay any damages which are awarded. In the case of solicitors and barristers, this is not problematic, as they are not allowed to practise without indemnity insurance policies. Insurance plays a major role in the operation of the tort system in general, and especially so in the area of professional negligence. Barristers are insured by a mutual fund, the Bar Mutual Indemnity Fund Limited. Solicitors also have insurance provided by a mutual scheme, the Solicitors Indemnity Fund.[28] In a mutual fund, the profession itself provides the fund by a levy on members of the profession. The Solicitors Indemnity Fund pays out millions of pounds each year to meet claims against the profession.[29] The largest category of claims made on the fund, both in terms of numbers and amount,

---

[25] *Al-Kandari v. J R Brown & Co* [1988] 2 W.L.R. 671.
[26] *Curran v. Docherty* (1995) S.L.T. 716.
[27] *Dickinson v. Jones Alexander & Co* [1993] 2 F.L.R. 521.
[28] Under s. 37 of the Solicitors Act 1974, the Law Society has power to makes rules requiring solicitors to take out indemnity cover. This can be done in by a system of approved insurers, a master policy with an insurance company, or a mutual fund.
[29] In 1996–97, gross claims paid amounted to £256,524,000. (Solicitors Indemnity Fund, *Tenth Annual Report* (1997), p.28.)

are in connection with residential conveyancing. Claims made by lenders, rather than consumers, are the most significant.[30]

There has been much criticism by the profession of the cost of the Solicitors Indemnity Fund to the profession as a whole. Individual firms are also complaining about their individual premiums, particularly the huge increase in premiums as a result of minor claims. Many firms claim that they would pay much less on the open market.[31] The large, city firms want an end to the mutual fund, and are pressing for a scheme of approved insurers. They claim that solicitors should be able to practise freely, subject only to the public interest. This requires no more than requiring practices to take out insurance cover against consumer claims.[32] This disquiet led to a consultation process by the Law Society, during the summer of 1998, on whether the compulsory, mutual scheme should remain, or whether there should be a choice of insurers on the open market. The profession is of the view that indemnity cover should be mandatory, but many favoured approved insurers, particularly among the large firms.[33] There is some discussion as to whether there can be a dual scheme without undermining a mutual fund. The Law Society commissioned research into whether a dual indemnity insurance scheme would be viable, and an experts' report on this has been received. The conclusion is that there could be a dual scheme, but the mutual fund would have to be protected in some way.[34] The Law Society has decided to retain the mutual found on a mandatory basis despite continued opposition from the profession.[35]

From the consumer's point of view, the main concern is that firms can meet any liability claims. Provided insurance is sufficient to meet these, it does not matter whether it is a mutual fund, master policy, or approved insurers. One advantage of the mutual fund is that it is not just concerned with meeting claims. It is also actively involved in promoting risk awareness in the profession, and it targets firms with poor claims records.[36] If this approach results in an improved service for consumers, this is a useful function, which may be lost if the mutual approach is abandoned.

---

[30] Solicitors Indemnity Fund, *Tenth Annual Report* (1997), p.11.
[31] R. Sayer, *The Law Society Gazette*, September 9, 1998, p.19.
[32] See *Law Society Gazette*, July 29, 1998, p.8.
[33] *Law Society Gazette*, September 9, 1998, p.1.
[34] The report, by insurance experts Aon, was sent to Council members in December 1998 (see *Law Society Gazette*, January 6, 1999, p.1).
[35] On March 2, 1999, the Law Society council voted to retain the Solicitors Indemnity Fund for all solicitors. There is now a ballot being conducted among the profession to decide whether firms can insure on the open market.
[36] Solicitors Indemnity Fund, *Tenth Annual Report* (1997), p. 6.

Problems with professional negligence claims

There are some advantages in using civil liability in contract and tort, as a means of regulating the legal profession. It ensures that the lawyer has a financial incentive to take care; the complainant receives financial redress; and it is a form of control which is external to the profession.[37] However, from the point of view of the consumer this is unlikely to be an avenue of redress. The problems associated with pursuing remedies through litigation are well known, and detailed discussion can be found elsewhere.[38] To put it briefly, the cost of litigation is "unpredictable, excessive and disproportionate".[39] This has resulted in the legal system being "simply too expensive ... to provide a meaningful forum for dispute resolution in the commonplace social interactions that fall within the confines of tort, contract and property".[40] Private litigation is an expensive way of providing compensation. It requires consumers to bring themselves within what are sometimes technical and narrow grounds for recovery. In addition, consumers must have evidence to establish the claim.

Most claims against lawyers concern professional negligence. Because the duty to take care arises from the contract for services, it is very difficult for non-clients to bring claims against solicitors. Such a duty of care has only been recognised in limited circumstances. Even if a duty of care is owed, the plaintiff needs to show that the conduct has not been reasonable. The burden of proof is on the plaintiff to show this, and it may not be an easy hurdle to overcome. Finally, the consumer will have to prove that the negligence caused the damage. The requirement to prove causation is likely to be a real problem for consumers. The rules are restrictive and formalistic. Causation must be proved on the balance of probabilities, and the burden of proof is placed on the consumer. In many cases, solicitors are prepared to admit negligence, but are not prepared to accept that the breach caused the loss which is claimed. In some countries, the burden of proving causation is reversed, to the consumer's advantage.[41]

There are also problems for consumers because of the limitation

---

[37] See C. G. Veljanovski and C. J. Whelan, "Professional Negligence and the Quality of Legal Services—An economic perspective" (1983) *Modern Law Review* 700–718.

[38] See Woolf, *Access to Justice: Final Report* (1996) [London: HMSO].

[39] A. A .S. Zuckerman, "Lord Woolf's Access to Justice: Plus ca change ... " (1996) 59(6) *Modern Law Review* 773–796, at p.773.

[40] S. Issacharoff, "Too Much Lawyering, Too Little Law" in *Reform of Civil Justice Procedure—Essays on "Access to Justice"* (A. Zuckeramn and R. Cranston eds., 1995), at pp.245–246 [Oxford University Press].

[41] J. A. Hayes and J. Poll, "Lawyer' immunity: the wider English and European framework" (1991) 7(4) *Professional Negligence* 184–187, at p.185.

period within which actions must be commenced. Claims in contract will be statute-barred six years after the breach has occurred. Actions in negligence must be commenced within six years of the damage occurring. The breach or the damage may not become apparent within this time. The Latent Damage Act is of no assistance for breach of contract, and, in the case of negligence, is subject to the "long-stop provision," so that no claims can be made after 15 years.

A case decided by the Legal Services Ombudsman[42] illustrates the problem. The complainant[43] was a disappointed beneficiary under a will. Joint wills had been prepared by a solicitor's firm. One will was witnessed correctly by the partner and a clerk in the firm, but the other was only witnessed by the partner. It was therefore invalid, and the complainant lost £57,480. The solicitors, supported by the Solicitors Indemnity Fund, denied liability, on the basis that the action was statute-barred. The will was made in 1977, but was not found to be invalid until 1993. This was beyond the 15 years provided for by the Limitation Act 1980.[44] If the limitation period were construed as running from the date when the will was executed, the action would be barred. In an action, the complainant would have to persuade the court that the limitation period should run from the death of the testator. The cause of action was, therefore, uncertain. The facts were not in dispute. The partner had simply failed to get the clerk to witness the will. The law was not in dispute. A solicitor who drafts a will is liable to the potential beneficiaries for negligence, even though they are not clients. The problem was the limitation period. In this case, the Ombudsman awarded the complainant £59,809 compensation. The Ombudsman cannot make legally binding awards, and the solicitor did not pay. The complainant was therefore left without a remedy.

Professional bodies may be of some assistance for consumers with small negligence claims against their lawyers. In the case of solicitors, the professional body can compensate complainants to a maximum of £1,000 for inadequate professional service.[45] As negligence is an aspect of inadequate professional service, this means that complaints of negligence involving a financial loss of up to that level could be dealt with by the professional body, without the need for court action. Where claims are for more than £1,000, complainants are told either to seek independent legal advice, or the professional body will refer the matter to the Solicitors Indemnity Fund, who will then investigate

---

[42] The Legal Services Ombudsman is dealt with in Chapter 6.
[43] See *Fourth Annual Report of the Legal Services Ombudsman 1994*, at p.23.
[44] s. 14B.
[45] This is dealt with in Chapter 5.

and deal with it.[46] The professional body has set up a panel of independent solicitors, who will give one hour's free advice to consumers who have negligence claims against their solicitors. Even so, many consumers who have had a bad experience with one solicitor may be reluctant to engage the services of another in order to progress their claim.

There are difficulties in trying to draw distinctions in some cases between matters that can properly be characterised as professional negligence and those which should be counted as instances of inadequate professional service.[47] Sometimes the professional bodies too readily claim that the matter concerns negligence, and is therefore outside their jurisdiction.[48] Whether a claim is about negligence or inadequate professional service is something that is not always clear cut. This distinction may have considerable practical importance for the consumer with a grievance, because of the problems in pursuing negligence claims. It is therefore important that the professional bodies do not interpret inadequate professional service too narrowly. Where low levels of loss are involved, the distinction can be subjective. In order to assist consumers, the Legal Services Ombudsman tries to persuade the professional bodies to deal with minor negligence and inadequate professional service without attempting to make a distinction between them.[49]

Using the private law to regulate the legal profession and to obtain redress for consumers is fraught with difficulty. The law itself is technical, and there are difficulties of proof and causation. Litigation is expensive and time-consuming. Limitation periods and the immunity from suit for actions in court prevent many claims being brought. Even when a case is successfully litigated, the outcome is directed to specific remedies, rather than broad structural reforms. The role of the professional bodies in preventing claims arising, and improving the quality of services is crucial. Private law is too problematic to be the main method of ensuring quality standards,[50] and other mechanisms are needed to regulate the profession in order to protect the interests of consumers of legal services.

---

[46] *First Annual Report of the Legal Services Ombudsman 1991*, at p.9.
[47] Mechanisms for dealing with complaints about inadequate professional service will be dealt with in Chapter 5.
[48] See *Seventh Annual Report of the Legal Services Ombudsman 1997*, at p.16; *Sixth Annual Report of the Legal Services Ombudsman 1996*, at p.29.
[49] *Fourth Annual Report of the Legal Services Ombudsman 1994*, at p.21.
[50] See M. Monti, "The liability of lawyers as suppliers of services," *New Law Journal*, October 6, 1995.

Chapter 3

The Statutory Framework

The legal profession, in common with other professions, operates within a statutory framework, and despite protestations of autonomy, a profession "necessarily derives its regulatory powers from the state".[1] As we saw in Chapter 1, the standard justification for intervention by the state in consumer matters is the failure of the market to provide adequate safeguards for consumers. Chapter 2 illustrated the way in which private law mechanisms for obtaining redress against the legal profession are problematic and fraught with difficulty. A strong regulatory framework can provide the necessary safeguarding of standards. However, intervention by the state in the control of the professions is not simply a consumer protection mechanism. In many respects, it is the price to be paid for professional closure. Thus, in return for the state's granting legally based privileges, which ensure monopoly provision by the profession, the profession accepts some regulation by the state. State regulation has additional benefits, in that it plays a part in providing reassurance for consumers on the services offered by the profession. Where lawyers are concerned this is particularly important, given the central role which law plays in democratic life.

Again, in common with other professions, the legal profession operates largely by means of self-regulation. The statutory framework is in a sense just that, a framework within which the legal profession performs its self-regulatory functions. Regulation of professions usually conforms to a pattern, whereby legislation creates and gives authority to a professional body, which is then empowered to regulate entry into the profession, and to lay down quality and ethical standards for practice. The appropriate balance between government regulation and self-regulation of the legal profession in protecting consumer interests

---

[1] R. Abel, *The Legal Profession in England and Wales* (1988), at p.29 [Oxford: Blackwell].

is a matter of debate. The succeeding chapters will evaluate the various mechanisms for consumer protection, and assess their effectiveness in ensuring that consumer interests are safeguarded. The purpose of this chapter is to set out the statutory framework on which self-regulation is based and, as such, lay the foundations for the succeeding chapters.

Although this chapter is concerned with the statutory framework for regulating the legal profession, there are, in fact, few statutory restrictions on non-lawyers undertaking legal work. Legislation does not prevent the giving of legal advice by any lay person. However, the few statutory restrictions which do exist are such as to make the effective provision of legal services by non-lawyers impossible. These statutory restrictions are discussed later in the chapter.

Solicitors

As discussed in Chapter 1, solicitors and barristers are two separate professions, and this has resulted in separate statutory frameworks for their governance. As we have seen, the solicitor's profession is far from homogeneous. However, all solicitors, whether employed or self-employed, whether salaried or partners, whether in the public or private sector, are governed by the same professional body, the Law Society. This is an independent body, which represents the interests of solicitors, but it is also the statutory body for their regulation.[2]

The Law Society obtained its Royal Charter in 1845, but its origins date back to 1739, when the Society of Gentlemen Practisers in the Courts of Law and Equity was founded. The present organisation was founded in 1826 as the Law Institution, and this received a Royal Charter in 1831 under the name of the Society of Attorneys, Solicitors, Protectors and others, not being Barristers, practising in the Courts of Law and Equity in the United Kingdom. Its present Royal Charter was granted in 1845, and this sets out its purposes as "promoting professional improvement, and facilitating the acquisition of legal knowledge". There has been a series of supplemental charters since then, in 1872, 1903, 1909, and 1954, and it was the supplemental Charter of 1903 which gave it its present name, the Law Society.[3]

---

[2] There is also an organisation called the British Legal Association, set up in 1964, with explicit trade union goals.

[3] For an account of the history of the Law Society, see D. Sugarman, "Bourgeois collectivism, professional power and the boundaries of the State. The private and public

Since 1845, the Law Society has acquired powers to regulate the profession, including keeping the register of Attorneys and Solicitors. It has also become responsible for the conduct of examinations for those wishing to enter the profession, and reporting charges of misconduct against solicitors to the court. Its source of authority to regulate derives largely, though not entirely, from statute. In 1907, it was given power to investigate the accounts of solicitors and to issue practising certificates. It was the Solicitors Act 1933 which first gave the Law Society power to make rules relating to solicitors' accounts and rules for regulating the professional practice, conduct and discipline of solicitors.

Membership of the Law Society is voluntary, although non-members are still regulated by the society. The majority of solicitors are members. The Law Society is governed by an elected Council of 75 members. Of these, 61 are elected by members on a constituency basis. These then elect a further 14, to represent categories of solicitors or areas of practice which are under-represented on the Council, or who have specialist knowledge on particular aspects of legal practice. Council members are elected for a four-year term of office. The Council is led by an elected President, who serves for a term of office of one year.

The Council meets eight times a year, but much of the work of the society is delegated to standing committees. The standing committees cover the following areas: training; professional standards; adjudication of complaints; practice development; courts and legal services; property law and commercial services; international affairs; finances and strategic policy. Membership of these standing committees is not confined to Council members, and members are also drawn from the profession as a whole. There is also a number of Law Society advisory committees.[4]

The Law Society is managed through a number of directorates and divisions, as follows:

1. co-ordination division;

2. communications division;

3. management division;

---

life of the Law Society, 1825 to 1914" (1996) 3(1/2) *International Journal of the Legal Profession* 81–135.
[4] The Law Society is about to undergo fundamental change to its structures. See R. Sayer, "Changing Times," *Law Society Gazette*, October 14, 1998, p.18.

4. legal practice directorate, which has an international subdivision;

5. professional standards and development directorate.

There is a management board, which consists of senior representatives from the divisions and directorates, together with the Secretary-General of the Law Society and the director of the Office for the Supervision of Solicitors. The annual income of the Law Society is over £55 million.[5]

The statutory framework for the regulation of solicitors

It is the Solicitors Act 1974, as amended by subsequent legislation, which provides much of the regulatory framework for the solicitors' branch of the profession. Section 1 of this Act makes it clear that no person is qualified to act as a solicitor unless he or she is admitted as a solicitor, has his or her name on the roll of solicitors, and holds a current practising certificate. This Act provides the Law Society with the power to make rules about accounts, and the regulation of professional practice, conduct and discipline.[6] The Act also gave powers to the Law Society to establish a compensation fund and to provide for professional indemnity cover. It extended the power of the Law Society to make regulations relating to the education and training of those wishing to be admitted as solicitors and in relation to training once admitted into the profession.[7]

No solicitor can practise as a solicitor without a current practising certificate. The power to issue these was granted to the Law Society in 1907. The 1974 Act removed the statutory maximum fee payable for practising certificates, and allowed for reduced fees to be paid in certain circumstances.[8] Further amendments were made to these regulations by the Courts and Legal Services Act 1990, which allowed for the broad powers in the 1974 Act to set reduced fees to be related to income from practice. The 1990 Act also made additions to the rules about the imposition of conditions to be attached to the granting of practising certificates, and to the imposition of conditions on a current certificate before it expired. The Law Society is also

[5] *Annual Report and Accounts of the Law Society 1997–98.*
[6] These are similar powers to those contained in the 1933 Solicitors Act
[7] s. 2.
[8] s. 6.

empowered to suspend a practising certificate where the solicitor is involved in fraud or serious crimes.

The Law Society also has authority to regulate solicitors by virtue of the Financial Services Act 1986. This is because the Law Society is one of a number of bodies authorised to regulate financial services under the regulatory regime set up under that Act.[9]

Consumer protection

It was the 1974 Act which extended the power of the Law Society to intervene in a solicitor's practice in order to safeguard a client's interest. Law Society was permitted to intervene if a solicitor[10] was suspected of dishonesty in connection with his or her practice or in the administration of any trust of which he or she was a trustee. Intervention can also occur where the conduct or incapacity of a solicitor could have a detrimental effect on his or her ability to provide services of a professional standard to clients. These include situations where a solicitor has been committed to prison, where there has been a failure to comply with rules relating to accounts or adequate professional indemnity cover, or where a solicitor is declared bankrupt. The Law Society can intervene in the practice of a sole practitioner, where the solicitor is so incapable, either through illness or accident, as to be unable to attend to his or her practice. This power is also available where the solicitor is made the subject of certain Mental Health Act powers, or where he or she is struck off or removed from the roll of solicitors.[11]

The Courts and Legal Services Act 1990 added further situations where there could be intervention in a solicitor's practice. The Law Society can now intervene where it is satisfied that a sole practitioner has abandoned his or her practice, or is incapacitated by age from attending to it. There can also be intervention where a sole practitioner is suspected of dishonesty, or if he or she has acted without having a practising certificate, or has failed to comply with a condition attached to a grant of such certificate.[12]

Another consumer protection mechanism provided by the 1974 Act was that which enabled the Lord Chancellor to appoint lay observers,

---

[9] The new proposals in relation to the regulation of financial services will have an impact on the Law Society's regulatory function in this respect.

[10] This includes employees of solicitors, and the personal representatives of deceased solicitors.

[11] s. 35, and Sched 1.

[12] s. 91.

paid out of public funds, to examine the handling by the Law Society of complaints against solicitors.[13] This provision resulted in the appointment of the Lay Observer, the forerunner of the Legal Services Ombudsman,[14] and it represents an acknowledgment that some lay input is necessary in complaint handling by the profession. The 1974 Act also provided for some lay input into other aspects of the regulatory functions of the Law Society, by allowing the Law Society to delegate some of its functions to committees which have non-solicitor members.[15]

The provision which allowed delegation to committees, did not go far enough, with the result that the Law Society had difficulty in meeting demands for greater lay participation in its regulatory work. At least half the members of such committees had to be members of the Council of the Law Society, and there was no power for the committees to appoint sub-committees. The Courts and Legal Services Act 1990 rectifies this, by allowing the Council to delegate its functions to committees, sub-committees, and individuals who need not necessarily be members of the Law Society or the Council, or even be solicitors. Some functions cannot be delegated. These include the making of rules and regulations about training, professional practice, conduct and discipline, accounts, the compensation fund, professional indemnity requirements, and fees for practising certificates or for removing or restoring a name on the roll of solicitors.

Remedies for consumers

Before 1985, the remedies available to clients who were dissatisfied with their solicitors were limited. If the matter involved professional misconduct it could be dealt with by the Solicitors' Disciplinary Tribunal. Matters of professional negligence could be pursued through a civil action in court. In the case of dissatisfaction with costs, the bill could be reduced in taxation.

Taxation is a method used to establish whether a solicitor's bill is fair and reasonable. It is the only method of checking a bill where there have been court proceedings, although it can also be used for other work. It does not involve the Law Society. It is a remedy sought from the court, which makes an assessment of the fairness and reasonableness of the costs charged by a solicitor. The client can make

---

[13] s. 7.
[14] The role of the Legal Services Ombudsman is discussed in Chapter 6.
[15] s. 79.

the application for taxation, or can instruct another solicitor to do so. It is a risky strategy because it could result in the client's paying court costs. If the result of the taxation is that the bill is reduced by less than 20 per cent, the client will almost certainly have to pay the solicitor's costs and his or her own costs of the taxation. The slightly reduced bill may be small consolation here. If the bill is reduced by more than 20 per cent, the solicitor will usually have to pay all the costs of the taxation.

In addition to the risk of having to pay costs as well as the original bill, there are strict time limits for implementing this procedure. To ensure that the court will order taxation, the application must be made within one month of receiving the bill. If the application is made between one and 12 months from the receipt of the bill, the court is not obliged to allow it. For applications made after 12 months from the receipt of the bill, or within 12 months, but after the bill has been paid, the client may have to prove to the court that there are special circumstances, before the application will be allowed. If the bill has been paid and over 12 months have elapsed, the court cannot order taxation. Solicitors have an obligation to advise clients of their right to use the taxation procedure.

Actions for professional negligence are discussed in Chapter 2, and the Solicitors' Disciplinary Tribunal is dealt with in Chapter 4. These mechanisms, together with taxation, did not however provide a complete remedy. They did not cover situations where the quality of service was inadequate, but the client had not suffered financial loss which was serious enough to justify negligence proceedings, or where the matter was not sufficiently serious to involve disciplinary proceedings.

The Benson Report[16] had recommended that, in addition to the power to deal with allegations of professional misconduct, the Law Society ought to be able to deal with complaints about bad professional work, irrespective of whether this would give rise to a claim in the courts. Measures to achieve this were provided by the Administration of Justice Act 1985, which inserted a new section 44A into the Solicitors Act 1974. The new remedy was to cover work which was "too shoddy to be paid for, without necessarily giving rise to negligence,"[17] for example undue delay, a failure to keep clients informed, or undue rudeness. It was the Law Society which requested the inclusion of these measures, but they were, in essence, a response

---

[16] *Report on the Royal Commission on Legal Services* (The Benson Report), Cmnd. 7648 (1979), para. 24.25.
[17] Lord Hailsham, H.L. Deb., vol. 458, col. 825, January 14, 1985.

to public dissatisfaction with the existing regime for disciplinary control of solicitors. The new section 44A provided for additional remedies for clients, by giving the Law Society powers to impose a wide range of sanctions, which were partly disciplinary and partly compensatory. These included waiving or repaying fees, or varying the costs which a solicitor could recover.

These provisions were amended by the Courts and Legal Services Act 1990,[18] which inserted a new section 37A and a new schedule into the 1974 Act. The result of the amendment is increased powers for the Law Society to direct payment of compensation to clients where a solicitor has provided inadequate professional service. In doing so it seeks to draw a distinction between complaints which involve the disciplinary functions of the Law Society and those where the issue is about the quality of service provided. How these provisions have been implemented will be discussed in Chapter 5.

Barristers

In contrast to solicitors, and indeed in contrast to the legal professions of other common law jurisdictions,[19] the Bar remained largely free of statutory regulation until the Courts and Legal Services Act 1990. Unlike the Law Society, the General Council of the Bar (the Bar Council), the regulatory body for barristers, had no statutory authority for its work. It was given statutory authority by section 31 of the Courts and Legal Services Act, which recognised it as the authorised body for barristers. Historically, it was the four Inns of Court which regulated the conduct of barristers. These were voluntary societies, and it was not until 1895 that the Bar Council was established, with responsibility for dealing with matters of "professional etiquette". These responsibilities were redefined in 1946, with the introduction of a new constitution.

In 1976 the Bar Council and the Senate, the governing body of the Inns of Court, combined to form the Senate of the Inns of Court and the Bar. This was disbanded in 1986, when it was replaced by the General Council of the Bar, and a separate Council of the Inns of Court. The Bar Council is the representative body for barristers, representing the general interests of the profession. It is also

---

[18] s. 93.

[19] A. Thornton, "The Professional Responsibility and Ethics of the English Bar" in *Legal Ethics and Professional Responsibility* (R. Cranston ed., 1995), at p.57 [Oxford: Clarendon Press].

responsible for the maintenance of professional standards. Since the mid-twentieth century, there has been a gradual erosion of the powers of the Inns, at the expense of the Bar Council. Their role in providing qualifications for practice is, however, preserved by the Courts and Legal Services Act. Under the Act no person shall have a right of audience as a barrister unless he or she has been called to the Bar by one of the Inns of Court.[20]

Because the Bar Council is not a statutory body, this has caused problems for enforcing the requirement that all barristers have to be current subscribers to the Bar Council. The Law Society can enforce the requirement for subscriptions because it has statutory authority to require all practising solicitors to have a practising certificate, and it can use the income from this to finance its activities. The Bar Council has no such authority, and, although only about 5 per cent of practising barristers do not pay, the legality of imposing a compulsory subscription was challenged during a disciplinary action.[21] The Council of the Inns of Court decided that the rule about compulsory subscriptions was lawful, but that it could not be enforced by disciplinary sanction. This was because it would be an unjustified restraint of trade, as the sanction could involve the loss of livelihood if the barrister was disbarred or suspended. The Bar Council has been unable to introduce a rule[22] to prevent barristers in default exercising rights of audience.

Barristers are sole practitioners, and are prohibited from conducting their profession in partnership. The Courts and Legal Services Act 1990 Act did provide for the introduction of multi-disciplinary and multi-national partnerships for barristers, but also allows the Bar Council to prohibit such partnerships.[23] There are, however, pressures in this country and in the European Union to encourage such practices. This will put pressure on the Bar Council to allow barristers some rights of association with other professionals, although it is felt that the Bar Council will be strongly opposed to permitting barristers to act in partnership with solicitors.[24] There are also proposals to

---

[20] s. 27(3).

[21] Report in *The Guardian*, October 2, 1990, of *S (A Barrister)*, a decision of a disciplinary tribunal of the Council of the Inns of Court, July 26, 1990.

[22] This was under the approval machinery of the Courts and Legal Services Act 1990, which is discussed later in the chapter.

[23] s. 66.

[24] A. Thornton, "The Professional Responsibility and Ethics of the English Bar" in *Legal Ethics and Professional Responsibility* (R. Cranston ed., 1995), at p.66 [Oxford: Clarendon Press].

allow more direct access to barristers,[25] so that it would cease to be an exclusively referral profession.[26]

Until 1980, the Bar had no written code of conduct, such matters being based on tradition. There is now a Code of Conduct, which sets practising standards, and the Bar Council is responsible for promoting amendments to the Code, and for investigating disciplinary complaints. The Bar Council is not directly controlled by the state, but, as a result of the Courts and Legal Services Act 1990, rules of conduct, education and training have to conform to the requirements of the Act. The statutory approved rules of conduct must be observed by barristers when exercising rights of audience as barristers. The 1990 Act also brought the work of barristers within the regulatory framework of anti-discrimination legislation, by making pupillages and barristers' chambers subject to the Sex Discrimination Act 1975 and the Race Relations Act 1976 for the first time.[27]

Restrictive practices

There are few statutory restrictions on the carrying out of legal services, and there is no general monopoly on the giving of legal advice.[28] The statutory restrictions concern the preparation of certain documents for reward. For example, it is an offence for an unqualified person to prepare the necessary documents connected with the transfer of title to property.[29] This restriction does not cover the preliminary stages of conveyancing, but it has the effect of ensuring effective protection over the conveyancing business for solicitors.[30]

There are no restrictions on non-lawyers preparing wills, but only

---

[25] At present, barristers are instructed by "professional clients". These are mainly solicitors, but also include patent agents, licensed conveyancers, the Government Legal Service, and the legal departments of local and public authorities (if these are headed by a solicitor or barrister). (S.Bailey and M. Gunn, *Smith and Bailey on the Modern English Legal System* (3rd ed., 1996), at p.152 [Sweet and Maxwell].

[26] There are a number of proposals, ranging from preserving the status quo; access for certain licensed bodies, for example, trade unions, and financial institutions; and complete access for private individuals.

[27] s. 64.

[28] The Government has acknowledged the role of those not qualified as lawyers in the advice sector. It believes that the "existence of alternative forms of provider is generally in the public interest". However, it does not rule out some form of regulation in the giving of legal advice, where this would be in the public interest. There are, for example, proposals to regulate those who provide advice about immigration and asylum issues (*Modernising Justice*, White Paper, Cm.4155 (1998), paras. 2.19–2.20).

[29] Solicitors Act 1974, s. 22.

[30] Since 1985, this monopoly has been extended to licensed conveyancers.

qualified persons can prepare the documents for a grant of probate or letters of administration. These formal documents only account for a small part of the work involved in the administration of an estate. The effect of them, however, is usually to ensure that all the work involved in administering the estate of a deceased person is done by solicitors.[31] The right to issue a writ, for the commencement of court proceedings, is restricted to solicitors, and in general only solicitors and barristers have rights of audience, allowing them to act as representatives in court.[32]

Although few in number, these monopolies became the "principal protectors of the exclusivity of the legal profession," and they were effective in reserving most legal work for barristers and solicitors.[33] When a Royal Commission on Legal Services was set up in 1976 to examine the structure, organisation, training and regulation of the legal profession, it also examined the monopolies enjoyed by the profession. The Commission concluded that all was well, and made no recommendations for major change.[34] It concluded that the divided profession was in the public interest, and that fusion of the solicitors' and barristers' branches of the profession would lead to a decline in standards. It recommended that the Bar's monopoly of advocacy in the higher courts should be retained, as this was a means of protecting standards, and that the conveyancing monopoly should also be retained. In its unreserved acceptance of the status quo, it missed an opportunity to protect the interests of consumers. It appeared to have an almost "unseemly desire ... to protect the interests ... of the legal profession".[35]

The immense relief of the profession "at this outcome of the first major inquiries into its activities"[36] was short-lived. In 1983, a Private Members Bill to abolish the conveyancing monopoly was

---

[31] Barristers are not prohibited by statute from undertaking probate (or conveyancing) work, but in practice they do not do so.

[32] Section 11 of the Courts and Legal Services Act 1990 allowed the Lord Chancellor to provide for unrestricted rights of audience in case of debt, housing and small claims procedures in the county court. Representation in these cases can be by non-lawyers. The only restriction is that the county court can exclude representatives who are unruly or demonstrably unsuitable. The Institute of Legal Executives can now also grant limited rights of audience in the lower courts to its Fellows.

[33] R.White, *A Guide to the Courts and Legal Services Act 1990* (1991), at p.2 [London: Fourmat].

[34] *Report on the Royal Commission on Legal Services* (The Benson Report), Cmnd. 7648 (1979).

[35] M. Stephens, "Law Centres and Citizenship: The Way Forward" in *Law in the Balance. Legal services in the 1980s* (P. Thomas ed., 1982) [Oxford: Martin Robertson].

[36] M. Zander, "The Thatcher Government's Onslaught on the Lawyers: Who Won?" (1990) 24 *The International Lawyer* 753–785.

introduced.[37] Although the Bill was not successful, the Government decided to back the proposal, by making the necessary provisions in Part II of the Administration of Justice Act 1985. The provisions,[38] introduced at a late stage in the process of the legislation, allowed for the extension of the conveyancing monopoly to licensed conveyancers, thus allowing competition with solicitors. The provision was little debated, and one effect of it was to determine the extent of the monopoly, by giving it a statutory definition.

The extension of the monopoly was heralded as a triumph for consumers. However, only a modest number of licensed conveyancers have set up in practice. The introduction of a new group of professionals into the market seems however to have made conveyancing work more competitive. Research has shown that the introduction of competition into this area of the market for legal services has brought significant benefits for consumers. Price discrimination has been reduced, conveyancing costs have fallen in real terms, and there has been a measurable improvement in consumer satisfaction.[39] There is, however, some concern in the profession that very low price conveyancing means corner-cutting. This raises the likelihood of mistakes, which can affect both the reputation of the profession and the cost of indemnity insurance.[40] There has been a reduction in the numbers of solicitors undertaking conveyancing work. In 1989, there were some 22,000 solicitors engaged in residential conveyancing work. This had reduced to about 15,000 in 1997.[41] Anecdotal evidence suggests that it is high street firms in small towns, which have lost business to the small numbers[42] of licensed conveyancers.

---

[37] By Austin Mitchell, M.P.

[38] ss. 9 and 10.

[39] See S. Domberger and A. Sherr, "The Impact of Competition on Pricing and Quality of Legal Services" in *The Regulatory Challenge* (M. Bishop, J. Kay and C. Mayer eds., 1995) [Oxford: Oxford University Press].

[40] S. Bailey and M. Gunn, *Smith and Bailey on the Modern English Legal System* (3rd ed., 1996), at p.131 [Sweet and Maxwell].

[41] B. Cole, *Solicitors in Private Practice. Their Work and Expectations*, Findings from the Law Society Omnibus Survey, Research Study No. 26 (1997) [Research and Policy Planning Unit: The Law Society].

[42] By 1995, there were about 350 licensed conveyancers in practice, together with about 450 more in employment (S. Bailey and M. Gunn, *Smith and Bailey on the Modern English Legal System* (3rd ed., 1996), p.131 [Sweet & Maxwell]).

Rights of audience and the conduct of litigation

Rights of audience are the rights "to exercise any of the functions of appearing before and addressing a court including the calling and examining of witnesses".[43] A right of audience, the right to act as an advocate, was traditionally the preserve of barristers in private practice, except for formal or unopposed matters. A right to conduct litigation involves the issuing of writs to start legal proceedings and the other preparatory work connected with such proceedings. This is the preserve of solicitors. As a result of these restrictions, consumers were obliged to engage the services of two lawyers, if the matters had to be dealt with in the higher courts. There is, of course, no bar to persons representing themselves. Nor are there any restrictions on rights of audience in the small claims procedure in the county court, or for certain tribunals.

The justifications for restricting rights of audience to lawyers have been well rehearsed.[44] The main argument is that, in an adversarial system, judges rely on independent and expert presentation of evidence and argument, as they are unable to investigate cases themselves. Untrained advocates could not be relied on to perform this function. This might have adverse consequences not only for the party employing an untrained advocate, but also for the other party, the courts, and the wider public. It could undermine the operation of the system of justice. It could involve delays and unnecessary appeals. It could interfere with the efficiency and cost-effectiveness of the court system.[45]

These are arguments for restricting rights of audience to lawyers. They do not justify their restriction to one branch of the legal profession, barristers. After solicitors lost the conveyancing monopoly, rights of audience became an issue for contention, with solicitors calling for the same rights as those enjoyed by barristers. As a result, a joint committee of the Bar Council and Law Society[46] was set up to look at the work of the profession. It became clear, however, that there was an irreconcilable conflict between the two branches of the profession on the issue of rights of audience in the higher courts,

---

[43] Courts and Legal Services Act 1990, s. 119.

[44] See *The Work and Organisation of the Legal Profession*, Green Paper, Cm.570 (1989).

[45] See *Rights of Audience and Rights to Conduct Litigation in England and Wales: The Way Ahead*, Lord Chancellor's Department (1998), pp.6–7.

[46] The Marre Committee.

which was the main issue before it. Not surprisingly, when it reported in 1988,[47] it had failed to reach agreement about this.

The Bar has used several justifications for preserving the monopoly of rights of audience in the higher courts for barristers in private practice. One of the main arguments is that it is only barristers who are sufficiently independent to do so. This independence is a function of the fact that they are self-employed, and therefore have no financial obligations to partners or employers. It is also argued that this is the only way to guarantee quality, and that only the independent Bar has the breadth of experience to appear in the higher courts. A final but least convincing argument is that to extend these rights would jeopardise the viability of the Bar as an independent profession.[48]

None of these arguments convinced the previous Government, and the Courts and Legal Services Act 1990 made provision for allowing rights of audience in the higher courts to be available to a wider range of lawyers.[49] Before this Act, barristers in private practice had full rights of audience in all courts. Solicitors had rights of audience in the lower courts, the county courts and magistrates' courts. Employed[50] barristers had similar rights to those enjoyed by solicitors.[51] One of the purposes of the Act was to extend rights of audience in the higher courts to solicitors and employed barristers. The mechanisms put in place by the Act to achieve this, which are discussed later in the chapter, have achieved very little. Although the Law Society has been able to grant rights of audience in the higher courts to solicitors since 1993,[52] less than 700 solicitors, out of more than 70,000, have done so. Barristers have retained an effective monopoly.

The present Government is unhappy with this situation, which is felt to be against the public interest.[53] It wants to make services by lawyers more affordable, for private clients and taxpayers, principally by eliminating unnecessary restrictive practices which reduce choice

---

[47] *Report of the Committee on the Future of the Legal Profession: A Time for Change*, July 1988, Bar Council and Council of the Law Society.

[48] *Rights of Audience and Rights to Conduct Litigation in England and Wales: The Way Ahead*, Lord Chancellor's Department (1998), at pp. 9–14.

[49] Since April 1998, the Institute of Legal Executives has been able to grant limited rights of audience in the lower courts to its Fellows.

[50] This term applies to barristers who provide legal services to an employer, rather than the public at large, as is the case with barristers in private practice. Typical employers are commercial companies and Government, particularly the Crown Prosecution Service.

[51] Rule 402.1(c) of the Bar's Code of Conduct limits the right of employed barristers to exercise rights of audience.

[52] Solicitors who are granted these rights have to meet the training requirements approved for this purpose.

[53] *Rights of Audience and Rights to Conduct Litigation in England and Wales: The Way Ahead*, Lord Chancellor's Department (1998).

and competition. It is particularly concerned about the restrictions on employed lawyers,[54] which prevent their appearing in the higher courts. The Government is proposing therefore that, in future, all barristers and solicitors will in principle be qualified to appear in the higher courts. Professional bodies will still be able to set additional training requirements. However, once a lawyer is granted these rights they should not be restricted if the lawyer transfers from one branch of the profession to the other or if he or she becomes employed.[55] In order to achieve these objectives, the Government is making radical changes to the regulatory framework set up by the 1990 Courts and Legal Services Act.[56] The changes to the regulatory process are discussed later in the chapter.

The right to conduct litigation has not caused as much controversy as rights of audience. Nevertheless, the Government proposes to extend this right to the Bar, and to the Institute of Legal Executives.[57]

Conditional fee arrangements

The Courts and Legal Services Act 1990 sought to increase access to legal services by modifying the restrictions on the way lawyers charge for services. In the past, lawyers were not allowed to charge conditional or contingency fees. Conditional fees are where fees are fixed in advance, but only charged if the case is won. Contingency fee arrangements are where the fees are calculated in accordance with the sum obtained in damages. The traditional argument against allowing fees to be based on outcome is that the lawyer's professional integrity may be compromised if he or she has a financial interest in the outcome of a case. There are, however, arguments in favour of such arrangements, in that they could result in an increase in access to legal services to those who would otherwise be unable to afford them.

Since 1991, it has been possible for solicitors to charge conditional fees,[58] in certain types of cases.[59] In practice, they are only used for

---

[54] A particular concern is employed barristers in the Crown Prosecution Service.

[55] *Modernising Justice*, White Paper, Cm.4155 (1998), para.2.27.

[56] The proposals are being implemented by means of the Access to Justice Bill, which was introduced into Parliament on December 2, 1998 in the House of Lords. It was given its second Reading on December 14, 1998, and it went to the Committee stage on January 19, 1999. It began its process through the House of Commons in April 1999.

[57] Access to Justice Bill, clause 34.

[58] Courts and Legal Services Act 1990, s. 58, and the Conditional Fees Agreements Order 1995, S.I. 1995, No. 1674.

[59] These are personal injury, insolvency and human rights claims.

personal injury cases.[60] Under conditional fee arrangements, if the case is lost, the client pays nothing or pays only for disbursements. If the case is won, the client agrees to pay a "success" fee. In successful cases, the losing party is usually ordered to pay the costs of the other party. This will include the "normal" costs charged by the lawyer. Under conditional fee arrangements, the successful client will therefore have to pay the additional "success" fee from whatever damages have been awarded. Success fees cannot be more than 100 per cent of the solicitor's normal fee. Most solicitors have agreed that the success fee should not be more than 25 per cent of any damages recovered. The practice of charging contingency fees is still prohibited. It is difficult to see why, given that lawyers have a financial interest in the outcome in conditional fee arrangements, but there appears to be no plan to allow them.[61]

In 1998, the Government announced that the conditional fee arrangements would be extended to all money and damages actions. There would then be a withdrawal of legal aid for such actions.[62] The freedom to use conditional fees where appropriate was welcomed by the profession, but there was concern about the withdrawal of legal aid.[63] As a result of the criticisms,[64] the proposals were modified to restrict the withdrawal of Legal Aid to personal injury cases, excluding medical negligence.[65] Since July 1998, conditional fee arrangements can apply in all civil cases, except family proceedings. In the future, they will apply to the property aspects of family proceedings, but not for child-care or domestic violence cases.[66] There are also proposals to enable the courts to include the "success" fee and any other excess fees (for example, any insurance premium) in the award of costs against the losing party.[67]

---

[60] S. Yarrow, *The Price of Success: Lawyers and Conditional Fees* (1997), at p.12 [Policy Studies Institute: London].

[61] M. Zander, "The Government's Plans on Legal Aid and Conditional Fees" (1998) *Modern Law Review* 538–550, at p.547.

[62] This radical move was first proposed by the Conservative Government in its Green Paper, *Legal Aid — Targeting the Need*, Cm.2854 (1995), and the White Paper, *Striking the Balance — the Future of Legal Aid in England and Wales*, Cm.3305 (1996). It was opposed by Labour in opposition.

[63] See *Law Society Annual Report and Accounts 1997–98*, at p.7.

[64] For a discussion of the debate see M. Zander, "The Government's Plans on Legal Aid and Conditional Fees" (1998) *Modern Law Review* 538–550

[65] It appears that there is still some doubt about whether the proposed Access to Justice Bill will remove personal injury cases from the scope of legal aid. See *Law Society Gazette*, November 25, 1998, at p.1.

[66] Access to Justice Bill, clause 27. See also, *Modernising Justice*, White Paper, Cm.4155 (1998), para.2.43.

[67] Access to Justice Bill, clause 28. See also, *Modernising Justice*, White Paper, Cm.4155 (1998), para.2.44.

The extension of conditional fee arrangements may provide legal services for consumers who would otherwise be unable to pay for them. However, it has been argued that they may not be entirely in the consumer interest. Lawyers may exaggerate the extent of the risk in bringing an action, and thus inflate the success fee. The main criticisms of the proposals however relate to the linking of conditional fees with legal aid, and using the changes as a reason to withdraw it.[68]

The Courts and Legal Services Act 1990

As has been indicated throughout this chapter, major changes to the regulation of the legal profession were brought about by the Courts and Legal Services Act 1990. This was a major piece of legislation, containing 125 sections, 20 schedules, and 201 pages. It has been described as "one of the most important pieces of legislation affecting the delivery of legal services" and one of the "great reforming statutes of the second half of this century".[69] It is largely an enabling Act providing the framework for regulation, with the regulations themselves to be provided by the authorised bodies and other schemes provided by the Act. It follows very closely the principles listed in the White Paper, in which the Government's two aims were set out. These were first, that there should be the widest range of choice in legal services, compatible with the maintenance of standards, and second, that the courts should have quick and cost-effective procedures, making them both accessible and fair. The overall aim was to improve access to good quality legal services, the courts and "ultimately to justice".[70]

The Bill was first debated in the House of Lords. When it was introduced, the then Lord Chancellor, Lord Mackay, said that the Government's "keynote" was to improve access to justice for all who needed it. There were three elements to this: a just and efficient court system; sufficient legal services of the right kinds to meet clients' needs both in relation to the courts and more generally; and an efficient and effective scheme to make public funds available to those who needed legal services and could not meet the costs themselves. This last aim had been tackled by means of the Legal Aid Act 1988, which had set up a new system for the operation of the legal aid

---

[68] M. Zander, "The Government's Plans on Legal Aid and Conditional Fees" (1998) *Modern Law Review* 538–550, at pp.548–549.

[69] R White, *A Guide to the Courts and Legal Services Act 1990*, (1991) [London: Format].

[70] *Legal Services: A Framework for the Future*, White Paper, Cm.740 (1989), at p.4.

scheme. The newly formed Legal Aid Board[71] had been charged with examining new and better ways of delivering legal services to those unable to fund such services themselves.[72] The first aim, the provision of a just and efficient court system, is dealt with in Part I of the Act. This deals with procedure in the civil courts, and largely implements the provisions of the *Civil Justice Review*.[73]

It was the second aim of the Act, the provision of sufficient legal services, which resulted in far-reaching changes for the regulation of the legal profession. The Lord Chancellor said that the Bill did not attempt to create a ready-made and immutable template for the way in which legal services were to be provided. Rather, this aim was to be achieved by creating "a framework" which would "foster evolution in legal services, allowing them to be more varied and better adapted to clients' needs". The importance of the consumer input was emphasised, with the aim being "to ensure that the voice of the user of legal services" would be heard when questions of the provision of legal services were decided. In addition, the widening of the provision of legal services emphasised the central importance of maintaining and improving the professional quality of those services.[74]

The Act was certainly an inroad into the self-regulation concept, and the Government was accused of engaging in "an exercise in the political dogma of competition" which would damage "one of our oldest professions" and the administration of justice.[75] On the other hand, however, others welcomed the Act, because, in enhancing competition, it was felt to enhance "the drive of legal services to serve the consumer". It was thought to help to establish a basic principle, that "the legal system is a service industry working to serve the people, particularly the consumer of legal services, rather than the self-interest of those who operate it".[76] Others have described the Act as

---

[71] The administration of legal aid is to be changed again, because the reforms did not achieve the objectives. The Government wants to control legal aid, by targeting it on real need, within a budget the taxpayer can afford. To this end, the Legal Aid Board is to be replaced with a Legal Services Commission. This will be charged with developing local, regional and national plans to match the delivery of legal services to identified needs and priorities. It will also manage the Community Legal Services Fund, which will replace legal aid (*Modernising Justice*, White Paper, Cm.4155 (1998), para.1.4). These proposals have been included in the Access to Justice Bill which is now progressing through Parliament.

[72] H.L. vol.514, col.122, December 19, 1989, second reading.

[73] *Civil Justice Review*, Report of the Review Body on Civil Justice, Cm.394 (1988).

[74] H.L. vol.514, cols.126,128, December 19, 1989, second reading.

[75] Lord Benson, H.L. vol.514, December 19, 1989.

[76] Austin Mitchell, M.P., H.C. vol.170, col.1521, April 18, 1990.

another manifestation of the Thatcher government's political crusade against restrictive practices in all areas of economic activity.[77]

The background to the 1990 Act

In order to understand the rationale of the Act, it is necessary to consider the impetus for these changes. During the 1970s and 1980s the rhetoric of professional privilege, with its emphasis on self-governance and autonomy began to be attacked. Pressures for external, state-driven regulation came as a result of the rise in the number and amount of claims made on the Law Society's compensation fund, with calls for more effective regulation to prevent frauds. Criticisms were made of the high costs of legal services, the poor standards of service, and the fact that there was an unmet need for legal services, particularly among those too poor to seek legal advice. The existing monopolies enjoyed by those delivering legal services were also the subject of attack.[78] It is true that the conveyancing monopoly of solicitors ended in 1985,[79] but it was only extended to licensed conveyancers. It was still an offence for any other person to draw up or prepare documents connected with the transfer of title to property for payment.

It is against this background that Green and White Papers on the legal profession were published by the then Conservative Government. There were three Green Papers,[80] which have been described as "short, sharp and to the point," a reflection of the Government's preference for action not words, and based more on "policy preferences than research".[81] They reflected the Conservative Government's ideology of the discipline of the market, and a belief that competition between the providers of legal services would ensure that consumers would be provided with an efficient and effective network of legal services at the most economical price. If the profession were subject to market forces, it was argued, legal services

---

[77] See, A. Thornton, "The Professional Responsibility and Ethics of the English Bar" in *Legal Ethics and Professional* Responsibility (R. Cranston ed., 1995) [Oxford: Clarendon Press].

[78] See R. White, *A Guide to the Courts and Legal Services Act 1990* (1991), at pp.2–3 [London: Fourmat].

[79] Administration of Justice Act 1985, s. 11.

[80] *The Work and Organisation of the Legal Profession*, Cm.570 (1989); *Contingency Fees*, Cm.571 (1989); *Conveyancing by Authorised Practitioners*, Cm.572 (1989).

[81] R. White, *A Guide to the Courts and Legal Services Act 1990* (1991), at p.8 [London: Fourmat].

would become more efficient, and value for money would be ensured.

The Green Papers represented an attack on the core values of the legal profession.[82] In particular, *The Work and Organisation of the Legal Profession* used the rhetoric of free competition between providers, and the tone was one of deregulation of the profession. Indeed the central tenets of the proposals seemed to espouse the "virtues of competition achieved through deregulation, deprofessionalisation and demystification," and the primacy of the consumer interest.[83] There was some acknowledgment that the public must also be assured of the competence of the providers of legal services, and there is one chapter in the Green Paper which specifically deals with the maintenance of professional standards. Despite the general deregulation rhetoric, this chapter set out the Government's belief that it should be the duty of the professional body to ensure standards of competence and professional conduct, in order to secure protection for clients. It was for the profession itself therefore to ensure that services were offered efficiently; that the providers had expertise; that complaints were investigated promptly, efficiently and impartially; and that there were sanctions for professional misconduct.[84]

The Green Paper[85] proposed that the Lord Chancellor's advisory committee on legal education be reconstituted to form an advisory committee on legal education and conduct. Its main functions were to advise on the arrangements for legal education and training and on codes of conduct. On advice from the committee, the Lord Chancellor would authorise new professional bodies, provided they could ensure appropriate education and training. Professional bodies would also have to demonstrate sufficient control over their members to ensure that satisfactory standards of conduct and behaviour were maintained and enforced. The Green Paper thus proposed that rule making powers be effectively passed to the Lord Chancellor.

The reaction from the legal profession to the Green Papers was largely negative. Indeed, Zander concludes that probably no other event in the history of the profession has ever provoked such a

---

[82] See J. Flood, "Cultures of Globalisation: Professional Restructuring for Internal Markets," in *Professionalism, Competition and Professional Power. Lawyers and the Social Construction of Markets* (Y. Dezalay and D. Sugarman eds., 1995), at p.148 [London: Routledge].

[83] C. Stanley, "Enterprising Lawyers: Changes in the Market for Legal Services" (1991) *The Law Teacher* 44, at p.45.

[84] *The Work and Organisation of the Legal Profession*, Cm.570 (1989), chapter 4, generally, and paras.4.1, 4.2.

[85] *The Work and Organisation of the Legal Profession*, Cm.570 (1989).

"fierce" and "broadly based" negative reaction.[86] The judges in particular were very critical, expressing the view that the proposed functions of the advisory committee in relation to advocacy rights were a breach of the doctrine of the separation of powers. The proposals were described as a threat to "the administration of the law on which our civilisation depends,"[87] and the Green Paper which proposed them as "one of the most sinister documents ever to emanate from Government".[88]

The Bar was critical, calling the proposals a threat to the quality of justice, to the continued existence of the Bar, and to the independence of the judiciary and profession.[89] The Bar was especially critical of the proposals to establish a new advisory committee. It believed that the committee's proposed role in relation to questions of conduct, standards and discipline was a challenge to self-regulation. These should remain matters for the profession and the judges. Not surprisingly, the Bar felt that rights of audience should be controlled by the judges, rather than the proposed advisory committee

The Law Society's initial response was to welcome the Green Papers. It indicated that the Green Paper's stated aims — to raise standards, to offer choice to consumers and to allow fair competition — was in line with the philosophy of the Law Society. Pressure from its members however caused it to respond more critically. In its response, *Striking the Balance*, the Law Society argued that the proposals did not provide adequate protection for the public. The Law Society was not opposed in principle to an advisory committee. It felt that there should be a body to advise on such matters as qualifications, conduct and discipline, which had a lay chairman and a majority of lay members. It was felt, however, that such a body should have its own secretariat, and be independent of Government. If it were not independent, there would be a "dangerous accumulation of powers in the hands of a Government Minister". As for rights of audience, the Law Society felt that this was a matter for primary legislation.[90]

Representatives of consumer interests were generally supportive of the Government's proposals. The Consumers' Association[91] is generally opposed to restrictive practices, believing them to be against

[86] M. Zander, "The Thatcher Government's Onslaught on the Lawyers: Who Won?" (1990) 24 *The Law Teacher* 753–85, at p.752.

[87] Sir Stephen Brown, President of the Family Division, *The Times*, February 23, 1989.

[88] Lord Lane, the Lord Chief Justice, *The Guardian*, February 17, 1989.

[89] Mr Desmond Fennell, Q.C., Chairman of the Bar, *The Guardian* January 26, 1989.

[90] *Striking the Balance* (1989) The Law Society.

[91] Consumers Association, *The Work and Organisation of the Legal Profession: Memorandum from Consumers' Association in response to the Government's Green Paper (Cm 570) of January 1989* (1989).

the interests of consumers. The association agreed with Government philosophy that competition was a means through which the interests of consumers were protected. The National Consumer Council[92] supported most of the proposals, although it wanted an independent council, rather than an advisory committee, to oversee standards and complaints. It did not feel that it was appropriate that the Lord Chancellor should make decisions on these matters. The Director General of Fair Trading[93] was supportive of the overall objective of the Green Papers, but was opposed to some of the proposals. For example, he, too, wanted an independent body, rather than the Lord Chancellor, to decide on rules of conduct and standards, and he was opposed to the sudden ending of the restrictive practices in relation to rights of audience.

When the White Paper[94] was published, it was evident that the Government had changed its emphasis. Although "in content the proposals actually gave little ground on key points,"[95] ideas of competition and the discipline of the market had given way to notions of the need for legal services to be responsive to the needs of clients. The White Paper confirmed that the Government continued to believe that some sort of advisory system was required to ensure that matters of public concern and interest were properly and publicly considered in a reasoned way. It was also necessary to ensure that advice was available to Parliament, the Lord Chancellor, the judiciary and the professions. A forum was therefore needed for the different branches of the profession, to ensure the standards of conduct and competence for those who provided legal services, and to give co-ordination between the practising profession and the academic legal profession.[96]

The policies in the White Paper became the basis of Part II of the Courts and Legal Services Act, which was concerned with legal services.[97] This is the part of the Act which provided for the extension of rights of audience, and for additional providers of litigation, conveyancing and probate services. It also established the

---

[92] National Consumer Council, *Response to the Lord Chancellor's Department's Green Paper* (1989).

[93] Office of Fair Trading, *Green Papers on: The Work and Organisation of the Legal Profession; Conveyancing by Authorised Practitioners; Contingency Fees — Comment by the Director General Of Fair Trading* (1989).

[94] *Legal Services: A Framework for the Future*, White Paper, Cm.740 (1989).

[95] R. White, *A Guide to the Courts and Legal Services Act 1990* (1991), at p.9 [London: Fourmat].

[96] *Legal Services: A Framework for the Future*, White Paper, Cm.740 (1989), para 7.4.

[97] It is this part of the Act which is the main concern of this book. Other parts of the Act are concerned with civil procedure, judicial appointments and arbitration.

office of the Legal Services Ombudsman[98] to deal with complaints
made against the legal profession. It established the new regulatory
framework for the delivery of legal services. Central to this regulatory
framework was the new advisory committee, the Lord Chancellor's
Advisory Committee on Legal Education and Conduct. In the debate
on the Act, the emphasis shifted away from the need for such a
committee to the composition of the committee, especially the lay
element. The Lord Chancellor defended the lay majority, on the basis
that the committee existed primarily to represent the views of the
consumer.

The Lord Chancellor's Advisory Committee on Legal Education and Conduct

Central to the new regulatory framework was the Lord Chancellor's
Advisory Committee on Legal Education and Conduct. This body has
been described as an "enormously significant body" which, although
only technically advisory in function, was in effect "a national legal
services commission" which would be a "key body in shaping legal
services delivery systems".[99] It was criticised by the profession from its
inception. The profession had wanted an independent committee, and
felt that the proposed committee would be incapable of performing its
role because of its lay member majority. One of the major problems
for the profession had been the committee's proposed functions in
relation to conduct. Solicitors and barristers had never considered that
there was a need for an outside body to give advice on the way they
conducted themselves.[1] The overriding concern, however, had been
the feeling that the proposed committee represented a transfer of
power from independent professions and the judiciary, to the
executive, as it was felt that the committee would not be fully
independent of the government.

The committee was established by section 19 of the Courts and
Legal Services Act, and has 17 members, the majority of whom are
lay people. It is chaired by a Lord of Appeal in Ordinary, or a judge
of the Supreme Court. The other members are required by the Act to

---

[98] This is dealt with in Chapter 6.
[99] R. White, *A Guide to the Courts and Legal Services Act 1990* (1991), at p.45 [London:
Fourmat].
[1] See Woolf, "The Lord Chancellor's Advisory Committee" (1989) *The Law Teacher*
132.

be a Circuit Judge, two practising solicitors, two practising barristers,[2] two teachers of law and nine others who must not be practising lawyers. All members are appointed by the Lord Chancellor, after wide consultation. Members are appointed for three years and are eligible for re-appointment after their term expires.

It was given a general duty to assist in the maintenance and development of standards in the education, training and conduct of those offering legal services.[3] One of its main functions was to advise the Lord Chancellor on applications from professional or other bodies who were seeking rights of audience or a right to conduct litigation for their members. The committee had also to keep under review the education and training of the providers of legal services, including continuing education and training. It supervised the rules about education, training and conduct of those seeking the new rights given by the Act. Its supervisory function applied not only to new providers in the area of legal services, but also to rule changes proposed by the Bar and Law Society. Much of the work of the Committee has been in relation to the rules about rights of audience. The Advisory Committee presents an annual report on its work to the Lord Chancellor, which he then lays before Parliament.

Under the revised plans for the regulatory framework[4] the Advisory Committee will be abolished and replaced by a Legal Services Consultative Panel.

The regulatory framework

The "statutory objective" of the 1990 Act is the development of legal services, by making provision for new or better ways of providing them, and a wider choice of persons providing them, while maintaining the proper and efficient administration of justice.[5] This objective applies to all areas of legal services governed by Part II of

---

[2] This is because the two existing authorised bodies at the time of the Act, the Law Society and the Bar Council, were allowed two representatives on the committee. As more bodies become authorised, they too will presumably require two representatives. This would then require an additional number of lay members to preserve the balance between the professional and lay elements of the committee. See *Rights of Audience and Rights to Conduct Litigation in England and Wales: The Way Ahead* (1998), p.22, Lord Chancellor's Department.

[3] s. 20 and Sched 2.

[4] See *Rights of Audience and Rights to Conduct Litigation in England and Wales: The Way Ahead* (1998), at p.22, Lord Chancellor's Department; *Modernising Justice*, White Paper, Cm.4155 (1998), para.2.30; and the Access to Justice Bill, clause 29.

[5] s. 17(1).

the Act. Where the issue is about the granting of rights of audience or rights to conduct litigation to new providers, the "general principle" is that this should be decided according to a limited number of criteria. These are concerned with educational and training qualifications, and membership of an appropriate professional body. In the case of advocacy rights, additional criteria are the professional body's rules about non-discrimination[6] in taking on clients. It has also to be established whether the rules of conduct are appropriate in the interests of the "proper and efficient administration of justice".[7]

The new regulatory framework provides the mechanisms for widening the provision of legal services. In order to encourage diversity of provision, mechanisms are provided for extending the traditional monopolies[8] previously enjoyed by solicitors and barristers to new classes of professionals. This is achieved by setting out procedures for bodies representing professions or practitioners to be recognised as "authorised" under the Act. Once established as "authorised bodies," they can apply for their members to have the rights to provide specified legal services. This was a direct attack on the restrictive practices of the legal profession.

Solicitors and barristers were, however, given an advantageous position by the Act. The Law Society and the Bar Council were automatically recognised as existing authorised bodies. There was a new body created by the Act, the Council of Licensed Conveyancers, which is empowered to make rules and supervise the entry, training and discipline of the new profession of licensed conveyancers.[9] Any newly authorised professional body will have to be recognised according to the approval machinery of the Act. In order to be approved, the body will have to demonstrate that it has appropriate rules of education, training and conduct for its members, and that these rules are enforceable and enforced. So far, only one other body has been authorised, the Institute of Legal Executives.[10]

After becoming an "authorised body," the professional body then has to apply for the rights to conduct the legal services specified in the Act. Neither the Bar Council nor the Law Society had to apply for their existing rights in relation to audience and the conduct of litigation. The Bar Council was deemed to have in force qualification

---

[6] This is the so-called "cab-rank" rule, whereby barristers are prevented from refusing to act for any client provided that the fee is appropriate and they are not otherwise committed.

[7] s. 17(3).

[8] These are: the right to conduct litigation; rights of audience; conveyancing; probate.

[9] s. 53.

[10] This was designated as an authorised body with effect from April 23, 1998. The Chartered Institute of Patent Agents formally applied for authorisation in June 1998.

regulations and rules of conduct relating to the rights of audience already existing for barristers.[11] Thus, barristers who are qualified in accordance with the Bar's rules have rights of audience before all courts and tribunals. There is a similar provision for the Law Society, which is recognised as the authorised body in relation to the rights of audience already enjoyed by solicitors.[12] The Law Society is therefore able to recognise a solicitor as qualified as an advocate, subject to the rules on education, training and conduct. The Law Society is similarly recognised in relation to the rights of solicitors to conduct litigation.[13] Only one other body has been authorised under the Act to grant rights of audience to its members, the Institute of Legal Executives, which can grant limited rights of audience in the lower courts to its Fellows.

The recognition of new authorised bodies, the extension of rights of audience and litigation, and rule changes by authorised bodies have all to be approved according to a procedure set out in Schedule 4 to the 1990 Act. This procedure involves the Lord Chancellor, the Advisory Committee on Legal Education and Conduct, the Director General of Fair Trading, and four judges. Applications have to comply with the "statutory objective" and "general principle," outlined above.

Rule changes

After the 1990 Act professional bodies are still free to make whatever changes they deem necessary to their rules. However, if the rule change relates to education and training or the conduct of litigation and advocacy, it must be approved using the procedure set out in the Act. This procedure requires the relevant authorised body to seek the advice of the Lord Chancellor's Advisory Committee on any proposed new rules or amendments to rules. This may lead to the proposals being modified. The authorised body then makes a formal application to the Lord Chancellor. The formal application is referred back to the Advisory Committee for formal advice. It is also referred to the Director General of Fair Trading, whose remit is to advise whether

---

[11] s. 31.

[12] s. 32.

[13] s. 33. The Law Society is the only body authorised to allow its members to conduct litigation generally. Some other professionals, such as patent agents, have limited rights to conduct litigation in their areas of specialisation. The Access to Justice Bill will enable the Bar Council and the Institute of Legal Executives to grant rights to conduct litigation to their members.

the application has the potential for being anti-competitive. If so, that is a possible reason for refusal.

The formal advice of these two bodies is referred back to the authorised body for comments. The Lord Chancellor considers the advice, and informs the designated judges whether any application should succeed. These designated judges are the Lord Chief Justice, the Master of the Rolls, the President of the Family Division and the Vice-Chancellor.[14] Each of the designated judges, acting individually and taking into account the advice received, must decide whether to approve the application or not. If any of the four judges, or the Lord Chancellor, decides against the application, it fails and may not take effect.

This procedure led Lord Benson, during the debate on the Bill, to declare that control of the legal profession would be

> "in the hands of 11 bodies: the Bar Council; the Law Society; the Lord Chancellor's Department; the advisory quango; the designated judges; the Director General of Fair Trading; the Solicitors' Disciplinary Tribunal; the conveyancing quango; the conveyancing appeals tribunals, and two ombudsmen."[15]

The process has been described as "cumbrous and very slow",[16] causing delays and frustration, which could lead, some feel, to "regulatory stagnation in some areas".[17] This increase in statutory intervention, and the laborious process of approval is considered to be ironic "in an Act which was heralded as deregulating legal services".[18] Such is the pressure for some rule changes that a fast-track system had to be introduced for considering minor amendments.

The Government has recognised that these approval procedures are

---

[14] The 1990 Act provided that four designated judges must agree before professional bodies will be authorised as suitable for their members to be allowed to have rights of audience and to conduct litigation. Their role in this respect was a response to some of the criticisms of the proposed advisory committee. Their role was a safeguard against the committee's potential for threatening the independence of the profession.

[15] H.L. vol.514, col.174, December 19, 1989, second reading.

[16] A. Thornton, "The Professional Responsibility and Ethics of the English Bar" in *Legal Ethics and Professional Responsibility* (R. Cranston ed., 1995), at p.62 [Oxford: Clarendon Press].

[17] A. Crawley and C. Bramall, "Professional Rules, Codes, and Principles Affecting Solicitors (Or What Has Professional Regulation to do with Ethics?)" in *Legal Ethics and Professional Responsibility* (R. Cranston ed., 1995), at p.101 [Oxford: Clarendon Press]. The quickest time between a new rule being approved by the Council of the Law Society and finally made under the Schedule 4 procedure is eight to nine months. The longest time is two years nine months.

[18] A. Crawley and C. Bramall, "Professional Rules, Codes, and Principles Affecting Solicitors (Or What Has Professional Regulation to do with Ethics?)" in *Legal Ethics and Professional Responsibility* (R. Cranston ed., 1995), at p.101 [Oxford: Clarendon Press].

"much too complicated, cumbersome and slow" and are a "major factor which has led to the frustration of the intention of the 1990 Act to extend the provision of legal services".[19] This has particularly been the case in one of the major areas of debate, that of extended rights of audience for solicitors. The approval machinery proved to be neither conclusive nor speedy.[20] Rather, it was an obstacle to the achievement of the statutory objective.[21]

A brief description of the process will illustrate the problem. In April 1991, the Law Society began the process of seeking approval for a rule change to enable solicitors either in private practice or employed by the Crown Prosecution Service or the Government Legal Service to have full rights of audience.[22] There was a similar application for employed barristers to have full rights of audience. A year later, after a period of public consultation, the Lord Chancellor's Advisory Committee on Legal Education and Conduct advised that the rights should not be extended. The Law Society was advised to amend the application to exclude employed solicitors. In May 1992, the Law Society made an amended application to meet the concerns about employed lawyers. The Advisory Committee's response indicated that there were still reservations about employed lawyers.

Despite this, the Law Society formally submitted its amended application to the Lord Chancellor in November 1992, for approval to change its rules to enable it to grant rights of audience in the higher courts to all solicitors. The application was referred to the Advisory Committee and the Director General of Fair Trading, as required by the 1990 Act. After discussions with the Advisory Committee, the Law Society submitted amended proposals in February and May 1993. In July that year, the Advisory Committee formally advised that the application was satisfactory only in relation to solicitors in private practice. Employed solicitors should only have rights of audience in the higher courts in civil cases. The Director General of Fair Trading's advice was that the application would widen consumer choice and might lead to efficiency gains. In December 1993, the Lord Chancellor and the designated judges announced that they had approved the application in so far as it related to solicitors in

---

[19] *Rights of Audience and Rights to Conduct Litigation in England and Wales: The Way Ahead* (1998), at p.24, Lord Chancellor's Department.

[20] See A. Thornton, "The Professional Responsibility and Ethics of the English Bar" in *Legal Ethics and Professional Responsibility* (R. Cranston ed., 1995), at pp.62–63 [Oxford: Clarendon Press].

[21] *Rights of Audience and Rights to Conduct Litigation in England and Wales: The Way Ahead* (1998), at p.27, Lord Chancellor's Department.

[22] See the Lord Chancellor's Advisory Committee on Legal Education and Conduct, *Annual Report for 1993–1994*, Cm 665, at pp.12–14.

private practice. These solicitors were able to exercise rights of audience in the higher courts from 1994. The whole process had taken over two and a half years.[23]

This did not resolve the problem of employed solicitors, particularly Crown prosecutors, who were still prevented from appearing as advocates in the Crown Court. Further discussions about this took place with the Law Society, the Bar Council, the Crown Prosecution Service, and the Government Legal Service. Not surprisingly, the Bar Council, which is dominated by representatives from independent practice, is opposed to attempts to extend rights of audience to Crown prosecutors. In 1995, the Advisory Committee advised that to extend rights of audience in the higher courts to employed solicitors would be incompatible with the proper and efficient administration of justice, and that the application should be refused.

The Law Society formally applied to the Lord Chancellor for approval, and, once more, this was formally sent to the Advisory Committee and the Director General of Fair Trading for advice. The Advisory Committee recommended rejection and the Director General recommended approval. The Law Society claimed that the Advisory Committee had departed from its statutory remit, and the validity of its approach had in fact been challenged by half of its members. The Lord Chancellor appeared to be in a difficult position. Whatever the decision, there was a possibility of a request for judicial review. Finally, in February 1997, it was decided that the application should be approved, but subject to restrictions. The result is that employed solicitors can appear in the higher courts, but only in preliminary hearings.[24]

As a result of the problems in relation to extending rights of audience, the Government is planning to alter and streamline the process of authorising new bodies, and approving rule changes.

The way ahead: the new regulatory framework

The 1990 Act gave the Lord Chancellor's Department a more direct role[25] in supervising the legal profession, through the statutory

---

[23] *Rights of Audience and Rights to Conduct Litigation in England and Wales: The Way Ahead* (1998), at pp.48–49, Lord Chancellor's Department.

[24] *ibid.*, at pp.49–51.

[25] The Lord Chancellor's Department has responsibility for overseeing the system of formal dispute resolution. It administers the judicial system and has responsibility for judicial appointments. As such, it has always had a role in regulating the operation of the legal profession. The 1990 Act gave the Lord Chancellor, assisted by the Advisory Committee, a more direct role.

approval process for rule changes and authorising new bodies to deliver legal services. The Government now feels that the current regulatory framework has been an impediment to the extension of legal services. The laborious process has been used to frustrate and delay the extension of rights of audience. The Government has concluded that the process allowed too much opportunity for obstruction, and is an "obstacle to the achievement of the statutory objective".[26]

The Government is proposing simpler procedures for approving changes to the professional body rules affecting rights of audience or rights to conduct litigation, and for authorising new bodies.[27] In this new procedure, the Advisory Committee is to be replaced by a smaller, more focused body, a Legal Services Consultative Panel.[28] Unlike the Advisory Committee, the new panel is not likely to need a permanent office, and will probably consist of a Chair and ten members. They would not represent the profession or interest groups, but would be a pool of expertise, from which the Lord Chancellor can seek advice. In future, applications for new authorised bodies will be made directly to the Lord Chancellor. This will be referred to the new panel and the Director General of Fair Trading for advice.[29] The designated judges will also be consulted, but the Lord Chancellor need only have regard to their advice. They will no longer have a veto.

Applications for rules changes will also be made directly to the Lord Chancellor. If he thinks it is appropriate, he will inform the designated judges of the decision he proposes to take and request their views. If the Lord Chancellor thinks the proposal deserves wider consideration, he will refer the application to the new consultation panel or the Director General of Fair Trading or both, for advice. All requests for advice will be subject to a timetable. The final decision will be for the Lord Chancellor.[30]

One of the more controversial proposals is the fall-back mechanism to remove unduly restrictive rules. This would allow the Lord Chancellor to "call in" a professional body's rule for scrutiny if it is

---

[26] *Rights of Audience and Rights to Conduct Litigation in England and Wales: The Way Ahead* (1998), at pp.24–27, Lord Chancellor's Department.

[27] *Modernising Justice*, White Paper, Cm.4155 (1998), para.2.26.

[28] *ibid.*, para.2.30. The Legal Services Consultative Panel is to be appointed by the Lord Chancellor. Its purpose is to assist in the maintenance and development of standards in the education, training and conduct of those offering legal services. It is also to give advice about particular matters (Access to Justice Bill, clause 29).

[29] As under the present procedure, the Director General of Fair Trading advises about the competition implications of the application.

[30] *Rights of Audience and Rights to Conduct Litigation in England and Wales: The Way Ahead* (1998), at pp.28–30, The Lord Chancellor's Department.

felt to be counter to the statutory objective or general principle. This would occur, for example, where it unduly restricted the exercise of the rights of audience. Once a rule is "called-in," the professional body will have three months to justify it or propose an acceptable alternative. If the Lord Chancellor, having consulted the designated judges, is not satisfied that the rule should be retained, he will be able to replace it, or strike it out.[31]

Not surprisingly, these proposals have met with a mixed response. The Law Society regards the replacement of the Advisory Committee with a more focused panel to be a step towards streamlining the procedure for advocacy rights applications. However, there is concern that the new powers given to the Lord Chancellor will hamper self-regulation. The Law Society is not convinced that there is a need for any external approval mechanisms for rule changes beyond the professional bodies.[32] The Bar is concerned about independence and standards, and claims that the new powers would dilute its independence.[33] A large number of senior judges are opposed to the Lord Chancellor's having the power to make rules on rights of audience, on the basis that this is a threat to the separation of powers.[34] Some of these criticisms echo the earlier fears expressed when the Advisory Committee itself was proposed. In the event, the Advisory Committee proved to be more an obstacle for change, than a facilitator.

Conclusion

The legal profession, although sharing characteristics of many of the other professions, is in a sense in a unique position. Lawyers are officers of the court, and an integral part of the system of justice. They cannot be simply the paid servants of their clients. There is therefore a public interest, over and above the consumer interest, in the quality of their work. The recent increase in statutory regulation is really a recognition that self-regulation must operate within bounds defined by a wider public interest. This is not unlike many other self-regulatory agencies (particularly in the area of financial services),

---

[31] *Modernising Justice*, White Paper, Cm.4155 (1998), para.2.31.
[32] See *Law Society Gazette*, September 23, 1998, p.20; September 16, 1998, p.3.
[33] *Law Society Gazette*, September 23, 1998, pp.20–21.
[34] *ibid.* October 21, 1998, p.4. It is claimed that 98 high court judges, and 36 Court of Appeal judges are opposed to this extension of the Lord Chancellor's powers.

which have to submit their regulatory regime for approval by independent public agencies.

There is no doubt that the Courts and Legal Services Act made major changes to the regulation of the legal profession, and serious inroads into the concept of self-regulation. As we have seen, the legislation provides the framework for control of the profession, and much of the detail is handled by the professional bodies themselves. Indeed, it would be impossible to regulate the profession (or any profession) without these self-regulatory mechanisms. The purpose of the Act was to allow the professional bodies to continue to regulate their members, but within a framework provided by the Act.

Competition and the extension of legal services was provided for by the ability to approve new providers of services. Although allowing a large measure of self-regulation, the public interest was to be protected by the Lord Chancellor's role in relation to rule changes and authorisation of other professional bodies to deliver legal services. The Government's new proposals make further inroads into self-regulation, particularly in relation to the extension of rights of audience. The question to be addressed in the succeeding chapters is whether the mechanisms, statutory and self-regulatory, are adequate to protect the consumer and public interests.

Chapter 4

Self-Regulation, Standards and Discipline

As we saw in the previous chapter, the legislative mechanisms for regulating the legal profession provide a framework within which the professional bodies perform their self-regulatory functions. It is the role of the professional bodies to regulate entry into the profession and to establish quality and ethical standards for members. As a corollary of this, the professional body is able to discipline members who are found to be in breach of the rules, and ultimately to expel them. These standards of conduct must be described and evaluated in order to assess whether they are appropriate for the protection of consumers. In addition, it is also necessary to see whether the mechanisms used for implementing the standards are adequate. As discussed in the previous chapter, there are two branches of the legal profession, solicitors and barristers. They have different professional bodies, different quality standards, and different mechanisms for enforcing those standards.

Professional bodies

The Law Society is the professional body which has statutory responsibility for the regulation of solicitors, and as such governs their professional conduct. In addition to this regulatory function, the Law Society also provides a range of services for the profession, for example, providing help and advice on ethical matters, as well as on matters of law and practice, and it runs a pension scheme and a recruitment scheme for the profession. It also plays a part in influencing legislation. It thus performs a dual function, that of representing the interests of the profession and of individual solicitors, and also policing the profession, exercising disciplinary sanctions and guarding standards in the public interest.

As we saw in Chapter 3, the Law Society is an independent body, which was established by Royal Charter in 1845. All solicitors are subject to regulation by the Law Society, whether they are in private practice or employed as in-house solicitors in the public or private sector. There is no obligation for solicitors to be members of the Law Society, but they are subject to its regulatory powers whether they are or not. There is no fee for being a member, but there is a cost to be admitted to the roll of solicitors, and a student membership fee. Solicitors who do not practise pay a fee to the Law Society of £15 per annum to stay on the roll. In 1998, the number of solicitors on the roll was 95,521, of whom 75,072 were in practice.

The Law Society operates through its Council, and various committees, sub-committees, departments and divisions. Some of these operate to represent the interests of, and provide services for, the profession, but many are concerned with regulation and good practice. As we saw in the previous chapter, there are a number of statutory sources governing solicitors' professional conduct. The Law Society's self-regulatory mechanisms include control over entry into the profession, mechanisms to ensure that solicitors remain competent throughout their professional lives, and the making and enforcement of practice rules and standards.

The Bar Council, a non-statutory body, regulates barristers. The Courts and Legal Services Act 1990 designated it the authorised body for barristers. It is responsible for complaints and discipline, ethics and standards, education and training, equal opportunities and pupillage. The work of the Bar Council is carried out by a number of committees. It is also the representative body for the interests of the profession and individual barristers. It provides a wide range of services for its members, including a service for collecting outstanding fees. It validates the institutions authorised to provide professional training, and provides advice to new entrants and recruitment literature. There are 9,698 barristers in private practice, and about 2,500 employed barristers.[1] The Bar Council is dominated by barristers in private practice, and the regulatory mechanisms are mainly concerned with the work of independent barristers.[2]

---

[1] These figures are for October 1, 1998. The actual figure given for employed barristers was 2,472.

[2] This is not surprising, given that the primary functions of the Bar, as a profession are "the services which it offers through independent practitioners by way of advice and advocacy in contentious work" (*Blueprint for the Bar. Report of the Bar Standards Review Body* (1994), at p.1, Chairman: The Lord Alexander of Weedon).

Control of entry and training

The one restrictive practice, which all professions share, is that of limiting entry to those who obtain certain qualifications.[3] Both the Law Society and the Bar Council control entry into their respective branches of the legal profession. Only by conforming to the requirements set out by these professional bodies can a person be admitted as either a solicitor or barrister, and thus engage in those areas of work which are reserved for the legal profession.[4]

A qualifying law degree is the basic requirement which is common to both branches of the profession. This is a law degree which has been approved by the professional bodies as satisfying their requirements.[5] Graduates without a qualifying law degree must pass the common professional examination.[6] After graduating, there are different post-graduate training requirements for each branch of the profession. Intending solicitors must take the Legal Practice Course, which is normally a year of full-time study. The equivalent for barristers is the Bar Vocational Course, which also lasts a year. The relevant professional bodies validate the vocational courses, which are provided by educational establishments, and thus retain control over this aspect of the qualification.[7]

Since the Courts and Legal Services Act 1990, any changes to the rules in relation to legal education are subject to the overall supervision mechanisms of the Act. This means that the professional bodies are not in sole control of the kind of legal education which is thought appropriate for solicitors and barristers. Under the Act, the Lord Chancellor's Advisory Committee on Legal Education and Conduct has a statutory duty to assist in the "maintenance and development of standards in the education, training and conduct of those offering legal services".[8] This was discharged by advising on changes to qualification regulations in so far as they related to rights of

---

[3] "Selective entry based on the fulfilment of certain educational requirements is one of the distinguishing features of all the professions" (M. Zander, *Lawyers and the Public Interest* (1968), at p.21 [London: Weidenfeld and Nicolson]).

[4] These are: conveyancing, probate, rights of audience, and rights to conduct litigation.

[5] The Law Society and Bar Council publish a joint statement setting out the regulations for degrees which qualify. The latest of these is the Joint Announcement on Qualifying Law Degrees of 1995.

[6] It is possible for non-graduates to become solicitors by becoming members of the Institute of Legal Executives, which has its own qualification requirements.

[7] Some believe that common education for barristers and solicitor advocates should be encouraged, as this would have the advantage of giving maximum flexibility to students. See *Blueprint for the Bar. Report of the Bar Standards review Body* (1994), at p.58, Chairman: The Lord Alexander of Weedon.

[8] Courts and Legal Services Act 1990, s. 20

audience and rights to conduct litigation. After its proposed abolition,[9] the new legal services consultative council, which is to replace it, will take on this function.

The Advisory Committee also had a wider role in relation to legal education, involving research and reviews of the system of legal education. This aspect of its work will not be directly replicated by the new legal services consultative council. The Government does not consider that the Advisory Committee's work on the wider issues in legal education has been helpful to it, the profession, or academic institutions.[10] Effective legal education and training is, however, essential to the Government's proposals for modernising the justice system.[11] It is proposed therefore that the new consultative panel will have a role in encouraging "appropriate and high quality" legal education, and it will work with universities and other providers of legal education to achieve this.[12] The Lord Chancellor's Department will also take over the function of organising the Standing Conference on Legal Education, which was within the Advisory Committee's remit.[13] The Department will also continue to have contacts with the professional bodies and providers of legal education.[14] Thus, although the Government does not consider it to be within its remit to prescribe the details of the education and training available for lawyers, it does have an interest in its quality and suitability.

After the relevant vocational courses, intending barristers and solicitors must complete a period of practical training before they can practice. Successful completion of the Bar Vocational Course does qualify a person as a barrister. However, in order to practise at the Bar, with rights of audience, there must be a period of training with a practising barrister, known as pupillage. This lasts for a year and after six months, rights of audience will be granted. No fees can be earned

---

[9] The Access to Justice Bill, which is progressing through Parliament.

[10] *Rights of Audience and Rights to Conduct Litigation in England and Wales: the Way Ahead*, (1990), at p.38, Lord Chancellor's Department. The Advisory Committee's *First Report on Legal Education and Training*, published in April 1996, recommended a major restructuring of legal professional training, with a new qualification, which would be common to both barristers and solicitors. The proposals were not well received by the professional bodies, and were never adopted.

[11] *Modernising Justice*, White Paper, Cm.4155 (1998), para.2.33.

[12] The Lord Chancellor, Access to Justice Bill, second Reading, H.L. Deb., col. 1110, December 14, 1998.

[13] *Rights of Audience and Rights to Conduct Litigation in England and Wales: the Way Ahead*, (1990), at p.37, Lord Chancellor's Department. The Standing Conference on Legal Education meets twice a year, and includes representatives of the professional bodies and providers of academic and vocational legal education.

[14] *Rights of Audience and Rights to Conduct Litigation in England and Wales: the Way Ahead*, (1990), at p.39, Lord Chancellor's Department.

during these first six months. After pupillage, a barrister must obtain a tenancy in a set of chambers, from where he or she will practise.

Successful completion of the Legal Practice Course does not qualify a person as a solicitor. Before being entered on the roll of solicitors, a two-year training contract with a firm of solicitors must be completed. Trainees are paid a salary during their contract.[15] In addition to these educational and training requirements, intending solicitors and barristers must satisfy the relevant professional bodies that they are of good character.

In order to gain entry into the legal profession, intending lawyers must thus show themselves to be educated and trained to a high standard. Such requirements are usual for professional practice, and, in ensuring that practitioners are competent, they protect the interests of consumers. The professional bodies have little control on the number of places on qualifying law degree courses. They are therefore unable to place limitations on the initial, academic, stage of entry into the profession. There is some control over the number of places on vocational courses.[16] An important limiting factor on entry to the profession is financial. Intending lawyers must have the means to finance themselves through the period of vocational training. The other limitation is the ability, or willingness, of the profession to take on trainees, as this is an essential component of gaining entry into the profession.

Control of practice

No-one can practise as a solicitor unless he or she holds a current practising certificate.[17] This rule applies to employed solicitors, as well as those in private practice. Practising certificates are issued each year, and the current fee is £440.[18] Legislation allows the fee to be reduced

---

[15] The Law Society stipulates a minimum wage of £10,850 per annum for trainees, but firms can be exempted from this.

[16] In April 1997, there was a moratorium on new and additional Legal Practice Course places. This was lifted in January 1998, because it was no longer necessary given the reduction in students enrolling on and passing the course. There will be an annual review each autumn on the relationship between the number of Legal Practice Course places taken up, the number passing, and the number of training contracts available (*Law Society Annual Report and Accounts 1997–98*, at p.4). The Bar Council has limited the number of places on the Bar Vocational Course for the time being.

[17] Section 1 of the Solicitors Act 1974 provides that no-one is qualified to act as a solicitor unless admitted as a solicitor, unless they have their name on the role of solicitors, and unless they have in force a practising certificate.

[18] This is for 1997–98, and represents a reduction from the previous year, when the cost was £470.

for solicitors in Government or other public service, or with low earnings. The fee can also be reduced in the first three years of practice. These fees are a valuable source of income for the Law Society. In the year ending December 31, 1997, the total income of the Law Society was £55.2 million, £33.4 million of which was income from practising certificates. At present, the Bar does not issue practising certificates. It may do so in future, as a method of ensuring compliance with the new continuing professional development rules. These are discussed later in the chapter.

Solicitors must be qualified for three years before they can practise as sole practitioners or supervise an office. There is a similar rule of conduct for barristers, who are not allowed to practise in their first three years unless they are in chambers with a barrister who has practised for more than five years. These rules recognise that some support is needed for newly qualified lawyers. Whether they actually provide adequate supervision is not clear. For the Bar, it has been recommended that newly qualified barristers should be supervised by more experienced barristers, and that chambers should have procedures to ensure that barristers do not undertake work where they lack experience or competence.[19]

At one time, it was forbidden for solicitors to practise in corporate form, and thus all firms were either partnerships or sole practitioners. Since 1985, the Law Society is allowed to make rules permitting solicitors to practise in corporate form.[20] In 1988 rules were made[21] setting out the circumstances in which it would be possible for solicitors to practise as limited companies. These rules provide that the corporate body must have a registered office in England and Wales and that all the shareholders and directors have to be solicitors. The relevant legislation was brought into force on January 1, 1991, and it is now possible for solicitors to incorporate provided they comply with the 1988 rules. There is also a proposed draft bill which will allow limited liability partnerships for solicitors firms.[22]

Legislation does not prevent solicitors or barristers conducting their profession in multi-disciplinary partnerships with other professionals.[23] However, the relevant professional bodies can prohibit such practices,

---

[19] *Blueprint for the Bar. Report of the Bar Standards Review Body* (1994), at pp.61–64. Chairman: The Lord Alexander of Weedon.
[20] Administration of Justice Act 1985, s. 9
[21] The Solicitors Incorporated Practice Rules 1988
[22] See *Law Society Gazette*, September 23, 1998, p.1.
[23] The Courts and Legal Services Act 1990, s. 66, provided for such practices.

and, so far, they remain prohibited.[24] The Law Society was opposed
to such practices, on the grounds that they could undermine "the
fabric and integrity of the profession". The interests of clients would
need to be considered before they were allowed.[25] This view was
endorsed by the Scottish Law Society, which felt that multi-
disciplinary partnerships would be "contrary to the interests of justice
and would put at risk the public's confidence in the legal
profession".[26]

It appears, however, that the rule about multi-disciplinary
partnerships will have to be relaxed.[27] In October 1998, the Law
Society issued a consultation paper, and it seems that the result will be
an acceptance of them, with conditions to safeguard standards.
Safeguards would be needed to eliminate the risk of undermining the
lawyer's independence. Regulations would be needed for situations
where there could be conflicts of interests. There would need to be
some assurance that there would be no erosion of confidentiality and
client privilege.[28] Consumer organisations feel that the move to multi-
disciplinary practices are long overdue. Provided that the rules
governing the various professionals are those which conform to the
highest regulatory standards, it is felt that they will be for the benefit
of consumers.[29]

Barristers are still prevented by their professional rules from
practising in partnerships, even with other barristers. There are
pressures to relax this, to allow some association with other
professionals.[30] Some of these pressures arise because of the funding of
litigation through conditional fee arrangements, which has implications
for the future structure of the Bar.[31] Barristers practise as a referral

---

[24] The rules do not prevent solicitors firms sharing profits with employees who are not
solicitors. Solicitors can now also practice in partnership with foreign lawyers (Multi-
National Legal Practice Rules 1991).
[25] *Strategy for the Decade*, 1990, The Law Society.
[26] *The Lawyer*, June 23, 1992.
[27] *Law Society Gazette*, December 16, 1998, at p.22. Research has found that six out of
ten solicitors believe that multi-disciplinary practices will be an integral part of the
profession in the next two years (*Law Society Annual Report and Accounts 1997–98*, at
p.4).
[28] See *Law Society Gazette*, June 3, 1998, at p.8.
[29] Both the Consumers Association and the Office of Fair Trading are in favour of
multi-disciplinary practices. See A. Holmes, Head of Legal Affairs at the Consumers
Association, *Law Society Gazette*, October 21, 1998.
[30] See A. Thornton "The Professional Responsibility and Ethics of the English Bar" in
Legal Ethics and Professional Responsibility (R. Cranston ed., 1995), at p.66 [Oxford:
Clarendon Press].
[31] The Bar Council has received a report on the future structure of the Bar, with
proposals to allow barristers to practice as corporate bodies, partnerships, or contractual
joint ventures.

profession, taking instructions from solicitors,[32] rather than having direct access to members of the public. These rules too are being examined, and there are proposals to relax them, so that the Bar would cease to be an exclusively referral profession.[33]

Continuing professional development

It is essential that practitioners remain competent to practise their profession. The professional bodies, therefore, have requirements for continuing professional development after being admitted to the profession. The Law Society requires solicitors in practice to complete a number of hours of professional development each year. For the first three years after admission to the profession, 16 hours must be completed each year. After three years, solicitors must complete 48 hours of continuing professional development during a three-year period.[34] This post-admission training and development can include attendance at approved courses and conferences, and legal research, writing and teaching. There is an obligation to keep a record of these hours, which must be produced for the Law Society on demand. This requirement is enforced by requiring solicitors to sign a declaration that they have complied with the regulations for the preceding year when they apply for renewal of their practising certificate.

In October 1997, the Bar Council introduced continuing professional development requirements for barristers in independent practice.[35] The programme applies to new practitioners, that is, barristers who commence independent practice on or after October 1, 1997. Barristers who commence employed practice on or after October 1, 1998 who exercise or intend to exercise rights of audience must also comply with the requirements. The requirement is to complete a minimum of 42 hours of continuing education in four prescribed areas by the end of their first three years of practice. A scheme for established practitioners has recently been approved by the

---

[32] They also take instructions from other "professional clients," for example, trade mark agents, patent agents and the Government Legal Service.

[33] The proposals have a number of options, from preserving the present position, to complete access for individuals. It may be that licensed access is the favoured option. Certain bodies, for example, trade unions and financial institutions, would be licensed to have direct access to barristers.

[34] These provisions have been phased in over a number of years. Initially, it was only recently qualified solicitors who were obliged to complete them. They now apply to all solicitors.

[35] *The New Practitioners' Programme*, Education and Training Department. The General Council of the Bar.

Bar Council.[36] The established practitioners programme will be introduced in stages from 2001. By 2004, all practitioners will be obliged to take part in the programme.[37] The requirement will be to complete 12 hours of continuing professional development each year. The regulations about continuing professional development are a mechanism for attempting to ensure the competence of solicitors and barristers once they have been admitted into the profession. They ought to apply to all practitioners throughout their working lives. This is now the case with solicitors. It is commendable that the Bar has now decided to extend its continuing professional development scheme to all practitioners.

Competence and specialisms

Another mechanism for trying to ensure the competence and quality of work is by means of special panels. Once solicitors have qualified and are entitled to practise, there is no general restriction on the type of work which they can do, and they may thus practise in any area where they are competent.[38] Under their professional rules they do have an obligation to ensure that they are competent to take on work in a particular area. The Law Society has, however, set up specialist panels to which solicitors can belong who practise in certain areas of work. These cover areas of practice which are considered to require some particular accreditation, either because the clients are especially vulnerable, or because a particular expertise is required. The Law Society also keeps registers indicating solicitors with interest and experience in certain areas. It may be considered odd for a professional body to create a class of members who are held out to the public as being more competent in specific areas than other members.[39] However, the Law Society believes that to neglect this

---

[36] This is the outcome of a Working Party, chaired by Richard Southwell Q.C., which prepared a policy statement on continuing professional development for practising barristers.

[37] New practitioners will start in 2001; barristers called in or after 1990 will start in 2002; those called between 1980 and 1990 will start in 2003; barristers called before 1980 will start in 2004.

[38] There are some areas of work which are regulated in such a way that solicitors must be licensed before they can engage in this type of work. These include insolvency and financial services.

[39] In many parts of Europe, apparently, this would not be possible. See J. Hayes, "Protecting the public and Serving the Profession". Paper presented at Manchester University on May 14, 1994, *Legal Professions in Transition Conference*, at p.9. Centre for Law and Business, Centre for Social Ethics and Policy, the University of Manchester.

method of accreditation would be to ignore evidence of incompetence. Furthermore, large buyers of legal services might themselves set up their own accreditation schemes, if the Law Society failed to do so.[40]

The Law Society has established specialist panels[41] to cover children,[42] mental health, personal injury, medical negligence,[43] and planning. There is also a specialist panel for rights of audience in the higher courts.[44] A specialist panel deals with the licensing of insolvency practitioners, and the Law Society also has a diploma in local government law and practice. The children panel and mental health panel were the first to be set up, and they resulted from public interest concerns and the vulnerability of these types of clients. The Law Society is in the process of forming a panel in family law, and developing panels for immigration, criminal law, employment and housing law.[45]

In order to become a member of a panel, an application form has to be completed, interviews are held, and references are sought. The Law Society assesses the application by evaluating the experience of the applicant, in terms of the number of years of practice and the percentage of the workload in that area. Solicitors also have to demonstrate knowledge of all the core areas of work, expertise in the specialised area,[46] and knowledge of related areas of law. They may also have to provide evidence of particular training in the area. There is no requirement to pass an examination,[47] although this is being considered for some new schemes. Some panels require attendance at

---

[40] J. Hayes, "Protecting the public and Serving the Profession". Paper presented at Manchester University on May 14, 1994, *Legal Professions in Transition Conference*, at p.10. Centre for Law and Business, Centre for Social Ethics and Policy, the University of Manchester.

[41] See Karen Mackay, "Specialisation Schemes" in *Report of the Consultative Seminar on Standards and Regulation of Immigration Advice*, (1997) The Lord Chancellor's Advisory Committee on Legal Education and Conduct.

[42] This is the largest panel, with some 1,660 members.

[43] These panels have 400, 2,500 and 120 members respectively.

[44] This is for those solicitors who have the necessary qualifications to appear as advocates in the higher courts.

[45] The Family Law Accreditation Scheme is to be launched in January 1999 (*Law Society Annual Report and Accounts 1997–98*, at p. 7)

[46] For example, in order to be licensed to undertake prescribed types of insolvency work, applicants must have accumulated a minimum of 600 chargeable hours of technical insolvency work during the three years preceding the application and have successfully completed the Joint Insolvency examination.

[47] An examination must be passed to be a licensed insolvency practitioner.

an approved training course.[48] Membership normally lasts for three to five years, after which there is a further assessment of competence to be a member of the panel. The panels are self-financing, and charge fees ranging from £150 to £500 for the membership period.

These panels perform one method of accreditation and regulation. They represent an acknowledgment that entry qualifications alone do not ensure competence throughout a practitioner's working life. They are a means used by the Law Society to accredit practitioners' practical experience and knowledge against recognised standards for each area of work. They are thus a mechanism for raising standards. There are also advantages for the profession. Membership of panels confers a number of benefits. It is a useful marketing tool.[49] Solicitors are able to use it to attract clients, and referral agencies find it useful in identifying experienced solicitors in particular areas of work. From the consumer perspective, these panels help to ensure that there is the appropriate focus on client vulnerability and the legal complexity of certain areas of work. However, except for the few areas which require certification, there is no requirement to be a member of one of these panels before practising in that area of work.

The quality of legal advice in immigration matters is a particular area of concern. Clients here are particularly vulnerable and liable to exploitation.[50] Some countries regulate this area of work by having a statutory scheme to which practitioners must belong.[51] The Government has decided to set up a statutory scheme[52] to regulate immigration advisers. There was resistance from the profession against additional regulation for solicitors practising in this area of law. When the proposals were being discussed, regulating legally qualified advisers was not ruled out. Last year the Law Society finalised its immigration accreditation scheme, as a method of providing the necessary quality

---

[48] For example, in order to be a member of the children panel, solicitors must attend two one-day courses. For the mental health review tribunal panel there is a one-day approved training course. The Law Society's diploma in local government law and practice requires completion of the course.

[49] Membership of the personal injury panel has the additional advantage of providing advantageous insurance arrangements related to conditional fee arrangements.

[50] The concern was such that the Lord Chancellor's Advisory Committee on Legal Education and Conduct set up an inquiry into the standards of education and training of those providing advice and representation in this area. It organised a consultative seminar to bring together others concerned with practice in this area. See *Report of the Consultative Seminar on Standards and Regulation of Immigration Advice* (1997) Lord Chancellor's Advisory Committee on Legal Education and Conduct.

[51] M. Garlick, "The Australian Model" in *Report of the Consultative Seminar on Standards and Regulation of Immigration Advice* (1997). Lord Chancellor's Advisory Committee on Legal Education and Conduct.

[52] The Immigration and Asylum Bill, currently going through Parliament, will require official registration of immigration advisers.

assurance by self-regulation. It hoped that this specialist panel would strengthen its case that additional regulation is unnecessary.[53] Under the new Act, statutory regulation will only be necessary for non-legally qualified advisers, and the law society will retain the right to regulate solicitors in immigration law firms.

There are external influences on quality, which operate in a similar way to specialist panels and accreditation schemes. For example, legal aid franchising arrangements provide a mechanism for accreditation which aims to ensure the quality of work performed by solicitors who undertake legal aid work. It may be that in the future, panel membership, together with practice management standards, will become an alternative to these franchising arrangements. Under the proposed new arrangements for the public funding of legal services, funding contracts may only be given to solicitors who demonstrate competence in the specialised areas. For example, funding for medical negligence may only be available to solicitors who are members of the medical negligence panel, or other suitable panel.[54]

One area where joint or "co-"regulation by the profession and by external forces has improved standards is in relation to advice given in police stations. In the 1980s, there were a number of research reports, which were critical of the standards of criminal defence work, particularly legal advice given in police stations. The Royal Commission on Criminal Justice, set up to examine miscarriages of justice, commissioned further research on custodial legal advice. It recommended that both the Law Society and Legal Aid Board should endeavour to improve standards. This resulted in an accreditation scheme, which is administered by both the Law Society and the Legal Aid Board. Although the Law Society sets out the detailed standards and requirements for this type of work, the Legal Aid Board enforces the requirements by restricting payment to those accredited. This financial incentive is considered to be an effective way of enforcing standards.[55]

There is no system of compulsory specialist panels for barristers. A working party of the Bar did investigate whether there should be specialisation and accreditation for barristers, but concluded that a compulsory system by a panel would be impractical and possibly

---

[53] See *Law Society Gazette*, July 29, 1998, at p.1.

[54] For example, that maintained by the Association for the Victims of Medical Negligence. See *Access to Justice with Conditional Fees*, Consultation Paper issued by the Lord Chancellor's Department. March 1998, at p.20.

[55] L. Bridges, "Teaching Appropriate Conduct: The Example of Police Station Advisers" in *Proceedings from the Annual Research Conference 1998: Governing the Profession* (1998), at pp.15,19, The Law Society: Research and Policy Planning Unit.

unlawful.[56] The report of the Bar Standards Review Body agreed with this conclusion. It felt that one of the values of the Bar is that practitioners can often transcend defined specialisms, and that this broad perspective is desirable. Consequently, it recommended that the Bar should not adopt a system of compulsory accreditation of specialisms.[57] There are, however, specialist Bar associations for some areas of specialist practice. These include commercial law, criminal law, employment law, family law, planning and revenue law.[58]

The Bar is a referral profession, with little exposure to lay clients. Instructing solicitors, the professional clients of the barrister, are often in a better position than lay clients to form a view of the services performed by barristers. It is sometimes argued that solicitors are a spontaneous form of quality control for the Bar.[59] Not only do solicitors monitor barristers for their efficiency as advocates, but they are also in a position to judge whether they are competent in the area of work for which the solicitor seeks specialist advice. It is therefore not as important for consumers that barristers operate a specialist accreditation system. Such a system may become necessary if the Bar ceases to be a referral profession.

Financial protection

The professional bodies are concerned to provide financial protection to the consumers of legal services. Where solicitors are concerned, this involves strict rules about clients' money, and the ability to intervene in the affairs of firms where there are indications that clients' money may be at risk. This kind of regulation is not necessary for barristers, as they do not handle clients' money. Solicitors must contribute to the compensation fund, which makes grants to clients who have suffered as a result of the dishonesty of a solicitor. Both solicitors and barristers must have professional indemnity insurance, to indemnify them against negligence claims. In addition, solicitors who offer financial services are subject to special regulation.

Solicitors offering financial services are subject to the regulatory regime set up by the Financial Services Act 1986. The Law Society is

---

[56] Bar Council Working Party on Specialisation and Accreditation, chaired by Hugh Bennett Q.C.

[57] *Blueprint for the Bar. Report of the Bar Standards Review Body* (1994), at p.61, Chairman: The Lord Alexander of Weedon.

[58] See R. Baldwin, *Regulating Legal Services* (1997), p.36, Lord Chancellor's Department Research Series No. 5/97.

[59] See *First Annual Report of the Legal Services Ombudsman 1991*, at p. 19

a recognised professional body under the Act, which can authorise solicitor's firms to carry out investment business.[60] Recognised bodies, which authorise firms, must have adequate resources for monitoring and investigating malpractice.[61] In order to comply with this the Law Society has a training and competence scheme for solicitors who are financial advisers, as required by the Securities and Investment Board. Although the Law Society authorises firms for investment business, the scheme is actually based on individual members of the firm, and these individuals must undertake or supervise all the investment work conducted by the firm.

Individual solicitors become authorised by the Law Society's authorisation casework committee. There is an extensive application form to be completed, and applicants must demonstrate prior knowledge and experience of this type of work. If applicants do not possess the required prior experience, they have to pass examinations in the subject. The Law Society sets its own examination, and runs a foundation course. Alternatively, applicants may pass an approved course accepted by the financial services industry. Applicants must also provide references, which are checked thoroughly, before becoming authorised. If the application is from a non-solicitor in a firm, there are additional requirements, including attendance on a conduct and rules course. This system appears to work well, and the Law Society's monitoring has shown that the competence of advisers has increased since the introduction of the training and competence scheme.[62] The Office for the Supervision of Solicitors undertakes regular monitoring of those solicitors who have qualified status.

This area of work forms a large part of the Law Society's regulatory powers. The proposals to alter the regulatory framework of financial services will affect this aspects of the Law Society's regulatory functions. Under these proposals, financial services will be authorised by a new Financial Services Authority. This authority, rather than the Law Society, will directly authorise solicitors who offer financial services. This proposal has been described as the "beginning of the end of self-regulation".[63] It is opposed by the Law Society, on the basis that, as it regulates all aspects of solicitors work, it would make

---

[60] See Bob Butler, "The Financial Services Act Model" in *Report of the Consultative Seminar on Standards and Regulation of Immigration Advice* (1997) Lord Chancellor's Advisory Committee on Legal Education and Conduct.
[61] Financial Services Act 1986, Sched. 3.
[62] It is, perhaps, worth noting that since the Personal Investment Authority Ombudsman took office in 1997, not one solicitor regulated by the Personal Investment Authority has been the subject of a complaint (*Law Society Gazette*, June 17, 1998, at p.8)
[63] *Law Society Gazette*, July 22, 1998, at p.29.

little sense to create a separate regulatory body just for investment business. The Financial Services and Markets Bill, which will introduce these changes, has not yet been enacted.

Indemnity insurance

Solicitors and barristers must have indemnity insurance to cover claims for professional negligence. For barristers, the insurance scheme is the Bar Mutual Indemnity Fund. As we saw in Chapter 2, advocates have immunity from negligence actions in connection with the presentation of a case in court. This means that negligence claims against barristers are restricted to work which is not covered by the immunity. Solicitors also have a mutual scheme, the Solicitors Indemnity Fund. This was set up under the Solicitors Act 1974, section 37 of which enabled the Law Society to make rules concerning indemnity against loss from claims against solicitors. The purpose of the fund is to indemnify practitioners against claims of negligence,[64] and there is no right of claim against the fund itself.

The Solicitors Act allowed for the provision of indemnity in a number of ways. There can be a mutual fund, established by the Law Society. Alternatively, the Law Society is permitted to take out a master insurance policy. Another method is to require solicitors to maintain insurance with authorised insurers. From 1975 until 1987, the Law Society operated an indemnity scheme using a master policy. This was changed in 1987, when the Solicitors Indemnity Fund was established. Solicitors must subscribe to the fund. In 1996, new indemnity rules were introduced, which were designed to ensure that negligent and high risk practitioners paid more.

As we saw in Chapter 3, the Law Society's decision on the appropriate arrangements for indemnity are being challenged by means of a postal ballot. Many solicitors are concerned at the rising cost of the fund, and wish to have a system of approved insurers.[65] It did seem likely that in the near future, the mutual fund would be replaced, or that there would be a choice of systems for solicitors. The Law Society has, however, decided to keep the mandatory mutual fund. The purpose of indemnity insurance is to benefit clients by ensuring that solicitors are financially able to compensate clients.

---

[64] The Fund does not cover claims due to dishonesty (see *Abbey National plc v. Solicitors Indemnity Fund Ltd* [1997] P.N.L.R. 306, Q.B.D.). These claims must be made to the Compensation Fund, discussed below.
[65] See *Law Society Annual Report and Accounts 1997–98*, at p.1.

Indeed, the principal purpose of section 37 of the Solicitors Act 1974 was to enable the Law Society to safeguard the lay public.[66] The Law Society must therefore ensure that the system enables practitioners to meet any liability claims. Provided this is done, it is for the profession to decide on the most appropriate system of indemnity cover.

Compensation fund

The compensation fund is a trust fund which the Law Society is required by statute to maintain.[67] It is a mechanism for ensuring that clients receive compensation when solicitors have acted dishonestly. The supervision of the fund comes within the remit of the Compliance and Supervision committee of the Law Society Council, and it is administered by the Office for the Supervision of Solicitors.[68] Its purpose is to replace client money that a solicitor has misappropriated or misused within the course of his or her practice.

Contributions to the fund are payable annually by solicitors after they have been in practice for three years. Full contributions are paid by solicitors who hold clients' money. Most principals in private practice and some in-house solicitors receive or hold clients' monies, and thus few solicitors will escape this liability. Employed and assistant solicitors in private practice and public service, who do not hold client money, pay a reduced amount. Solicitors in their first three years of practice make no contribution. The amount payable varies from year to year, and it includes a basic contribution, plus a special levy, which was introduced because of the large amounts of claims made against the fund. The present basic contribution is £100 for all solicitors who hold client money, that is, partners and sole practitioners.[69] The reduced fee for employed solicitors is £30.[70]

In order for a grant to be authorised from the fund, the application must come within the statutory provisions. Applicants must show that they have suffered loss because of the dishonesty of a solicitor, or have suffered hardship as a consequence of a failure to account. Applications must be made using the appropriate application form, and should be made within six months of the loss. This time limit can be

---

[66] *Swain v. The Law Society* [1983] A.C. 598 at 618.
[67] Solicitors Act 1974, s. 36.
[68] This is discussed later in the chapter.
[69] Only half of this is payable for solicitors applying for their fourth, fifth or sixth practising certificate.
[70] Only £15 is paid by employed solicitors in the fourth, fifth and sixth years of practice.

extended in exceptional circumstances. Grants are made at the discretion of the Law Society, and there is no right of appeal against refusal. The Law Society must, however, administer the fund in a fair and consistent manner and its decisions are subject to judicial review. The fund is one of last resort and applications will be refused where there is another remedy, for example, where the loss is covered by insurance. Professional negligence is not covered by the fund. No grant will be made where there is no evidence of dishonesty, or, in the case of a failure to account, where the applicant is not suffering material hardship.

Applications to the fund are divided into those which are over, and those which are under £5,000. Those under £5,000 tend to be simple, and are dealt with fairly quickly, grants sometimes being made within a few weeks. Some staff within the Office for the Supervision of Solicitors have delegated authority to authorise payments up to £50,000 and to reject applications below £5,000. Applications for over £5,000 are usually more complicated, and sometimes have to be referred to the Compliance and Supervision Committee. This happens where there is a decision to reject an application for more than £5,000 or where the proposed grant is for over £50,000. If the issues are particularly complex the matter will also be referred to the committee.

In 1997, there were 1,074 applications for grants, with a total value of £20.4 million. The total value of the grants authorised in that year was £10.75 million.[71] Altogether 73 per cent of the applications were for sums under £5,000. The remaining 27 per cent, 293 applications in total, had a combined value £19 million, some 93 per cent of the total. Of these 293, 47 were from lending institutions in respect of mortgage fraud, and had a total value of £5.6 million. Indeed, the applications from mortgage lenders, while accounting for 4 per cent of the number, accounted for 27 per cent of the value of all the applications. During the 16-month period to the end of December 1998, there were 2,299 grants made, with a total value of £17.4 million. The value of grants for 1998 was £12.8 million, an increase of 20 per cent on the previous year.[72]

Applications for grants usually occur in relation to firms which have been the subject of interventions by the Office for the Supervision of Solicitors.[73] The vast majority relates to sole practitioners. Both applications and grants have decreased over the past few years. The

---

[71] The Law Society Compliance and Supervision Committee *Compensation Fund: Annual Report 1997 and Contributions 1998–99.*

[72] Office for the Supervision of Solicitors, *Annual Report 1997–1998*, at p.11.

[73] This is discussed later in the chapter.

Office for the Supervision of Solicitors suggests that the reason for this is that the improved intelligence network can better target firms which may be having problems.[74] Some applications are withdrawn. In 1997, 290 were withdrawn, and this is attributed to the fact that many lending institutions apply under the compensation fund, while at the same time pursuing claims in negligence. When a settlement is reached under the indemnity fund, the application for a grant is not pursued. Not many applications are totally rejected, but many do not receive the total amount claimed. The compensation fund provides a useful mechanism of last resort in those cases which come within its provisions. However, as the figures indicate, many of the beneficiaries of the scheme are lending institutions, rather than consumers.

Fees and costs

The cost of legal services is a source of much dissatisfaction for consumers. It is of concern to the Government, because many legal services are financed from public funds. It is also of concern to the private client. The previous Legal Services Ombudsman spoke of the "widespread fear of legal costs," noting the Civil Justice Review's conclusion that it was this fear which deterred people from using the courts to resolve their disputes.[75] There are no scales of charges for either solicitors' or barristers' fees. The Bar's code of conduct allows barristers to charge on any basis deemed appropriate. Solicitors' professional rules provide that their charges should be fair and reasonable.

Solicitors' charges are usually worked out according to the time spent on the matter. This is usually an hourly figure, which has to cover overheads and salaries. This hourly figure is then subject to a mark-up, which is often referred to as "care and conduct" or "uplift". This is a percentage of the costs, which is usually added as a lump sum to the bill. It is, in effect, a responsibility allowance to reflect the complexity, difficulty and skill associated with the work. It is normally between 10 and 15 per cent. The Legal Services Ombudsman has commented on the "mysteries" of this "uplift" for care and attention, on the basis that most clients assume that they are already paying for this in the standard fee for the work.[76] The "uplift", together with the

---

[74] *First Annual Report of the Office for the Supervision of Solicitors* 1996/97, at p.15.

[75] *Second Annual Report of the Legal Services Ombudsman 1992*, at pp.14–15.

[76] *Seventh Annual Report of the Legal Services Ombudsman 1997*, at p.14; *Third Annual Report of the Legal Services Ombudsman 1993*, p.19.

addition of value-added tax and disbursements, can greatly increase the expected cost of the services. For example, in one case referred to by the Ombudsman,[77] a complainant was quoted an hourly rate of £85. After the inclusion of a mark-up for care and attention and value-added tax, the actual hourly rate was £150.[78]

According to the National Consumer Council, there is no reason to believe that solicitors make unreasonable charges. The main problem is that clients have little idea about the charges. This lack of information hinders competition, as consumers cannot make price-sensitive choices.[79] One safeguard for consumers, therefore, is regulation to ensure that clients are aware of the cost of services. The Law Society has taken action to deal with "ambush charging" by solicitors. This is where solicitors provide little or no information about their charges. Clients are then "ambushed" at a later date by being presented with a bill which, although reasonable for the work done, is far more than the client expected.[80]

Professional standards now require that solicitors should inform clients of the likely costs of their services. This involves giving the best possible information, in writing, about likely costs. Where the matter is protracted, there should be regular updates of the fees, and at least every six months, clients should be told the approximate costs to date.[81] Where the requirements on information about costs have not been complied with, this is evidence of inadequate professional service.[82] In the absence of the required written information, any dispute about costs will be resolved in favour of the client.[83]

Despite these safeguards for clients, there is evidence that the provisions about costs are not widely enforced. Until this is done, the Legal Services Ombudsman believes that lack of accurate costs information will remain a widespread source of dissatisfaction for clients.[84] The Ombudsman gives an example of the reluctance of solicitors to tell clients how much the case is likely to cost. In one case, the solicitor was instructed in connection with a number of

---

[77] *ibid.*, at p.14.

[78] In this case, the Ombudsman recommended that the solicitors pay compensation of £300 to the complainant, for failing to make their charging arrangements transparent.

[79] *Ordinary Justice: Legal services and the courts in England and Wales: a consumer view* (1989), at p.163, National Consumer Council.

[80] *Third Annual Report of the Legal Services Ombudsman 1983*, at p.9.

[81] *Second Annual Report of the Legal Services Ombudsman 1992*, at p.15.

[82] *Third Annual Report of the Legal Services Ombudsman 1993*, at p.9.

[83] The Law Society has recently amended the Practice Rules to require solicitors to give information about costs, which must not be inaccurate or misleading. They will come into operation on September 3, 1999 (see *Law Society Gazette*, April 21, 1999 at pp. ii–iii).

[84] *Sixth Annual Report of the Legal Services Ombudsman 1996*, at p.4.

commercial and property transactions. It was agreed that the costs could be taken from the proceeds of sale of the client's flat. Nothing more definite was arranged about costs, and it therefore came as a shock to the client to receive bills totaling £30,000. Although the solicitor had done a great deal of work, there had been inadequate information about costs. The Ombudsman recommended that the solicitor pay the complainant £5,000 compensation for the distress and inconvenience caused to him by being taken by surprise by such a large bill at a late stage in the transaction.[85]

The Government has now entered the arena of costs and charges. It has announced that it intends to make legal bills more predictable by ensuring that lawyers provide full and clear information to their clients about the likely cost of taking a case. There is also an intention to make legal services more affordable by regulating, where appropriate, the cost which lawyers can charge their own clients or recover from the other side.[86]

There are regulations which enable clients to challenge the charges made by solicitors. If clients are dissatisfied with the amount charged, the fees can be reviewed in two ways. They can be taxed by the court, as outlined in Chapter 3. As we saw then, this procedure is risky and could involve the client paying court fees in addition to the original bill, if the application is not successful.

The other method is the remuneration certificate procedure, which is administered by the Law Society.[87] The purpose of this is to establish whether the fees charged are reasonable, and if not, what reduction should be made. This procedure is free. It can only be used in matters which do not involve court proceedings. Only the client of the solicitor can apply, except in the case of wills where the solicitor is the only executor. In this case, applications can be made by residuary beneficiaries. A remuneration certificate can only be granted if the bill has not been paid, and is less than £50,000. The application has to be made within one month of the solicitor informing the person in writing of the right to apply for a remuneration certificate.[88] Where this has not been done, an application can be made within three months of receiving the bill.

The application has to be made by the solicitor on behalf of the client. If the bill is unpaid, the solicitor can ask for 50 per cent of it to be paid. The solicitor then completes an application form, and

---

[85] *Seventh Annual Report of the Legal Services Ombudsman 1997*, at p.14.
[86] *Modernising Justice*, White Paper, Cm.155 (1998), para. 2.34.
[87] It is administered by the Law Society's remuneration certificate department, which is one of the functions of the Office for the Supervision of Solicitors.
[88] This information is usually printed on the bill.

sends it with the file to the remuneration certificate department. The department sends a copy of the completed form to the client for comment. Where possible the department will try to resolve the dispute. If this is not possible, the matter is examined in more detail, and a provisional assessment is prepared. If both the solicitor and the client agree to the provisional assessment, a remuneration certificate is issued for that amount and this will have to be paid.

If the whole bill has not been paid, interest can be charged on the amount outstanding from one month after the bill was sent. To avoid this, the client can pay the bill and inform the solicitors that it is only paid on condition that they obtain a remuneration certificate. Solicitors are not obliged to accept the payment on this basis. In the year ending August 31, 1997, there were 1,300 applications for remuneration certificates, compared with 1,798 in the previous year. There were 1,008 certificates issued, and more than half resulted in a reduction in favour of the client.[89] In the 16-month period ending on December 31, 1998, there were 1,614 remuneration certificates issued, just over 70 per cent of which resulted in a reduction of the bill in favour of the client.[90]

Although this procedure is a useful mechanism for clients, there are two particular problems for consumers. Firstly, the right to apply for a remuneration certificate is forfeited if the client pays the bill first. There is no obligation on the solicitor to warn the client that paying the bill will have such a consequence. If remuneration certificates exist for the protection of clients, all clients need to know about them.[91] Consumer interests would be safeguarded by making disclosure of their existence, and their limitations, compulsory.[92]

Another problem is that the procedure cannot be used where there is a formal agreement with the solicitor about charges. These agreements are known as non-contentious business agreements.[93] They usually involve an agreement about the hourly rate to be charged by the solicitor. They ought, therefore, to make the client's liability for costs clear. Unfortunately, they can obscure the true position, because often the client has no real idea of the hours that may be involved. An hourly rate is meaningless without this information. Where a client signs such an agreement, the right to a

---

[89] *First Annual Report of the Office for the Supervision of Solicitors 1996/97*, at p.10.

[90] Office for the Supervision of Solicitors, *Annual Report 1997–1998*, at p. 14. A review of the remuneration certificate procedure is planned for 1999.

[91] The Office for the Supervision of Solicitors has found that, in a significant number of cases, solicitors had not given proper notice to clients of their rights to a remuneration certificate (*OSS Bulletin*, April 1998, at p.4).

[92] *Seventh Annual Report of the Legal Services Ombudsman 1997*, at p.18.

[93] Such agreements are allowed by s. 57 of the Solicitors Act 1957.

remuneration certificate is lost. These agreements therefore can give the appearance of offering protection, while actually weakening the client's position to challenge a bill. The Legal Services Ombudsman believes that solicitors should not be able to by-pass the remuneration certificate procedure in this way, and that the effect of entering a non-contentious business agreement should be clearly explained to clients.[94]

Professional conduct and standards

It is in the nature of professions that they produce codes of conduct, which have to be observed by their members. The existence of such a code is often seen as one of the most important characteristics which distinguish professions from other occupations. The Green Paper[95] specifically charged the professional bodies with ensuring standards of competence and conduct, and of guaranteeing that the services their members provided were economic and efficient. New professional bodies will be recognised[96] as authorised to provide legal services only if they can ensure that they will be able to maintain and enforce appropriate standards of conduct and behaviour for their members.

The Law Society publishes the *Guide to Professional Conduct of Solicitors*, which sets out the principles and rules governing the conduct of solicitors. It is very comprehensive, covering all the statutory and non-statutory regulations for solicitors, and it had its origins in *A Guide to the Professional Conduct and Etiquette of Solicitors* published in 1960. It is published about every three years and between these times, a bulletin is published which acts a supplement to it. The latest *Guide* was published in 1996, and runs to almost 700 pages. It is subdivided into seven parts, and each section sets out basic principles, together with a commentary and annexes of relevant statutory regulations, Council statements and other published guidance.[97]

Part I of the *Guide*, Solicitors in Practice, deals with the rules and principles of professional conduct. Practice Rule 1 sets out the general principle for guiding the conduct of a solicitor. The rule states that solicitors are not to do anything in the course of their work which

---

[94] *Sixth Annual Report of the Legal Services Ombudsman 1996*, at p.15.

[95] *The Work and Organisation of the Legal Profession*, Cm.570 (1989).

[96] Under the procedure set up by the Courts and Legal Services Act 1990.

[97] Practice rules and other regulations are made by the Council of the Law Society. These matters, however, come within the province of the Standards and Guidance Committee and the Professional Standards and Development Directorate, which also have responsibility for updating the *Guide*.

compromises or impairs their independence or integrity. Solicitors must not act in a way which interferes with a person's freedom to instruct a solicitor of his or her choice. They must always act in the best interests of the client. They must not compromise their good reputation or that of the profession, or their proper standard of work or duty to the court. The commentary to this rule advises that it should be given a common-sense interpretation.

Part II of the *Guide* is concerned with international aspects of practice, which means practice outside England and Wales. Part III deals with the relationship with clients, for example taking instructions, client care, conflict of interests, confidentiality and standards of work. Solicitors must cease to act for a client if a conflict of interest arises, and in conveyancing matters they may not normally act for both sides to a transaction. Part IV deals with relationships with non-clients, for example, third parties, other lawyers and other professionals. Part V is concerned with particular areas of practice, for example litigation and advocacy, conveyancing and property selling, investment business, alternative dispute resolution, insolvency practice, and the administration of estates. The financial regulations governing solicitors' practices are dealt with in Part VI.[98] Part VII of the *Guide* deals with complaints and the disciplinary process, including the Office for the Supervision of Solicitors and the Solicitors Disciplinary Tribunal.

The General Council of the Bar produces the *Code of Conduct of the Bar of England and Wales*, which regulates how barristers may practice.[99] The rules are elaborate and wide-ranging. Like the rules relating to solicitors, the independence of the barrister is stressed, and also the protection of the lay client's best interests. Many of the rules are concerned with advice and advocacy in contentious work. For example, barristers in independent practice must comply with the "cab-rank rule". This means that a barrister is obliged to accept any brief, provided it is within his or her range of competence, he or she is not otherwise engaged, and an appropriate fee is paid.

There are also rules about barristers' relationships with the courts, tribunals, other barristers and professional and lay clients. The *Code* deals with such matters as returning briefs, and the conduct of the case in court. It covers practice overseas, and the rules governing practice in this country by foreign lawyers, and practice in the European Union. Because barristers do not hold money on behalf of clients,

---

[98] As an important safeguard for consumers, clients' money must be kept in a separate account.

[99] This was first published in 1981. Before this time, there was no written code to cover conduct.

there is no need for rules of conduct to guard against fraud or mismanagement. In addition to the *Code of Conduct* itself, there are *Written Standards for the Conduct of Professional Work* and *Chambers Administration Guidelines*, which is a practising handbook.

Although it is a function of the professional bodies to make rules of professional conduct,[1] the Courts and Legal Services Act 1990 provided for some state intervention. Since that Act, legal education and professional conduct rules relating to litigation, advocacy, and rights of audience, have been subject to the overall supervision mechanisms created by the Act. These are described in Chapter 3. The result is that, in practice, many changes to the codes of practice of both the Law Society and Bar Council have to be approved in this way. There is thus a large measure of state intervention in the detailed regulatory powers of the professional bodies. This development was acknowledged by the Law Society in 1990, when it spoke of the "continuing encroachment on self-regulation by governmental bodies" which would result in the regulation of the profession becoming increasingly complicated.[2]

The guides and codes of conduct provide as comprehensive an account as is possible about the rules and regulations covering the professional conduct of barristers and solicitors. They ought therefore to be useful in establishing whether the correct practice has been followed in a particular instance. Indeed, the White Paper[3] suggested that certain areas of practice were of such fundamental importance that there should be clear written statements of the practice which must be followed. These statements should be set out in ways which were accessible to lawyers and clients. Unfortunately, it appears that the regulations are not always clear, nor are they particularly accessible. The previous Legal Services Ombudsman considered that the Law Society's *Guide* was "tangential in its approach rather than incisive and to the point". The 1993 edition, some 845 pages long, was an "extremely difficult reference book to use," and was "frequently opaque and obscure". Rather than setting out clear written statements of practice, it appeared that some of the principles and commentary had been drafted "with the intention of allowing maximum scope for interpretation".[4]

The present edition[5] has been reduced to 670 pages. Despite having

---

[1] The Solicitors Act 1974 provided that many of the conduct rules made by the Law Society had to be approved by the Master of the Rolls.

[2] *Strategy for the Decade* (1990), The Law Society.

[3] *Legal Services: A Framework for the Future*, White Paper, Cm.740 (1989), para. 4.8.

[4] *Fifth Annual Report of the Legal Services Ombudsman 1995*, at p.9.

[5] The 7th edition, published in 1996.

the objective of being comprehensive yet manageable, it is still "not an easy reference book to use" and the rules often require "interpretation or subjective judgments".[6] It is still so detailed that "most practitioners cannot possibly be aware of all of its rules," and it may be that some rules are broken "through inadvertence" because of their "sheer bulk".[7] The National Consumer Council has also expressed concern that it is not always clear whether some practices may be regarded as professional misconduct.[8] It may be that part of the problem is that the *Guide* seeks to combine the functions of a rule book and a manual of good practice.[9]

Enforcement of professional standards

Codes of conduct are only as good as the mechanisms in place to enforce them. There is evidence that some of the rules are widely flouted and not enforced. For example, the cab-rank rule is said to be so widely flouted as to be seen by some as a "joke".[10] Even if this has not been proved, it is of concern that this is a widely-held view.

The first Legal Services Ombudsman was critical on a number of occasions of the way professional bodies dealt with cases involving allegations of breach of the code of conduct. In his first annual report in 1991, he emphasised that professional bodies must ensure compliance where there had been a clear breach of the rules. He warned that "technical" breaches and flexibility in interpreting the rules would lead to a decline in standards.[11] He also felt that detailed reasons for decisions should be given in conduct cases, so that complainants could have confidence that cases of professional misconduct were dealt with without any inherent bias in favour of solicitors.[12]

Later reports highlighted that there seemed to be a reluctance to discipline solicitors in cases where there had been a breach of the rules. The rules were too liberally interpreted, particularly where there

---

[6] *Sixth Annual Report of the Legal Services Ombudsman 1996*, at p.7.

[7] A. Sherr, "Inculcating Professional Codes and Professional Behaviour" in *Proceedings from the Annual Research Conference 1998. Governing the Profession* (1998). The Law Society: Research and Policy Planning Unit.

[8] *Ordinary Justice. Legal Services and the Courts in England and Wales: a consumer view (1989)*, at p.204, National Consumer Council.

[9] *Fifth Annual Report of the Legal Services Ombudsman 1995*, at p.9.

[10] *Blueprint for the Bar. Report of the Bar Standards review Body* (1994), at pp.24–25, Chairman: The Lord Alexander of Weedon.

[11] *First Annual Report of the Legal Services Ombudsman 1991*, at p.17.

[12] *Fifth Annual Report of the Legal Services Ombudsman 1995*, at p.11.

was a direct contravention of the rules of conduct in relation to conflicts of interest.[13] The Ombudsman was also concerned that there was an unwillingness to declare that there had been a breach of professional conduct in cases which required a value judgment. There was also an over-reliance on reports by independent solicitors in making decisions about these matters.[14] Because of the lack of confidence in the professional bodies' ability to deal with conduct issues, the previous Ombudsman dealt with a number of them himself. He awarded compensation to the consumer, rather than leaving it to the professional body to impose some disciplinary sanction.[15]

These criticisms were directed against the Solicitors Complaints Bureau.[16] The present Ombudsman has not highlighted any particular difficulties with conduct issues in her annual report. It may be that the Office for the Supervision of Solicitors, the successor to the Solicitors Complaints Bureau, is being a "stronger champion of the rule book than its predecessor was inclined to be".[17]

Codes of conduct and practice must be enforced if consumers are to have any confidence in their ability to protect their interests. If professional bodies are too ready to allow technical breaches to go unchecked, or allow a flexible interpretation of the rules, consumers may conclude that the rules exist to protect the profession, rather than the consumer's legitimate interests. As the Ombudsman has noted, there seems to be "little point" in the Law Society going to the trouble of producing such a detailed *Guide* if it is to be interpreted so freely that clear breaches of the rules go unchecked.[18]

The Office for the Supervision of Solicitors

The practice rules and other regulations of the Law Society are enforced through the Office for the Supervision of Solicitors.[19] This was set up by the Law Society on September 1, 1996, as the organisation responsible for regulating the profession, guarding

---

[13] *Sixth Annual Report of the Legal Services Ombudsman 1996*, at p.8.

[14] *Fifth Annual Report of the Legal Services Ombudsman 1995*, at p.11.

[15] *Sixth Annual Report of the Legal Services Ombudsman 1996*, at p.7.

[16] This was replaced by the Office for the Supervision of Solicitors, which is discussed later in the chapter.

[17] The Ombudsman urged the Office for the Supervision of Solicitors to be so, if it were to retain its initial credibility (*Sixth Annual Report of the Legal Services Ombudsman 1996*, at p.7).

[18] *Sixth Annual Report of the Legal Services Ombudsman 1996*, at p.10.

[19] Serious cases are referred to the Solicitors Disciplinary Tribunal, which is discussed later in the chapter.

professional standards and investigating complaints about service and conduct. Its mission is to work for "excellence and fairness in guarding standards", and it is committed to providing high levels of service as well as impartial and effective mechanisms to resolve complaints.

It replaced the Solicitors Complaints Bureau, and its new name reflects more accurately its overall role which is to regulate the profession, rather than simply deal with complaints.[20] Despite its name, the Solicitors Complaints Bureau never did have the sole function of dealing with complaints against solicitors. It had a wide range of regulatory functions, which have now been taken over by the Office for the Supervision of Solicitors.[21] Disciplinary and regulatory matters form the vast majority of its work, and it has a major role in enforcing professional standards and regulating the profession.

The work of the Office for the Supervision of Solicitors is clearly demarcated into client complaints and regulatory matters, and its organisational structure reflects these two separate aspects of its work. The two main divisions, the Office for Client Relations and the Office for Professional Regulation reflect the dual functions of the new body. The former is concerned with the level of professional service provided to clients by solicitors, and this is discussed in detail in Chapter 5. It is the Office for Professional Regulation which deals with regulatory matters, enforcing professional standards and allegations of serious professional misconduct. Its work encompasses the regulation of practising certificates, interventions into solicitors' practices, and prosecutions before the Solicitors Disciplinary Tribunal. It also runs the Law Society's compensation fund and the remuneration certificate procedure, discussed above.

As well as these two main divisions, the Office for the Supervision of Solicitors has a Front Office, which receives all new matters and tries to resolve complaints. If they cannot be resolved at this stage, it routes them to one of the two case-working offices, depending on whether the issue is concerned with inadequate professional services or conduct. Co-ordination of the Office for the Supervision of Solicitors is provided by the Director's Office, which is responsible for policy and committee business.

The Office for the Supervision of Solicitors is governed by a

---

[20] *Fifth Annual Report of the Legal Services Ombudsman 1995*, at p.8.

[21] These functions include responsibility for the inspection of solicitors' accounts; the imposition and removal of restrictions on practising certificates; interventions in a solicitor's practice; the administration of the compensation fund; the remuneration certificates procedure; prosecution in the Solicitors' Disciplinary Tribunal.

committee of the Law Society, the Compliance and Supervision Committee. It has 23 members, 10 of whom are non-solicitors. Of the solicitor members, eight serve on the Law Society Council, and five are non-Council members. The non-Council solicitors and lay members are appointed by the Master of the Rolls.[22] The lay members play an active role in policy making and the complaint handling process.[23] The committee is divided into two sub-committees, which also reflect the dual nature of the organisation. The Client Relations Sub-committee has a lay majority and lay chair.[24] The Professional Regulation Sub-committee has a solicitor majority and solicitor chair. It has a number of case-working sub-committees. These work in panels of three or five, and for professional regulatory work there is a solicitor majority and a solicitor chair.[25] This division of work into two distinct areas, with separate sub-committees, ensures that the profession retains its control over disciplinary matters.

The Office for Professional Regulation is divided into four units: solicitors practice unit; monitoring and investigation unit; legal services and compensation fund. The solicitors practice unit deals with casework relating to regulation and conduct matters. Most of the staff are legally qualified. Its work includes the imposition and removal of conditions on practising certificates, authorising inspections of accounts, and the investigation of serious professional misconduct. In the most serious cases, it could decide to intervene in a firm, or refer a matter to the Solicitors Disciplinary Tribunal.

The solicitors practice unit is the department which deals with the regulation of practising certificates. In 1997, 1,059 applications for practising certificates were referred before issue. This is done where solicitors have had a case referred to the Solicitors' Disciplinary Tribunal. Referrals are also made where solicitors failed to give satisfactory explanations about an issue of conduct or service. Failing to deliver an accountant's report on time, or bankruptcy, is also a

---

[22] These are now selected by an open and transparent process. In March 1997, the Office for the Supervision of Solicitors advertised for new lay and solicitor members. As a result, one solicitor and three lay members joined the committee. Three further lay members were selected during the year. The selection process followed the guidelines set out in the code of practice established by the Commissioner for Public Appointments (*First Annual Report of the Office for the Supervision of Solicitors 1996/97*, at p.5).

[23] See *First Annual Report of the Office for the Supervision of Solicitors 1996/97*, at p.5: *Sixth Annual Report of the Legal Services Ombudsman 1996*, at p.6.

[24] Its work is discussed in Chapter 5.

[25] The Compliance and Supervision Committee sits about 20 times each year as a full committee to discuss policy issues or as panels of its two casework committees. About 40 adjudicating panels meet in a full year (*First Annual Report of the Office for the Supervision of Solicitors 1996/97*, at p.8).

matter for referral. Typical conditions include the submission of half-yearly or quarterly accounts. There could also be a condition to work only in partnership or in approved employment. Sometimes practising certificates are granted only if the solicitor attends an approved course.[26] Solicitors may also be restricted from providing the full range of legal services, for example, by being prevented from holding clients' money or providing probate services. Decisions on conditions on practising certificates can be made by assistant directors in the department. The matter can also be referred to the Compliance and Supervision Committee. There is a right of appeal to the appeal committee of the Compliance and Supervision Committee,[27] and then to the Master of the Rolls.

The monitoring and investigation unit carries out the examination and inspections of solicitors' accounts. It used to consist of two separate departments, investigation accountants and monitoring. These were merged in May 1997 in order to provide a more systematic and co-ordinated approach to compliance and preventing dishonesty and fraud. It is staffed by trained accountants. By the end of August 1997, it had visited 308 firms in connection with accounts monitoring, and 149 firms for investment business monitoring. In the year ending August 1997, investigation accountants completed 583 inspections of accounts.[28] In 1998, 722 inspections were completed.[29]

The monitoring and investigation unit also operates the systems known as Red Alert and fraud intelligence. These are mechanisms by which solicitors can report concerns that fellow solicitors may be involved in professional malpractice. Solicitors are encouraged to do so, in the interests of the profession as a whole. In certain circumstances there is a professional obligation to do so. The procedure is a method for the profession itself to weed out those who may bring the profession into disrepute. It is a service available for use by solicitors and their staff. Causes of concern, which solicitors should report, are cheques being returned, or a sudden departure of employees from a firm. Solicitors should also report persistent failures to correspond or answer calls, and suspected mortgage fraud or suspected dishonesty. Matters reported are treated in confidence, the identity of those reporting is never revealed to the person about whom concern has been expressed, and even anonymous calls are taken. When the Office for the Supervision of Solicitors receives information through this method, it undertakes its own independent

---

[26] For example, an accounts course.
[27] This must be done within 28 days.
[28] *First Annual Report of the Office for the Supervision of Solicitors 1996/97*, at p.12.
[29] Office for the Supervision of Solicitors, *Annual Report 1997–1998*, at p.6.

investigation into the allegations made, before deciding on appropriate sanctions.

It is the fraud intelligence unit which processes information about possible dishonesty. This information can come from the profession (sometimes through Red Alert), or from other bodies, such as the police, regulatory bodies, the financial sector, and the public. Between May 1, and August 31, 1997 it uncovered a shortfall of £370,618 on client accounts in 11 firms.[30]

Sanctions

Sanctions which can be imposed by the Office for the Supervision of Solicitors for breach of the rules include the solicitor being "deprecated,"[31] or receiving various levels of "rebuke". The previous Legal Services Ombudsman considered these to be fairly low level sanctions, which amounted to "very little except perhaps injured pride".[32] Certainly the "rebuke" or "severe rebuke" involved no expense or inconvenience. It was only in the case of a Chairman's rebuke that expense and inconvenience was involved, as in this case, the solicitor had to present himself or herself before the Chair of the Compliance and Supervision Committee.

In the more serious cases of professional misconduct, the Office for the Supervision of Solicitors can intervene in a solicitor's practice, which in many cases means effectively closing down a firm. It is the legal services unit which authorises such interventions.[33] Intervention will occur where there is a suspicion of dishonesty by the solicitor, or there has been a failure to comply with the rules about accounts, or adequate professional indemnity cover. There can also be an intervention where the solicitor is adjudged bankrupt, or is in prison. Interventions can occur in the case of sole practitioners who cannot attend to their practices, either because they are incapacitated through illness or accident, or because they have been removed or suspended from the roll.

In 1996–97, there were interventions in 78 firms, 25 of which were for suspected dishonesty, and the remaining 53 for difficulties not relating to dishonesty. Altogether, 71 of the firms where interventions

---

[30] *First Annual Report of the Office for the Supervision of Solicitors 1996/97*, at p.13.

[31] There is a proposal to change the terminology to "disapprove of" (*First Annual Report of the Office for the Supervision of Solicitors 1996/97*, at p.12).

[32] *Fifth Annual Report of the Legal Services Ombudsman 1995*, at p.10.

[33] The legal services unit also conducts all litigation, costs recovery and prosecutions before the Solicitors Disciplinary Tribunal.

took place were sole practitioners. This is attributable to the fact that there is less scope for supervision of solicitors who practise without partners.[34] The trend for interventions is increasing.[35] There were 115 interventions from September 1, 1997 to December 31, 1998. Of these, 53 (46 per cent) were for suspected dishonesty. The remainder were concerned with such matters as mismanagement, and the ill-health or death of sole practitioners.[36]

One factor which limits the utility of the disciplinary mechanisms of the professional body is the standard of proof required in cases of professional misconduct. As we shall see in Chapter 5, in the case of complaints about inadequate professional services, the matter has to be proved on the balance of probabilities. But in misconduct cases, the matter has to be proved beyond reasonable doubt, which is a much more rigorous standard. This rigorous standard is appropriate where the solicitor's livelihood is at stake, as is the case in proceedings before the Solicitors Disciplinary tribunal, or where there is a possibility that a condition will be imposed on the practising certificate. But it is questionable whether natural justice requires the same standard of proof where there is only a low-level sanction, for example a rebuke. To have such a high standard of proof limits the cases where an effective disciplinary sanction can be imposed for a minor breach.[37] The Office for the Supervision of Solicitors has now decided to adopt a more flexible standard of proof in disciplinary matters. The more serious the allegation, the higher will be the standard of proof required.

Another problem with the effectiveness of the disciplinary sanctions is the time taken to deal with these matters. A streamlined process was introduced for the solicitors practice unit, with a target of dealing with 90 per cent of matters within three months. Only 59 per cent of the matters were concluded within this time in the third quarter of 1998. Of the remaining claims, only 61 per cent were concluded within five months. The target for this was 100 per cent.[38]

---

[34] *First Annual Report of the Office for the Supervision of Solicitors 1996/97*, at p.15. It has also been suggested that sole practitioners experience unique occupational hazards associated with unstable practices in "trouble" areas, for example criminal, personal injury, matrimonial cases. See B. Arnold and J. Hagan, "Self-regulatory responses to professional misconduct within the legal profession" (1994) 31(2) *Canadian Review of Sociology and Anthropology* 168–183, at p.171.

[35] *Compensation Fund: Annual Report 1997 and Contributions 1998–99*, at p.4, The Law Society.

[36] Office for the Supervision of Solicitors, *Annual Report 1997–1998*, at p.10.

[37] *Fifth Annual Report of the Legal Services Ombudsman 1995*, at p.10.

[38] *Law Society Gazette*, December 2, 1998, at p.3.

Solicitors Disciplinary Tribunal

If the Office for the Supervision of Solicitors believes that there has been a serious case of professional misconduct, the matter can be referred to the Solicitors Disciplinary Tribunal. Its function is to hear and determine applications about solicitors[39] relating to allegations about conduct, which include allegations of unbefitting conduct or breaches of the rules relating to professional practice, conduct and discipline. It is independent of the Law Society, and is composed of nine lay and 18 solicitor members, who are appointed by the Master of the Rolls. The solicitor members must have not less than ten years standing. Although independent of the Law Society, the Law Society provides the premises and staff for its work, and pays the expenses of its solicitor members.[40]

It is usually the Office for the Supervision of Solicitors which brings cases before the tribunal, but anyone may make an application to it. The complaint is heard by three members, two of whom must be practising solicitors, the other being a lay person. There is thus always a majority of the profession when these decisions are made, and this illustrates the importance the profession attaches to self-regulation in disciplinary matters.

The sanctions it can impose include striking the solicitor off the roll of solicitors, suspension from practice indefinitely or for a specified period, and payment of a fine of up to £5,000 for every allegation proved. Solicitors can also be excluded from legal aid work. Where the case is brought against a former solicitor, there can be a prohibition on his or her name being restored to the roll. The solicitor may also have to pay legal costs. There is a right of appeal by the solicitor to the High Court, the Court of Appeal, and ultimately the House of Lords, against the finding of the tribunal. The findings and orders of the Tribunal are reported in the *London Gazette* and the *Law Society Gazette*, and are often widely reported in the press.

Typical cases before the tribunal deal with allegations of unbefitting conduct, and failure to keep properly written-up accounts. Most cases concern the mishandling of funds, fraud, and the failure to account. There are also cases where there has been a failure to release files.

---

[39] The Courts and Legal Services Act 1990 provides that former solicitors may be required to appear before the Solicitors Disciplinary Tribunal to answer allegations about their conduct when they were solicitors.

[40] The expenses of the lay members are paid by the Lord Chancellor' Department. There has been a call for the tribunal to be completely independent of the Law Society, and funded by the fines it levies on solicitors. See *Law Society Gazette*, October 12, 1998, at p.3.

Criminal convictions can also lead to disciplinary action before the tribunal. All criminal convictions in England and Wales involving solicitors are notified to the Law Society. Where the criminal conviction relates to behaviour outside legal practice, there can be disciplinary sanctions if it will bring the profession into disrepute.

In 1996–97, there were 277 cases referred to the tribunal from the Office for the Supervision of Solicitors. The tribunal decided 207 cases. Of these, 45 solicitors were struck off the Roll, 32 were suspended from practising and 68 were fined.[41] In 1997–98 there were 200 applications, which represents almost a doubling of the caseload since 1975. In the 16-month period up to the end of December 1998, there were 395 referrals to the tribunal of which 284 were heard. These cases resulted in 67 solicitors being struck off and 42 suspended from practising. A total of 102 solicitors were fined.[42]

There is some evidence that the tribunal is too lenient in its dealings with some solicitors. Research[43] suggests that more than half of solicitors found guilty of misusing clients' money were not struck of the roll after a disciplinary hearing. The tribunal appeared to distinguish between those solicitors who had taken money for their own use, and those who had used it improperly by not keeping it in a separate client account. In the latter case, the tribunal decided that this was not sufficiently dishonest to justify being struck off. There were even cases where solicitors were making second appearances before the tribunal for dishonesty, who were allowed to continue in practice. One case concerned a solicitor, who had received a custodial sentence for conspiracy to defraud a building society, and who had not been struck off. These are serious findings, and cast some doubt on the effectiveness of the Solicitors Disciplinary Tribunal to enforce standards.

The Bar's disciplinary machinery

The Bar's disciplinary machinery is less complex than that relating to solicitors. Under the disciplinary system, complaints against barristers on the grounds of professional misconduct or breach of proper professional standards are handled by the Professional Conduct and

---

[41] *First Annual Report of the Office for the Supervision of Solicitors 1996/97*, at p.13.

[42] Office for the Supervision of Solicitors, *Annual Report 1997–1998*, at pp.8–9.

[43] This research was conducted by the Channel 4 programme, *Dispatches—Law and Disorder*, which was broadcast on December 3, 1998. A survey of 2,000 solicitors who had appeared before the Tribunal found that 78 of them had been found guilty of misusing clients' money. Over half of these had not been struck off.

Complaints Committee of the Bar Council. This has powers delegated by the Inns of Court to investigate complaints and impose minor sanctions. It consists mainly of barristers, who need not be members of the Bar Council, and some lay members.

If the investigation reveals no prima facie case of professional misconduct, but the conduct gives cause for concern, the committee can draw attention to this in writing and advise the barrister as to future conduct. If there is a prima facie case of inadequate professional service, the matter is dealt with under the new complaints procedure which is discussed in Chapter 5. If a prima facie case of non-serious professional misconduct has been disclosed, a barrister can be required to attend informally before a panel of the committee.[44] The matter can also be dealt with by the summary procedure. This is for less serious complaints. Under this procedure, there is a hearing before a panel of between two and four barristers and a lay representative. The barrister can be advised, admonished, fined up to £500 or suspended for up to three months. The barrister can also be ordered to repay fees or be excluded from legal aid work for a defined period.

Where there is a serious case of professional misconduct, the committee can bring charges against the barrister before a Disciplinary Tribunal of the Council of the Inns of Court. This tribunal consists of a judge as chair, three practising barristers and a lay representative. The Professional Conduct and Complaints Committee acts as the prosecutor. The powers of the tribunal include disbarment, suspension from practice for any period and a fine to a maximum of £5,000. If found guilty of professional misconduct, a barrister has the right of appeal to the Visitors of the Inns of Court. The appeal will be heard by at least three judges of the high court, nominated by the Lord Chief Justice.

At one time, these proceedings were held in private, and even the fact that they were taking place at all was not disclosed. Unless a barrister was suspended or struck off, the result of the proceedings were kept private. The Bar Standards Review Body recommended that hearings should be in public, unless the tribunal in its discretion decided otherwise, on the basis that other professions have public hearings for disciplinary matters. In addition, it was recommended that all findings of professional misconduct by both the disciplinary tribunal and summary procedure should be published.[45] The Bar has now recognised the need for transparency. Under the new complaints

---

[44] This panel consists of two or three barrister members of the committee and a lay member.

[45] *Blueprint for the Bar. Report of the Bar Standards Review Body* (1994), at p.77, Chairman: The Lord Alexander of Weedon.

system[46] disciplinary tribunal hearings are now held in public. In addition, where the Bar imposes a disciplinary sanction, the complainant will be informed of the outcome.[47]

Some of the complaints about barristers come from judges and relate to the barrister's conduct in court.[48] Because of the relatively small and homogeneous nature of the Bar, informal mechanisms of control of conduct are still important. Judges can report unsatisfactory advocacy to the attention of the Bar Council. They can also see barristers privately, to invite an explanation, and if not satisfied, they can write to the head of the barrister's chambers.[49]

Like the disciplinary procedures for solicitors, these procedures are directed to examining allegations of misconduct against barristers, and to punishing them if proved.[50] They have to give a proper measure of due process, and protection for the individual. The procedures must be rigorous, formal and impartial. They exist primarily for the benefit of the profession as a means of identifying possible breaches of the code of conduct. They are not designed to give satisfaction to the complainant, except perhaps for the satisfaction of seeing the barrister disciplined. The Legal Services Ombudsman has confirmed that it is a vigorous disciplinary system. Such an approach, however, inevitably leads to the letter of the code of conduct "being trumps over what a lay person might legitimately regard as its spirit".[51] Procedures which have evolved to discipline members of a small homogeneous profession may often lead lay complainants to feel as though they are minor players. At one time, the Bar did not make it a priority to notify a complainant even of the barrister's response to a complaint.[52] It is therefore welcome news that in future the Bar will inform complainants of the outcome of disciplinary hearings.[53]

---

[46] This is discussed in more detail in Chapter 5.

[47] Seventh Annual Report of the Legal Services Ombudsman 1997, at p.20.

[48] In 1987, the Bar Council estimated that 80 per cent of complaints came from members of the public, 15 per cent were from serving prisoners, and the rest were from judges, other barristers, solicitors and magistrates (Counsel, September 1987).

[49] Blueprint for the Bar. Report of the Bar Standards Review Body (1994), Chairman: The Lord Alexander of Weedon.

[50] Their purpose is not to provide compensation to complainants. However, in professional misconduct proceedings, the panels and tribunals can order all or part of the barrister's fees to be foregone or repaid.

[51] A. Abraham, "Prophet or High Priestess?" Counsel, December 1998, at p.18.

[52] First Annual Report of the Legal Services Ombudsman 1991, at p.12.

[53] Seventh Annual Report of the Legal Services Ombudsman 1997, at p.20.

Conclusion

It is the Government's view that the duty of a professional body is to ensure that the standards of competence and professional conduct of those who practice in the profession are sufficient "to secure adequate protection for clients".[54] The Law Society itself is of the view that the aim of its regulation procedures is to protect the client in a relationship that is inevitably unequal by virtue of the skills and knowledge possessed by the solicitor. The regulation procedures should promote high standards of competence and conduct, in order to serve effectively the administration of justice and promote confidence in the legal system.[55]

The regulatory framework for both barristers and solicitors controls entry into the profession and methods of practice. It also sets standards for competence and conduct. In the case of solicitors, many of the rules are to safeguard clients' money. Mechanisms for preventing fraud and mishandling of funds thus form a large part of the regulatory framework for solicitors. Professional misconduct can include dishonesty, serious failures to observe the ethics and rules of the profession, and serious failures of competence. The professional bodies have procedures for enforcing standards, with a range of sanctions. Ultimately, a practitioner can be expelled from the profession, and thus will no longer be able to provide legal services. In less extreme cases, there can be fines, reprimands, and restrictions on practice.

Although these disciplinary systems do protect the interests of consumers, their primary aim is disciplinary, and the emphasis is on punishment of the practitioner. Redress for the individual complainant is not the aim of the system.[56] Moreover, consumers do not even take part in the proceeding. They are not invited to attend disciplinary hearings. Their interests are not represented before disciplinary committees or tribunals, nor do they see any of the relevant documents or transcripts. Just as the victims of crime are now being given more status in the criminal justice system, so should consideration be given to the victims of professional malpractice. Consumers need to be at the heart of the disciplinary process, rather than marginal to it.

Because the procedure is disciplinary, there must be adequate

---

[54] *The Work and Organisation of the Legal Profession*, Cm.570 (1989), para. 4.1.

[55] *Strategy for the Decade* (1990), The Law Society.

[56] The Law Society has called on the Government to give it power to make costs awards against solicitors in conduct cases. At present, this can only be done for inadequate professional services (*Law Society Gazette*, March 10, 1999, at p.1).

safeguards for those accused. The usual standard in these matters is that the allegation must be proved beyond reasonable doubt. This is understandable and accepted in serious cases, which could result in the loss of livelihood. Such a standard is probably inappropriate in more minor cases, where the sanctions are not so serious. The fact that the Office for the Supervision of Solicitors has decided to be more flexible in the standard of proof required for less serious allegations is therefore to be welcomed.

Where the allegations are serious, and proved, it can be reassuring for consumers to know that miscreants can be prevented from practising. These are the infrequent cases of breach. It is often the minor breaches of the rules which need addressing, and it is here that the attention needs to be paid to the sanctions available. If practitioners feel that they have little to fear from minor breaches of the rules, it brings the system of self-regulation into disrepute. It is understandable that lawyers should respond to complaints about themselves like lawyers,[57] as due process and legal rigour is fundamental to the culture. Such an approach, however, is not appropriate for some consumer matters, where the spirit of the rules is more appropriate than a strict interpretation of the letter of the rule.

Disciplinary procedures are a valuable mechanism for the enforcement of standards. They have an important deterrent effect in reducing the incidence of shoddy work, dishonesty or other misconduct. They thus protect the interests of consumers. Their main problem is the lack of effective redress, and the standard required to prove allegations. Where the complaint is not about misconduct, but involves inadequate professional services, or shoddy work, other mechanisms are needed to provide redress for consumers. These remedies are discussed in the next chapter.

---

[57] A. Abraham, "Prophet or High Priestess?" *Counsel*, December 1998, at p.18.

Chapter 5

Client Complaints

In the previous chapter, we looked at the role of professional bodies in implementing standards of professional conduct. One of the chief claims made by the professions is that they provide assurance of quality of service[1], and one of the mechanisms for doing so is the ability to impose codes of conduct, with consequent sanctions for their breach. Disciplinary sanctions are, of course, important in maintaining quality, and they have always featured in the regulatory functions of professional bodies. Indeed, this ability to set standards and discipline members is seen as crucial to a concept of self-regulation. Mechanisms for dealing with complaints from clients which do not raise issues of a disciplinary nature, but which relate to the quality of service are, however, a comparatively recent phenomenon. In the past neither side of the profession paid sufficient attention to clients who had a grievance about the quality of the work done by a lawyer.[2]

Mechanisms for dealing with such complaints are an important aspect of regulation, and of guaranteeing quality. Both the Law Society and the Bar Council have self-regulatory procedures for handling complaints from dissatisfied clients of solicitors and barristers. They thus have a large degree of control over the way complaints are handled. Self-regulation does ensure that the legal profession bears the cost of complaint handling, rather than the taxpayer. There is also an incentive for the profession to deal with complaints effectively and efficiently, in order to keep the costs at a reasonable level.[3]

Since the Courts and Legal Services Act 1990, there is an additional tier to this complaint handling process. If the consumer is dissatisfied with the way that the professional body has handled the complaint, it

---

[1] M. Zander, *A Matter of Justice, the Legal System in Ferment* (1989), at p.74 [Oxford: Oxford University Press].

[2] *ibid.*, p.92

[3] *Fifth Annual Report of the Legal Services Ombudsman 1995*, at p.6.

can be referred to the Legal Services Ombudsman, an independent, statutory ombudsman.[4] This system of joint regulation[5] for consumer complaints provides for independent supervision of the self-regulatory process, and is therefore advantageous for consumers. However, in order to be effective, the self-regulation stage of the process must be consumer-friendly, fair and efficient, and able to achieve an acceptable level of complainant satisfaction. The public is generally suspicious of self-regulation, and if there is not a sufficient level of satisfaction, the two-tier model falls into disrepute.[6]

This chapter examines the mechanisms used by the two branches of the profession to deal with client complaints, and assesses whether they are achieving the standards required to make the two-tier model acceptable. The two branches of the profession have always had very different mechanisms for dealing with client complaints, and we shall deal with them separately.

Solicitors

There has been a continuing increase in the number of complaints about solicitors. In 1992, there were just under 20,000 complaints a year to the professional body. By 1997, this had increased to 26,445.[7] There was a dramatic increase in 1998 to 30,000 cases, and it is anticipated that there will be well over 30,000 in 1999.[8] In the 16-month period to December 31, 1998, 41,380 complaints were received.[9] The Office for the Supervision of Solicitors estimates that it is now receiving about 3,000 complaints each month.[10] Client complaints account for over 50 per cent of the complaints received, the balance coming from solicitors, organisations such as banks and building societies, and third parties.[11] It may be that the reason for the

---

[4] The role of the Legal Services Ombudsman is discussed in Chapter 6.

[5] M. Barnes, "Monitoring and Evaluating Methods of Regulation" in *Proceedings from the Annual Research Conference 1994: Profession, business or trade: Do the professions have a future?* (1994), at p.61, The Law Society's Research and Policy Planning Unit.

[6] *Fifth Annual Report of the Legal Services Ombudsman 1995*, at p.6.

[7] *Seventh Annual Report of the Legal Services Ombudsman 1997*, at p.11.

[8] *Law Society Gazette*, December 2, 1998, at p.3.

[9] Office for the Supervision of Solicitors, *Annual Report 1997–1998*, at p.5.

[10] *The OSS Bulletin*, April 1998, at p.2.

[11] Client complaints accounted for 52.2 per cent of new matters in 1996/97. The rest was made up as follows: solicitors, 21.1 per cent; organisations (including banks, building societies, the police, courts and the Legal Aid Board), 24.3 per cent; and others, including third parties, 2.4 per cent (*First Annual Report of the Office for the Supervision of Solicitors 1996/97*, at p.7).

rise in the number of complaints is increasing consumer awareness,[12] and rising expectations. It should not therefore be viewed entirely negatively.[13] Nevertheless, this is a large number of complaints, and represents one complaint made for every three practising solicitors.[14] Most of the complaints relate to poor standards of service, rather than negligence or disciplinary matters. The most common types of complaints from clients are about failures in communication, particularly in relation to costs; delay or inaction; and disregarding instructions.[15]

As we saw in Chapter 3, it was not until 1985 that the Law Society was empowered to provide remedies where there had been inadequate professional services.[16] Before this, complaints about solicitors were dealt with by the Professional Services Committee, a committee of the Law Society, which decided whether the solicitor had been guilty of professional misconduct. Although this could result in disciplinary sanctions, there was no provision to award compensation to the complainant. In order to obtain financial redress, the client had to pursue a professional negligence claim, or use the taxation procedure if the complaint related to the cost of services. The problems of using these remedies are discussed in previous chapters.[17] Most client complaints do not involve issues of professional misconduct, or serious financial loss which would justify a negligence action. These remedies are therefore irrelevant for the vast majority of complaints, which involve allegations of poor service and shoddy work.

It was therefore a welcome addition to consumer protection mechanisms when the Administration of Justice Act 1985 gave the Law Society the power to investigate complaints of inadequate professional services. The remedies provided by the Act included the power to reduce a solicitor's bill or to require work to be done again without charge.[18] It was clear during the passage of the 1985 Act that

---

[12] *First Annual Report of the Office for the Supervision of Solicitors 1996/97*, at p.7.

[13] T. Goriely and T. Williams, "A Review of Trends in Complaints and Complaint Handling" in *Governing the Profession, Proceedings from the Annual Research Conference* (1998), at p.3, The Law Society.

[14] *Seventh Annual Report of the Legal Services Ombudsman 1997*, at p.4.

[15] *ibid.*, at p.14.

[16] Section 44A of the Solicitors Act 1974, which was inserted by the Administration of Justice Act 1985. Although it was the Law Society which had requested the inclusion of these powers in the Administration of Justice Bill, this was done in response to public dissatisfaction with the existing regime.

[17] The problems with negligence actions are discussed in Chapter 2. As we saw in Chapter 3, taxation is a complicated remedy, which involves a certain amount of risk for the client, and for which legal advice is strongly recommended before an application is made.

[18] Section 93 of the Courts and Legal Services Act 1990 inserted a new S. 37A and a new schedule into the Solicitors Act 1974. This increased the powers of the Law Society, so that clients could also be provided with compensation.

the Government felt that client complaints were the "domestic concerns of the profession". It was for the profession itself to deal with them, as part of its "duties to the public to maintain the high levels of conduct, the standards of service and the collective discipline" that was expected of solicitors.[19]

The Law Society, in exercising its responsibility for investigating and resolving complaints, decided to adopt a model whereby its statutory powers were delegated to a body at arm's length from it, but still under its control. The original body, set up in 1986, was the Solicitors Complaints Bureau, which also dealt with regulatory matters. This was abolished in 1996, as a result of the mounting tide of criticism which was levelled against it during its ten-year history.[20] Before evaluating the present scheme for dealing with client complaints, it is probably helpful to examine why the Solicitors Complaints Bureau was deemed to be such a failure in its complaint handling function.

The Solicitors Complaints Bureau

The Bureau itself had been "born out of adversity" after the previous procedures for handling complaints had, "to some extent, fallen into ill-repute".[21] This was partly as a result of what became known as the Glanville Davies affair.[22] In this *cause célèbre*, the Law Society's professional purposes department, which was then responsible for complaints handling and giving ethical advice, was accused of mishandling a serious complaint by a member of the public against a council member. There was also a view that the complaint-handling procedure, before 1986, was slow and unresponsive, and lacked public confidence.[23] Even in 1979, the Royal Commission on Legal Services had found evidence of a general feeling of unease about the Law Society's handling of complaints, and a feeling that lawyers "look[ed] after their own".[24]

Because of the public disquiet about the existing procedures for handling complaints, the Law Society appointed management

---

[19] Lord Chancellor, H.L. Deb., vol 458, col. 779.

[20] It was replaced by the Office for the Supervision of Solicitors.

[21] *Solicitors Complaints Bureau, First Annual Report*, at p.2.

[22] In 1983, it was revealed in the High Court that for more than six years, senior Law Society officials had obstructed the investigation of complaints of gross professional misconduct against one of its own council members, Mr Glanville Davies.

[23] Coopers and Lybrand, *Review of the Law Society's Affairs* (1984).

[24] *Report of the Royal Commission on Legal Services*, Cmnd.7648 (1979)

consultants to advise on its regulatory functions.[25] In their report, the consultants advised that complaints and discipline should be administered separately from the Law Society, and that an independent statutory body should be set up to investigate and adjudicate on complaints against solicitors.[26] Despite this recommendation, the Law Society established a system whereby complaint-handling was dealt with by a committee of the Law Society. It did, however, accept the rationale for establishing a body which was removed from the Law Society, and decided that this could be achieved by separating complaints handling and discipline from its other functions. The Solicitors Complaints Bureau was thus established with a separate identity from the Law Society, and a separate physical location.

The fact that the Law Society, defying "the force of the argument and the persistence of the critics,"[27] had chosen not to introduce a truly independent system for handling complaints presented the newly established Bureau with a major credibility problem from the start. This perceived lack of independence from the Law Society was a constant source of criticism throughout its ten-year history. Despite the attempt by the Law Society to establish a body at arm's length from itself to deal with complaints, the Bureau was not given a separate legal identity, and its personnel remained Law Society employees. Its funding and budget were subject to the normal budgetary mechanisms of the Law Society. In addition, its adjudication and appeals committee was a standing committee of the Law Society and its chair was appointed by the Law Society and was also a member of the Law Society Council. To augment the presentational problems, the Bureau was obliged to describe itself on its letterhead as an establishment of the Law Society, and the director of the Bureau was a member of the board of management of the Law Society. The system was thus accused, with some justification, of lacking "structural propriety and public confidence".[28]

Before the Bureau was established, the National Consumer Council had concluded that a body independent of the Law Society was needed to deal with consumer complaints. It had grave doubts about the practice of solicitors investigating themselves, and was concerned about the conflict in the Law Society's dual role, in both furthering the interests of the profession, and upholding the interests of

---

[25] Coopers and Lybrand, *Review of the Law Society's Affairs* (1984).
[26] Coopers and Lybrand, *Exposure Draft Report* (1985), and Coopers and Lybrand, *Final Report* (1986).
[27] A. Newbold and G. Zellick, "Reform of the Solicitors' Complaints Procedures: Fact or Fiction?" (1987) *Civil Justice Quarterly* 25.
[28] *ibid.*, at p.26.

consumers.[29] Four years later, it was critical of the Solicitors Complaints Bureau. It suggested that if there were not substantial improvements, the Lord Chancellor should introduce an independent legal council.[30] Some five years after this, the National Consumer Council published the results of a research study, which found that the Bureau's procedures seemed to favour solicitors over complainants, and that consumers did not perceive it as independent.[31] Indeed, the Bureau's own investigation committee, which had a lay majority, had been critical both of the Bureau, and its own role within the system. It felt that the Bureau was only a "half-way house", which could not be seen to be truly independent of the Law Society. Further, the procedures had not achieved the impartiality and independence required.[32]

There was also some criticism at this time of the committee structure of the Bureau, particularly as to whether there was sufficient non-lawyer input. When the Bureau was first set up, it was responsible to two separate committees, the adjudication committee, which consisted of solicitors, and the investigation committee, which had a majority of lay members. The adjudication committee exercised the Law Society's statutory powers in relation to disciplinary matters. The investigation committee was responsible for overseeing the investigation work of the Bureau, and monitoring all complaints that went before the adjudication committee. Its role was to ensure that complaints from members of the public were investigated fully and fairly. The investigation committee did introduce an independent element into the complaint-handling process. It was supposed to ensure that the public interest was protected, as it was claimed that its majority of independently appointed lay persons would "ensure that the process of complaints investigation" was "both competent and fair".[33]

However, in 1991, without any consultation outside the Law Society, the Bureau was restructured, and the two committees were amalgamated to form one adjudication and appeals committee, with a majority (by one) of solicitors. The newly formed adjudication and

---

[29] *In Dispute with the Solicitor: consumers and the profession: a review of complaints procedures* (1985), National Consumer Council.
[30] *Ordinary Justice: Legal services and the courts in England and Wales: a consumer view* (1989), at p.218, National Consumer Council.
[31] *The Solicitors Complaints Bureau: A consumer view* (1994), at p.3, National Consumer Council.
[32] Submission to the Lord Chancellor's Department by the Investigation Committee of the Solicitors Complaints Bureau on the Green Paper *The Work and Organisation of the Legal Profession*, Cm.570 (1989), para. II.
[33] *Solicitors Complaints Bureau, First Annual Report*, at p.2.

appeals committee had two sub-committees, one of which dealt with inadequate professional services appeals. This had a lay majority and a lay chair. A Policy and Advisory Committee was established at the same time, consisting of six lay members and three solicitor members. It met at irregular intervals to discuss a "broad spectrum of issues relating to policy and procedures in complaints handling,"[34] but had less of a role to play in the handling of complaints. The National Consumer Council concluded that, although there may have been sound efficiency and management reasons for the changes, the effect was "to make the investigation process less independent and to reduce the influence of lay committee members".[35]

Of course, it does not follow that because staff and committee members are not independent of the Law Society, they are not impartial, but this inter-relationship does present problems of perception. Interestingly, although the first Legal Services Ombudsman had been critical of the Bureau, he never challenged its impartiality, and he went on record as saying that "some of the more extreme criticisms levelled at them were undoubtedly undeserved".[36] Indeed, in commenting on the National Consumer Council's findings[37] that the Bureau was not seen as independent but as favouring solicitors, he concluded that the research on which the report was based "was somewhat limited in scope".[38] It was not his view that the Bureau favoured solicitors, but that it genuinely set out to investigate complaints impartially.[39]

Another problem with the Bureau was in relation to its dual function. When it was first set up it had responsibility for the inadequate professional services jurisdiction provided for by the Administration of Justice Act 1985. It thus had responsibility for handling all complaints from consumers about solicitors. In addition, the Bureau carried out a wide range of regulatory activities on behalf of the profession. From its inception, then, and despite its title, the Solicitors Complaints Bureau was responsible for disciplinary and regulatory matters in relation to the profession. Dealing with client complaints was only a part of its work, and indeed, probably only 20 per cent of the Bureau's staff were engaged in dealing with complaints from the public.[40] This dual function of the Bureau led to a

---

[34] See *Solicitors Complaints Bureau Annual Report 1992*, at p.17.
[35] *The Solicitors Complaints Bureau: A consumer view* (1994), at p.87, National Consumer Council.
[36] *Sixth Annual Report of the Legal Services Ombudsman 1996*, at p.6.
[37] *The Solicitors Complaints Bureau: A consumer view* (1994), National Consumer Council
[38] *Fourth Annual Report of the Legal Services Ombudsman 1994*, at p.8.
[39] *ibid.*, at p.9.
[40] *Fifth Annual Report of the Legal Services Ombudsman 1995*, at p.8.

complicated committee structure, and was probably a source of confusion for consumers.

The profession itself was critical of the Bureau, and with a budget of £10.7 million in 1994,[41] it was a very considerable drain on revenues provided by the profession. A survey of solicitors' firms conducted in 1995[42] reported a perception that the Bureau was not providing value for money. Only 14 per cent of solicitors thought that the Bureau provided a good service relative to its cost, with another 20 per cent responding that it only provided average service. A total of 35 per cent thought that it was providing poor service, and almost one-third (31 per cent) of the respondents said that they were unsure or did not know whether it was providing good service. While these responses are not conclusive, they do not indicate that overwhelming support for the Solicitors Complaints Bureau existed at the time.

The Bureau's procedures, too, were cumbersome and slow, and thus a source of dissatisfaction. In 1989, during the early days of the Bureau's operation, the National Consumer Council found consumer dissatisfaction in relation to complaints about poor work and actions in negligence.[43] In a report five years later, it concluded that the system was "ineffective, slow and weighted against the complainants".[44] The White paper[45] in 1989 had also noted the public disquiet about the effectiveness of procedures for dealing with failures in professional competence. Research by the Law Society in 1990 had found that 60 per cent of complainants were dissatisfied with the way their complaint was handled by the Bureau, with only 31 per cent claiming satisfaction.[46] The Legal Services Ombudsman was also critical of the Bureau's office procedures.[47] These appeared to him to be too defensive on behalf of the Law Society rather than "a

---

[41] Solicitors Complaints Bureau, *100 Facts at a glance*,(1994). The newly established Office for the Supervision of Solicitors had a net expenditure of £12.8 million in 1996–97, its first year of operation.

[42] Research conducted by R. James and M. Seneviratne, by means of a postal questionnaire sent out in July 1995. The questionnaire was sent to 1,674 firms, 1,544 containing 20 partners or fewer, and which were randomly selected from *The Law Society's Directory of Solicitors and Barristers 1993*. There was a response rate of 23 per cent. Some of the results of the survey were published in R. James and M. Seneviratne, "Solicitors and client complaints" (1996) 6(3) *Consumer Policy Review* 101–105.

[43] *Ordinary Justice: Legal services and the courts in England and Wales: a consumer view* (1989), at pp.203–204, National Consumer Council.

[44] *The Solicitors Complaints Bureau: A consumer view* (1994), at p.104, National Consumer Council.

[45] *Legal Services: A Framework for the Future*, Cm.740 (1989).

[46] *A Survey of Complainants Satisfaction among Lay Complainants to the Solicitors Complaints Bureau* (1990), The Law Society.

[47] *First Annual Report of the Legal Services Ombudsman 1991*, at p.9; *Second Annual Report of the Legal Services Ombudsman 1992*, at p.10.

problem-solving mechanism for complainants".[48] He was also critical of the tendency by the Bureau to reject complaints too readily, observing that a "well-motivated complaints handling body...will not seize on the first indication that a complaint may be outside its terms of reference" in order to reject it.[49]

Proposals for reform

Given the breadth of these criticisms, it was clear that the Bureau could not continue as it was. There was no doubt that the Bureau faced a difficult task, and it was itself aware of the awkward position in which it was placed. It had, on the one hand, to work with the profession and maintain the confidence of solicitors who funded its operation. On the other, it had to deal fairly with an increasing number of complaints, and reassure the public that a firm line was being taken on poor quality work.[50] The Legal Services Ombudsman believed that the real difficulty for the Bureau resulted from its having to perform the two essentially incompatible functions of being a "policeman of the profession" and at the same time a "consumer-friendly complaints handler".[51]

There were various options for reform. One was to establish an independent system. This was an option favoured by the National Consumer Council, which, with three critical reports in 10 years about the way the Law Society dealt with consumers complaints,[52] had been a strong advocate of an independent system. It proposed setting up a new independent Legal Services Complaints Council to handle complaints and to help set and enforce standards of conduct and entry requirements for the profession. This Council would have a non-lawyer majority and a non-lawyer chair, and its members would be appointed by the Lord Chancellor. The Council would appoint an ombudsman or regional ombudsmen to deal with all complaints about solicitors, and would be able to award compensation of up to £5,000. It would thus fulfil the roles of both the Solicitors Complaints Bureau and the Legal Services Ombudsman, although it was envisaged that

---

[48] *Third Annual Report of the Legal Services Ombudsman 1993*, at p.8.

[49] *Sixth Annual Report of the Legal Services Ombudsman 1996*, at p.8.

[50] *Solicitors Complaints Bureau Annual Report 1993*, at p.6.

[51] *Fifth Annual Report of the Legal Services Ombudsman 1995*, at p.8.

[52] *In Dispute with the Solicitor: consumers and the profession: a review of complaints procedures* (1985); *Ordinary Justice: Legal services and the courts in England and Wales: a consumer view* (1989); *The Solicitors Complaints Bureau: A consumer view* (1994), National Consumer Council.

the ombudsman would "act for" the complainant in order to redress the "inevitable power imbalance".[53]

This was never going to be an option favoured by the Law Society. Ten years previously, in the mid–1980s, it had not accepted the rationale for establishing an independent body, and had chosen instead to retain control of the process of complaint handling. This reflected concerns about the funding of the system. The involvement of the profession was also seen as an essential aspect of self-regulation, which involved of necessity, a system of peer review.[54] In its own proposals for reform, the Law Society emphasised that it would not surrender its statutory responsibilities in the area of complaint handling. Nor should it surrender any other field of regulation, but it should rather work to improve and strengthen self-regulation.[55] The Law Society's consultation document specifically rejected the National Consumer Council proposals, just as it had done with the recommendations of Coopers and Lybrand in 1985. It felt that it was for the profession to take responsibility for the standard and conduct of its members. This, it claimed, was in the interests of the reputation of the profession as a whole. Any government intervention "would be inimical to the public and the professional interest" as solicitors often had professional responsibilities to oppose government policies or actions.[56] In addition, the Secretary-General of the Law Society completely rejected the idea that there is any conflict between the role of professional bodies as trade unions and disciplinarians, maintaining that "[r]eputation and regulation are inextricably linked".[57] The Law Society pointed out that, even if there were an independent body, it would still have to be funded by the profession.

Another option was to improve the public's perception of the Bureau. It could perhaps be given a different title, and its remit could be confined to handling complaints from consumers only, not from other members of the profession. In respect of the existing title, the first Legal Services Ombudsman felt that this was a misnomer. Only 20 per cent of the Bureau's staff dealt with consumer complaints, the other 80 per cent dealing with professional complaints, default,

---

[53] *The Solicitors Complaints Bureau: A consumer view* (1994), at p.4, National Consumer Council.

[54] Submission to the Lord Chancellor's Department by the Investigation Committee of the Solicitors Complaints Bureau on the Green Paper *The Work and Organisation of the Legal Profession* Cm.570, Annex B—Minority report of the two Council Members of the Investigation Committee.

[55] *The Supervision of Solicitors. The Next Decade*, Consultation Paper issued by the Law Society, July 1995, at p.2.

[56] *ibid.*, at pp.9,10.

[57] John Hayes, "Law Society compares professions," *The Lawyer*, January 6, 1995.

dishonesty and regulatory matters of one kind or other.[58] From a budget £10.7 million, just over one-third was spent on complaints handling and dealing with misconduct and regulatory breaches not caused by dishonesty.[59] The Bureau's main role had been very much that of a regulator of the profession, rather than dealing with complaints against solicitors.

The first Legal Services Ombudsman had been of the opinion that it would be preferable to separate the two functions of the Bureau. Regulatory functions, he asserted, should be under the direct control of the Law Society. The complaint handling function could then be dealt with by a separate body, which might even keep the name of Solicitors Complaints Bureau, because it would only be concerned with complaints handling and monitoring firms' own internal complaints procedures. The Ombudsman did not argue for a completely independent body to be set up (as the National Consumer Council had), but recommended that the Bureau should be given as much independence from the Law Society as possible. It should be in the control of a separate body, responsible to a council or committee, with a lay majority and a lay chairperson.[60]

The Law Society's reform package did not involve a radical alteration to the system. Instead, it recommended that the Bureau be replaced with an organisation whose remit and title would emphasise its role as a regulator of solicitors. This would change the perception that it existed wholly or principally to deal with client complaints. Like the Solicitors Complaints Bureau, it would have regulatory as well as investigation and adjudication functions, and it would still be under the control of the Law Society. The Council of the Law Society therefore decided to replace the Bureau with a newly formed Office for the Supervision of Solicitors. The rationale for this was that if there were to be any progress in improving standards, it was necessary to integrate the work of the bodies dealing with complaints, education, practice improvement, professional insurance and monitoring and setting standards. This task would be more difficult if complaints and other supervisory matters were dealt with by a body outside the Law Society's ambit. The Law Society was also concerned that if complaint handling were dealt with by an independent body, there would be pressure to transfer to that body the other regulatory functions of the Law Society.

---

[58] *Fifth Annual Report of the Legal Services Ombudsman 1995*, at p.8.
[59] Solicitors Complaints Bureau, *100 Facts at a glance* (1994).
[60] *Fifth Annual Report of the Legal Services Ombudsman 1995*, at p.8.

The Office for the Supervision of Solicitors

As was seen in Chapter 4, the Office for the Supervision of Solicitors
was established by the Law Society on September 1, 1996. Its remit is
the regulation of the profession and guarding professional standards, as
well as investigating complaints about service and conduct. The new
director of the Office was mindful of the troubled history of the
Bureau and the Legal Services Ombudsman's advice that the new
body needed to adopt a more consumer-friendly approach in order to
overcome many complainant's doubts about its impartiality.[61] He
therefore emphasised that the changes to the system were tangible,
rather than mere "window dressing".[62] The Office for the Supervision
of Solicitors was also keen to point out that it also existed to serve
solicitors, by acting as a guardian for professional standards. The goal
was, therefore, to serve both constituencies, solicitors and clients,
"fully, fairly and honestly".[63] The change in the system, it was
claimed, was not only a "wholesale revision of working practices" but
also a "change in culture".[64]

As discussed in Chapter 4, the Office for the Supervision of
Solicitor's work is overseen by the Compliance and Supervision
Committee, a standing committee of the Law Society's council. The
director of the Office for the Supervision of Solicitors is a member of
the Law Society's management team, but he is accountable to and
speaks in the name of the Compliance and Supervision Committee.
The work of the committee is clearly demarcated into regulatory
matters[65] and complaints handling. This latter is dealt with by a
branch of the organisation called the Office for Client Relations. It is
this which is examined in this chapter, as this is the branch which
deals with complaints about inadequate professional service and minor
misconduct. The Office for Client Relations is split into three teams:
case-working, remuneration certificates,[66] and compliance and client
care.

---

[61] *Fifth Annual Report of the Legal Services Ombudsman 1995*, at p.8.

[62] See "New deal for clients who complain about lawyers," *The Observer*, September 1,
1996.

[63] *This Is The OSS*, Office for the Supervision of Solicitors (1996).

[64] P. Pharaoh, Chairman of the Compliance and Supervision Committee, *First Annual
Report of the Office for the Supervision of Solicitors 1996/97*, at p.4.

[65] These are dealt with by the Office for Professional Regulation branch of the
organisation.

[66] This is a mechanism used for assessing solicitors' charges. It is discussed in Chapter 4.

Jurisdiction

The Office for the Supervision for Solicitors can investigate allegations of professional misconduct and inadequate professional service. This covers a wide range of activities of solicitors. Among the functions which the Office for the Supervision of Solicitors cannot perform is giving legal advice, or requiring a solicitor to stop acting for a particular client. Nor will they usually investigate a client matter which has not yet been completed.

The Office for the Supervision of Solicitors cannot deal with complaints about the fairness and reasonableness of a solicitor's costs. Solicitors are, however, obliged to provide clients with the best information they can about their charges, and failure to do so may constitute inadequate professional service. Thus, if information on costs is not given, consumers may have a valid complaint. The remit therefore covers the breach of the regulation concerning information about costs, but not about the actual level of costs. If consumers have complaints about the level of costs, they must either use the taxation procedure,[67] or the remuneration certificate procedure.[68] If there were an extreme case of gross overcharging it would be investigated, because that would be a conduct matter, which is within the Office's remit. However, a finding of gross overcharging is only likely to arise where a bill has been significantly reduced using the remuneration certificate procedure or taxation. Those procedures would therefore have to be used before a consumer could bring an allegation of gross overcharging, a factor which limits its usefulness for consumers.

The Legal Services Ombudsman has expressed concern that some complaints about solicitors' costs are being treated as beyond the Office's jurisdiction, when in fact they may not be simply complaints about the amount charged for work done. Sometimes such complaints actually involve a complaint that, contrary to the Law Society's written professional standards, there was no warning about the likely level of costs.[69]

---

[67] This is discussed in Chapter 3.

[68] This is discussed in Chapter 4. It is a Law Society function, which is administered by the Office for the Supervision of Solicitors, on the grounds that it forms part of the overall service to consumers. The Office for the Supervision of Solicitors provides an information leaflet about applying for a remuneration certificate.

[69] *Sixth Annual Report of the Legal Services Ombudsman 1996*, at p.8.

Complaints from non-clients

The Office for the Supervision of Solicitors is reluctant to entertain complaints from non-clients. The rationale for this exclusion is that solicitors owe no duty of care to non-clients. There can however be an investigation where there is an allegation of serious professional misconduct. This limitation drew some early criticism[70] from the first Legal Services Ombudsman on the grounds that a solicitor has a general professional obligation towards non-clients and therefore third parties could have legitimate complaints which should be heard.[71] There is in any event a special section in the *Guide to Professional Conduct* dealing with relationships with third parties. The broad obligation is for solicitors not to act towards anyone in a fraudulent or deceitful way, and not to use their position to take unfair advantage for themselves or another. The Office for the Supervision of Solicitors seems more prepared to entertain non-client complaints, but only in relation to conduct matters, rather than inadequate professional services.[72]

This limitation has consequences for non-executor beneficiaries of wills, who wish to complain about the solicitor dealing with the will. Beneficiaries of wills are not clients, and the solicitor is only accountable to the executors. The Legal Services Ombudsman has continually urged the Law Society and the complaints body to find ways of taking "more robust action against that... minority of solicitors" which display total disregard or outright hostility towards beneficiaries.[73] There has been more flexibility in this respect since 1994, when the Solicitors (Non-Contentious Business) Remuneration Order 1994 gave beneficiaries the right to obtain a remuneration certificate where the only executors were solicitors. This provides some protection against overcharging, but it only applies in a limited number of situations.

The problems caused for beneficiaries are often not in relation to costs, and the Ombudsman was very critical of the Solicitors Complaints Bureau's reluctance to deal with these problems, particularly where beneficiaries faced intractable delays. Although the Bureau had become more flexible, there were cases where it seemed to "seek refuge behind technical arguments,"[74] rather than trying to

---

[70] This was in relation to the Solicitors Complaints Bureau's practices.
[71] *Sixth Annual Report of the Legal Services Ombudsman 1991*, at p.10.
[72] This information was obtained in an interview with an officer at the Office of the Supervision of Solicitors by the author.
[73] *Fourth Annual Report of the Legal Services Ombudsman 1994*, at p.5.
[74] *Fifth Annual Report of the Legal Services Ombudsman 1995*, at p.12.

help the complainant. For example, in one case the mother of two infant beneficiaries was refused certain information from the solicitors administering the estate. The Solicitors Complaints Bureau made an initial inquiry of the solicitors, but took no further action because she was not the client. In another case, the beneficiary sought an explanation from the solicitors as to why her deceased mother's life policy had only yielded £7.37. The Solicitors Complaints Bureau's response to her complaint that the solicitors had given no explanation was that it was not for them to determine the value of the life policy. The Ombudsman felt that the Solicitors Complaints Bureau was misguided in suggesting that the beneficiary did not have standing to seek such information or to complain.[75]

The Office for the Supervision for Solicitors, on the other hand, seems to be more prepared to accept that beneficiaries do have standing and that it is legitimate for them to complain about delay and about the cost of administering the estate. However, this problem can really only be rectified if all beneficiaries are brought within the 1994 Remuneration Order, and if solicitors' obligations towards beneficiaries and intended beneficiaries are clarified, and extended.

The limitation on the ability of non-clients to complain is particularly problematic where the complainant is responsible for paying the costs incurred by the client. The remuneration certificate procedure can only be used by clients.[76] For those non-clients, who are responsible for another party's solicitor's bill, the only recourse is to ask the client to apply for a remuneration certificate, and if the client will not, use the taxation method. The Ombudsman gave an example of the hardship caused by the refusal to investigate complaints by third parties about charges.[77] The complainant's home was repossessed by her building society. She complained about the conveyancing charges of £1,200 which she had to pay to the society's solicitors in connection with the repossession, which she considered to be too high. The only way this could be challenged was for the building society to ask their solicitor to have the bill certificated, and the society was unwilling to do this.

---

[75] *ibid.*, at p.12.
[76] It can also be used by residuary beneficiaries under a will, where the solicitors are the only executors.
[77] *Fifth Annual Report of the Legal Services Ombudsman 1995*, at p. 12

Professional negligence

The Office for the Supervision for Solicitors will not investigate complaints of professional negligence, on the grounds that such matters are for the courts. If the complaint from the consumer is that the solicitor was negligent, no legal advice will be given, but the complainant will be referred to another solicitor. In order to assist consumers, the Office for the Supervision of Solicitors has set up negligence panels. These are lists of independent solicitors, who are experienced in negligence claims. They offer an initial one-hour consultation free of charge. They offer advice on whether the solicitor complained about was negligent, and if so, what the consumer should do. If it appears that the client may have a claim in negligence, the solicitor is notified, and he or she will refer the matter to the profession's insurers, the Solicitors Indemnity Fund.[78] The Solicitors Indemnity Fund carries out its own investigation and reaches a decision as to whether it is appropriate to settle. If not, the client will have to pursue the case in court.

There are understandable reasons why the Office for the Supervision of Solicitors is reluctant to become involved in matters of professional negligence. However, there is some degree of overlap between negligence and inadequate professional service. Negligence is always inadequate professional service, but the converse is not always true. It is not always clear whether the complainant is actually alleging negligence, or whether it is a complaint about inadequate professional service. Some complaints may involve issues of, for example, delay, as well as negligence. The Legal Services Ombudsman has advised that the professional body (at the time it was the Solicitors Complaints Bureau) should be prepared to investigate the non-negligence aspects of the complaint, rather than reject the complaint out of hand. He felt that a "well-motivated complaints handling body" would consider whether there were any aspects of a complaint which were within the remit, before rejecting the complaint.[79]

The Office for the Supervision of Solicitors seems to have heeded this advice, and has adopted a broader view of its remit in relation to negligence than the Solicitors Complaints Bureau was inclined to do. It will investigate allegations involving negligence where the amount claimed is small. However, it believes that there is no sense in making an award, when a professional negligence claim in the courts may

---

[78] This organisation is not connected to the Office for the Supervision of Solicitors. It acts on behalf of the solicitor against whom the complaint is made.

[79] *Sixth Annual Report of the Legal Services Ombudsman 1996*, at p.8.

result in damages in excess of £1,000. The Legal Services Ombudsman cautions, however, that this must not be used as an excuse for inaction. Care should be taken by the Office for the Supervision of Solicitors to distinguish the reliable estimate of a claim from the optimistic and ill-informed speculation of complainants. In addition, there is always the power to make an unlimited reduction in a solicitor's costs.[80]

Despite the general improvements, there are unfortunately cases where the Office for the Supervision of Solicitors appears to have retreated "behind the legalistic barricades" in the same way as its predecessor. One complainant complained that his solicitors had hung on to the proceeds of sale of his business lease. The amount in question was £15,000, and the Office for the Supervision of Solicitors claimed that appropriate remedy was negligence or breach of contract. The Ombudsman's view was that there should be an investigation, as a professional body ought to be concerned at an allegation that a solicitor has grown too attached to a client's money.[81]

Complaint handling

The initial contact a complainant will make with the Office for the Supervision of Solicitors is the "Front Office". It is here that the complaint will be evaluated, and there will be an attempt to settle it informally at this stage. As a first step towards resolving a complaint, complainants are advised to speak to the solicitor or partner who deals with complaints within the firm. The Office for the Supervision of Solicitors has produced a special complaint referral form, and consumers can telephone the help-line or write asking for the form. As well as being available from the Office for the Supervision for Solicitors, the form has been distributed to solicitors' firms and Citizens Advice Bureaux.

When the completed form is returned to the Office for the Supervision for Solicitors, it is analysed to ensure that it is a complaint about the service received from a solicitor, or about his or her professional behaviour. Before the Office for the Supervision of Solicitors will deal with the complaint, it must be sure that the solicitor concerned is aware of the complaint, and has had an opportunity to deal with it in-house. Even where this has been done, the Office for the Supervision of Solicitors will sometimes refer a

---

[80] *Seventh Annual Report of the Legal Services Ombudsman 1997*, at p.15.
[81] *ibid.*, at p.16.

complaint back to the solicitor, to ensure that the solicitor has done all that is possible to resolve the complaint.

Where a complaint cannot be resolved by the Front Office, the matter is referred to the appropriate case-working unit, depending on whether it is a matter of inadequate professional service, or regulatory.[82] The Office for Client Relations has two case-working teams who continue to try to resolve matters by means of conciliation and mediation. There are two further case-working teams in this office, and they concentrate on formal investigations. In accordance with the new approachable style of the Office for the Supervision of Solicitors, matters are dealt with wherever possible by telephone.

A new streamlined way of handling complaints was introduced on January 1, 1998,[83] after consultation with the Legal Services Ombudsman and consumer groups. It is applied to most complaints about poor service, and some cases about conduct. The procedure is designed to achieve a resolution in a very short time-scale, and telephone contact is utilised to facilitate this. On receipt of the complaint form, the complainant will usually be telephoned by the Office for the Supervision of Solicitors, and agreement reached on the exact nature of the complaint. During the following two weeks, there will be an attempt to conciliate the matter. Like the Solicitors Complaints Bureau which preceded it, the emphasis of the Office for the Supervision of Solicitors is on conciliation,[84] and it is committed to trying to resolve complaints without resorting to a formal investigation. It has found that, although conciliation can be successful, its effectiveness is reduced in proportion to the length of time taken to settle. It is for this reason that the two-week time-scale for conciliation has been introduced under the new procedure.

If the matter is not resolved within these two weeks, the solicitor will be invited to respond in writing to the complainant and will be asked to provide evidence (for example, correspondence, attendance notes) to support the response. The solicitor will be given three weeks in which to do this, and at the end of this period, the decision taken by the Office for the Supervision of Solicitors will be made on the

[82] Inadequate professional service and minor conduct matters are referred to the Office for Client Relations. Regulatory matters are referred to the Office for Professional Regulation. In the 16-month period to December 31, 1998 the Front Office dealt with 87 per cent of written enquiries. The remaining 13 per cent were passed to the case-working units (Office for the Supervision of Solicitors, *Annual Report 1997–1988*, at p.12).

[83] *The Bulletin—News update for the profession from the Office for the Supervision of Solicitors,* "New approach to complaints handling," December 5, 1997.

[84] There is an expanded network of local conciliation officers to help sole practitioners deal with client complaints.

information then available. This means that if the solicitor has failed to reply within 21 days, a decision will be made only on the information from the complainant.

The rationale behind these tight time-scales is that both parties will have to focus on resolving the issues and making their views known quickly. The Office for the Supervision of Solicitors is prepared to take a tough line where solicitors refuse to co-operate, on the basis that solicitors have a professional obligation to co-operate with its supervisory role and reply promptly and fully. It believes that it is in the interests of both solicitors and clients to address dissatisfaction by resolving complaints as quickly and effectively as possible. Failure or delay by solicitors to deal with correspondence from the Office for the Supervision of Solicitors will usually increase the distress and inconvenience caused to clients. Solicitors have therefore been warned that such conduct may be reflected by an increase in the compensation awarded to clients.

This new approach indicates a willingness by the Office for the Supervision of Solicitors to improve consumer satisfaction with the complaints process by reducing the time taken to conclude the matter. Where matters are taking some time to be concluded, the Office for the Supervision of Solicitors has undertaken to communicate with the complainant at least every six weeks to give an update on the progress of the complaint. However, the reality is that there are so many complaints to the Office, that many of them have to wait up to 26 weeks, before they can even enter the new streamlined procedure. This adds to the dissatisfaction of complainants.

First instance decisions on complaints are made by an assistant director at the Office for the Supervision of Solicitors. If the complainant is dissatisfied with the decision (which can include the amount of the award), there is a right of appeal to the Client Relations Sub-Committee, which has a lay majority. In 1996–97, there was a total of 209 appeals against first instance decisions.[85] Over 80 per cent were dismissed. In 8 per cent of the cases, the decision was varied and 7 per cent resulted in the decision being overturned.[86] In the 16-month period until December 31, 1998, there were 473 appeals against the 1,160 first instance decision made. Of these, 382 (81 per cent) were dismissed.[87] There is no charge for appealing, but there is a risk attached, as any compensation which has been awarded initially can be reduced as well as increased. The Ombudsman believes

---

[85] There were 537 first instance decisions made during this period.
[86] *First Annual Report of the Office for the Supervision of Solicitors 1996/97*, at p.9.
[87] Office for the Supervision of Solicitors, *Annual Report 1997–1998*, at p.13.

this system to be unfair, particularly if the compensation on the complainant's appeal is reduced where the solicitors were prepared to pay the original award.[88] The Office for the Supervision of Solicitors has no plans to change this rule, arguing that if there were a no-risk appeal, everyone would appeal. In practice, very few awards of compensation are reduced.[89]

Remedies

At the end of the investigation, if it is found that the solicitor is at fault, the Office for the Supervision of Solicitors has a number of remedies. It can reduce the solicitor's bill totally or partly, as well as ordering compensation of up to £1,000. The compensation is not for money lost but for the poor service provided. The solicitor can be required to correct the mistake at his or her own expense. A complaint may also result in disciplinary proceedings against a solicitor where there is evidence of misconduct. In 1996–97, there were 537 decisions on poor service complaints. In 151 cases there was an award of compensation, and 145 resulted in reduced or limited costs. There were 97 awards of costs reduction plus compensation. Disciplinary proceedings occurred in 33 cases, and 62 resulted in other action. In 49 cases, there was no finding of inadequate professional service.[90] For the 16-month period ending December 31, 1998, of the 1,160 first instance decisions, 395 resulted in an award of compensation. In 280 cases there was a reduction or limitation in costs, and in 262 there was a reduction in costs as well as compensation. In 65 cases there was no finding of inadequate professional service.[91]

Solicitors are obliged to comply with an award by the Office for the Supervision for Solicitors. There can be a problem, however, when there is a failure to comply because the solicitor concerned is bankrupt, has been struck off the Roll, is no longer in practice, or cannot be traced. In cases where the Office for the Supervision of Solicitors has directed that costs be refunded, the Law Society's Compensation Fund will normally refund the money. If, however, the direction is that compensation be paid, this is regarded as a personal debt of the solicitor, and the former client is left to pursue the matter

---

[88] *Sixth Annual Report of the Legal Services Ombudsman 1996*, at p.19.
[89] This information was obtained in an interview with an officer at the Office of the Supervision of Solicitors by the author. There are no published figures.
[90] *First Annual Report of the Office for the Supervision of Solicitors 1996/97*, at p.9.
[91] Office for the Supervision of Solicitors *Annual Report 1997–1998*.

through the courts, usually without much hope of success. This is an anomaly. The Law Society should ensure that clients actually receive the awards made. The previous Legal Services Ombudsman suggested that the Law Society make provision for both types of financial award to be paid. The payment could be made either by the Compensation Fund or the Solicitors Indemnity Fund.[92]

Evaluation of complaints handling by the Office for the Supervision of Solicitors

The previous Legal Services Ombudsman noted the "very definite change of style" when the new body was established. The Office for the Supervision of Solicitors looked and sounded much more like an organisation that existed to help people who had problems with their solicitors.[93] This was a promising start, and an improvement on its predecessor, whose procedures were criticised for being too defensive on behalf of the Law Society.[94] The previous Ombudsman, in his last annual report, felt that it might be necessary to wait "two or three years before a reliable picture of the performance" of the Office for the Supervision of Solicitors emerged.[95] It is now in its third year of operation, and some preliminary evaluation of its work can be made in relation to the complaint handling process.

Whether a grievance resolution mechanism is effective depends upon a number of factors. These include questions about whether the remit is wide enough to encompass consumer concerns, whether it is accessible, and whether its procedures are fair and user-friendly. It is also important that the system has effective remedies. The Office for the Supervision of Solicitors must be seen to be effective if it is to escape the criticisms that dogged the Solicitors Complaints Bureau.

The Office for the Supervision of Solicitors is more consumer-friendly in its approach. Only 6 per cent of complaints handled by the Office for the Supervision of Solicitors find their way to the Legal Services Ombudsman. On the face of it, this does not indicate a large measure of dissatisfaction by consumers on the way their case was handled. In over two-thirds (67 per cent) of these referrals, the Ombudsman found no reason to criticise or make a formal recommendation about the way the consumer complaint had been

---

[92] *Sixth Annual Report of the Legal Services Ombudsman 1996*, at p.10.
[93] *ibid.*, at p.7.
[94] *Third Annual Report of the Legal Services Ombudsman 1993*, at p.8.
[95] *Sixth Annual Report of the Legal Services Ombudsman 1996*, at p.1.

dealt with. There was a reduction in the number of adverse reports by
the Ombudsman from 27 per cent in 1995 to 23 per cent in 1996–
97.[96] However, this does mean that there were 434 cases where there
was a formal recommendation or criticism.[97]

The Office for the Supervision of Solicitors is more customer-
focused than the Solicitors Complaints Bureau, basing its approach on
market research and monthly satisfaction surveys of completed
complaints.[98] The results of this research have not been published, so
only the Office for the Supervision of Solicitors knows whether it is
achieving greater levels of consumer satisfaction. The Legal Services
Ombudsman has suggested that it may be defensible to withhold
publication as the survey established a baseline on which to build.
However, she would want there to be greater openness about this in
future, as such surveys are a key measure of quality assurance.[99]
Certainly any secrecy about the results of surveys leads one to believe
that all is not well.[1] Nor was it helpful that the Office for the
Supervision of Solicitors did not publish its second annual report until
spring 1999.[2] This made it difficult to make a meaningful assessment
of its work before this time.

There has been a streamlining of procedures within the office, in
order to try to reduce delay. This is clearly not working, as many
complaints are not even entering the streamlined procedure for many
months. It is seriously failing to meet its targets for response times,
and there are still too many examples of delay in the system.[3] Despite
an undertaking to conclude 90 per cent of cases within three months,
and the rest within five months,[4] the Office for the Supervision of
Solicitors only concluded 23 per cent of its streamlined matters in
three months, and only 44 per cent of the rest in within five months.[5]
Some of these delays may have been due to the flood at the Office's

---

[96] *First Annual Report of the Office for the Supervision of Solicitors 1996/97* at p.16.

[97] *Seventh Annual Report of the Legal Services Ombudsman 1997*, at pp.13, 27.

[98] *First Annual Report of the Office for the Supervision of Solicitors 1996/97*, at p.11. Market
research was conducted in March and April 1997.

[99] *Seventh Annual Report of the Legal Services Ombudsman 1997*, at p.12.

[1] "Supervision at arm's length," Editorial in *New Law Journal*, August 15, 1997, at
p.1229. The Office for the Supervision of Solicitors has recently released the results of a
survey of 303 complainants. The main areas of concern were the length of time taken
to process complaints and a need for improved communications (*Law Society Gazette*,
April 21, at p. 3).

[2] This is to bring its reporting year in line with the Law Society's accounting year.

[3] *Seventh Annual Report of the Legal Services Ombudsman 1997*, at p.13.

[4] *Law Socieety Gazette*, July 1, 1998, at p.1.

[5] *ibid.*, December 2, 1998, at p.3.

premises in April 1998,[6] but this cannot be a complete explanation. Despite its determined start, the Office for the Supervision of Solicitors is failing to live up to its promise. Complaints appear to be escalating out of control.[7] Although the Office for the Supervision of Solicitors should be judged on the way it responds to complaints rather than the volume it receives, the sheer volume of work at present seems to be overwhelming it.[8] This leads to delays with consequent dissatisfaction on the part of consumers and the profession.

There is certainly more lay involvement in the organisation than previously, and the lay members play a more active role in the main organisation, and in setting policy.[9] As for its independence, the Ombudsman has found "no sign of conscious bias," but noted the persistence of a tendency to see matters from the solicitor's point of view. The solicitor's version of events is often accepted without corroborating evidence, and there are too many instances where complainants are not given the benefit of the doubt. This gives the perception that it is not even-handed in its approach. The warning is clear. Any "suspicion of partiality" must be banished if self-regulation is to be credible.[10]

It is difficult for the Office for the Supervision of Solicitors to establish itself as fundamentally different from its predecessor. Although it has a different director, it operates from the same premises as the Solicitors Complaints Bureau, and has much the same staff. There is still the view that it has insufficient real and perceived independence from the Law Society.[11] Without this, it is difficult to maintain public confidence in the system. The critics within the profession have not been silenced either.[12]

The present Ombudsman's assessment is that the Office for the Supervision of Solicitors has "laid the foundations" on which to erect an effective complaints handling system, but that it still has "a long

---

[6] This happened during the Easter weekend, in April, when the river Leam in Leamington Spa burst its banks. The ground floor of the offices were flooded. 2,000 files were damaged, and work had to be transferred to other premises.

[7] "Deal with complaints in-house," New Law Journal, May 8, 1998, at p.651.

[8] There has been a 30 per cent increase in complaints in the last year. In 1998, the Office for the Supervision of Solicitors handled 30,000 cases. It is anticipated that there will be over 30,000 new matters in 1999 (Law Society Gazette, December 2, 1998, at p.3). The Law Society has allocated an extra £500,000 to the Office for the Supervision of Solicitors so that it can retain temporary staff helping to clear a backlog of 9,000 cases (Law Society Gazette, March 10, 1999, at p 1).

[9] First Annual Report of the Office for the Supervision of Solicitors 1996/97, at p..5

[10] Seventh Annual Report of the Legal Services Ombudsman 1997, at p. 17

[11] Editorial, New Law Journal, August 25, 1997.

[12] M. Mears, Law Society Gazette, December 10, 1997.

way to go".[13] But, however far it goes, and whatever efficiencies and streamlining it introduces, it will not necessarily improve public confidence in the system. As the Ombudsman has observed, the increasing volume of complaints and continuing delays at the Office for the Supervision of Solicitors are "symptoms of the problem, not the problem itself".[14] What is needed is for solicitors to be more concerned about client care, and more willing to settle complaints at the level of the firm. Solicitors need to have effective in-house complaints procedures.[15] They need to "shoulder the responsibility for client care" and accept that effective complaints handling "is an integral part" of this.[16] It is to this aspect of complaint handling that we now turn.

In-house complaints procedures and Practice Rule 15

It is probably true to say that most high street retailers see the value of resolving complaints by customers at the lowest possible level. The enlightened view is that dissatisfied consumers are not good for business, whereas satisfactorily resolved complaints are. Moreover, complaints are a positive aspect of business in so far as they can be used for management information, by highlighting failures within the system. Some solicitors however have been slow to adopt this positive view of complaints despite the fact that one disgruntled client could potentially cause the loss of many more.

In 1991, the Law Society introduced Practice Rule 15, requiring each firm of solicitors to have an internal procedure for dealing with client complaints. Before this, only about 20 per cent of firms had in-house complaints procedures.[17] Practice Rule 15 (Client care) provided that:

"Every principal in private practice shall operate a complaints handling procedure which shall, *inter alia*, ensure that clients are informed whom to approach in the event of any problem with the service provided."

The Law Society is clear that it can be a simple procedure. What the rule does require is that clients are informed whom to approach

---

[13] *Seventh Annual Report of the Legal Services Ombudsman 1997*, at p.12.
[14] *ibid.*, at p.13.
[15] *Fifth Annual Report of the Legal Services Ombudsman 1995*, at pp.8–9.
[16] *Seventh Annual Report of the Legal Services Ombudsman 1997*, at p.13.
[17] J. Jenkins, *Quality of Solicitors' Practice Management*, at p.46. (1993) Research Study No 10 (Research and Policy Planning Unit), The Law Society.

and that complaints are investigated promptly and thoroughly. Where clients are not satisfied, they should be informed of their right to complain to the professional body. Although not a requirement, the Law Society recommended that the procedure should be set out in writing.

It is probably true to say that Rule 15 was not wholeheartedly supported by the whole profession, and its implementation has been problematic. A survey conducted in 1993[18] discovered that the majority of clients were not informed about the existence of in-house complaints procedures. One quarter of the firms surveyed were not operating a complaints procedure, as they were required to do. The Law Society's own research, in 1993, noted that, although only 20 per cent of firms had complaints procedures before 1991, the introduction of the rule had not resulted in total compliance. Complaints procedures had tended to be adopted by the larger firms, with the sole practitioner and 2 – 4 partner firms having a poor record in this respect. The research also found that firms were not explaining the procedures to their clients, and that they had poor procedures for recording complaints.

A survey conducted in 1995[19], some four years after the introduction of the rule, found that 20 per cent of respondents had no defined procedure for handling complaints. Of these 76 firms, only seven had any plans to introduce such a procedure in 1995. Most of the rest of the respondents (53) said that such a procedure would not be necessary for their firm. Moreover, despite the fact that 80 per cent of firms in this survey had complied with Rule 15, only 60 per cent of firms said that they believed it was beneficial to their firm to have an internal complaints procedure. Although this indicates that the majority are convinced of the benefits of having internal procedures, there is still a large minority who remain to be persuaded of the benefits of this aspect of client care. This echoes the findings of earlier research, which concluded that it was "clear that the new complaints culture" had not yet reached solicitors. The idea that firms might encourage complaints or learn from complaints was "alien to the legal profession".[20]

The Law Society recommends that firms should inform clients about the possibility of taking the complaint to the professional body.

---

[18] N Harris, 'Do Solicitors Care for their Clients?' (1993) *Civil Justice Quarterly* 359; N. Harris, *Solicitors and Client Care* (1994), National Consumer Council.

[19] Research conducted by R. James and M. Seneviratne, by means of a postal questionnaire sent out in July 1995, referred to above.

[20] T. Goriely, "Quality of legal services: the need for consumer research" (1993) *Consumer Policy Review* 112–116, at p.116.

However, research[21] has found that only 62 per cent of firms informed clients about the possibility of doing so. Moreover, it appears that, even when firms do have internal procedures, they are not informing their clients of their existence. Research in 1995[22] found that over 80 per cent of clients had no recall of being told about how the firm dealt with complaints. The conclusion from this research was that "most firms, even those who have established a complaints procedure, have yet to adopt a culture of client care which is founded on the notion that it is beneficial to operate a complaints procedure and to use reports of clients' dissatisfaction as a feedback mechanism to improve the legal services offered".[23]

In theory, it ought to be cheaper and more effective for firms to deal with complaints directly with the client. If complaints are dealt with at this level, it should reduce the burden on the profession as a whole, which is financing the Office for the Supervision of Solicitors. Indeed, it has been suggested that one of the reasons for the introduction of Practice Rule 15 was the overwhelming workload being placed upon the Solicitors Complaints Bureau.[24] Complaint handling by firms can be seen as a delegation by the Law Society of part of its self-regulatory responsibility, and thus the Law Society should be offering support to firms in relation to complaint handling.

The Solicitors Complaints Bureau did take some responsibility for monitoring the adequacy of the internal complaints procedures. In 1993, it established a Rule 15 compliance officer to encourage greater compliance, and to ensure that the profession was aware of the benefits of following good client care principles. The compliance officer saw his work as "more pastoral than disciplinary".[25] One commentator has concluded that in appointing a compliance officer, the Law Society acknowledged "that there is a pervading negative attitude to good complaints handling within the solicitors' profession".[26] Despite this effort by the Bureau, only 15 per cent of firms surveyed in 1995[27] had ever been contacted by the compliance officer from the Bureau, and of these, three-quarters were firms which

---

[21] T. Goriely, "Quality of legal services: the need for consumer research" (1993) *Consumer Policy Review* 112–116, at p. 116
[22] J. Jenkins and V. Lewis, *Client Perceptions* (1995) Research Study No 17 (Research and Policy Planning Unit) The Law Society.
[23] *ibid.*, at p.56.
[24] C. Christensen, "The Client as Consumer" *New Law Journal*, June 5, 1998, at pp. 832–834.
[25] A. Baker, *Law Society Gazette*, February 23, 1994.
[26] C. Christensen, "Complaints are good for you," *Solicitors Journal*, June 17, 1994.
[27] Research conducted by R. James and M. Seneviratne, by means of a postal questionnaire sent out in July 1995, referred to above.

had complaints procedures. Some sixty firms (16 per cent of respondents) had not complied with Rule 15, and had not been contacted by the compliance officer.

The poor levels of implementation may be even more serious than originally thought. Another research study[28] conducted between September 1996 and December 1997, into the operation of Rule 15 found that the published procedures for handling complaints bore little resemblance to the actual procedures as they operated. Many firms had created written procedures in order to apply for a Legal Aid franchise or for other quality marks. All the firms in the empirical study had complied with Rule 15, and appointed a complaint-handling partner, but the response to complaints was unstructured. The firms had no central collection of complaint information and there were few positive outcomes from the process. The procedure was viewed negatively by all the participants. The clients felt that the system was not independent, and the complaint handler, under pressure because there were billing targets to meet, saw complaints as non-chargeable time. It was felt that the exhortation of the Office for the Supervision of Solicitors about Rule 15 was unrealistic. Practitioners felt that they did not have the time to handle complaints properly, and they needed to be convinced of the commercial benefits. The recommendation from the research is that the Law Society should adopt a more robust line on the implementation of Practice Rule 15.[29]

The Office for the Supervision of Solicitors does appear to be taking a strong line in relation to internal procedures, and will be expecting solicitors to use Rule 15 more effectively. Complaints will be returned if they have not been through the internal procedure.[30] The Office for the Supervision of Solicitors has introduced a new six-month time limit for clients to make complaints if attempts, to resolve them internally are unsuccessful.[31] It is prepared to make awards of compensation to clients where solicitors fail to operate an internal complaints handling system. Its view is that the rule is an integral part of the solicitor/client retainer, and failure to comply may amount to inadequate professional service and possibly misconduct. In order to encourage firms, it has produced a leaflet *Making Rule 15 Work for You*

---

[28] C. Christensen, "The client as consumer," *New Law Journal*, June 5, 1998, at pp. 832–834.
[29] *Law Society Gazette*, May 28, 1998, at p.1.
[30] Since May 1, 1998 the Office for the Supervision of Solicitors will only accept new matters which have already been subject to a firm's own in-house complaints procedure ("Deal with complaints in-house," *New Law Journal*, May 8, 1998, at p.651).
[31] There is a discretion to accept complaints outside this time limit.

in which "the benefits... of a positive approach to complaint handling" are emphasised. The emphasis in the leaflet is on the Office for the Supervision of Solicitors working with the profession to encourage effective complaints handling. It is emphasised that resolving complaints internally is good for the profession, being the cheapest, quickest and most effective mechanism.

The leaflet recommends that there is a clear procedure, which the client knows about from the outset, and that firms appoint a complaints-handling partner with the authority to take action to resolve complaints. In the case of sole practitioners, it is recommended that reciprocal arrangements are made with a local colleague, or the local law society is approached. All staff should be trained in the procedure and should know who the complaints handling partner is. Complaints should be dealt with as objectively as possible, and the aim of the procedure should be to resolve the complaint without involving the Office for the Supervision for Solicitors. There is a promise that, if there is a genuine attempt to try to resolve the complaint in a "professional, reasonable manner," and if the client appears unreasonably to reject this, the Office for the Supervision of Solicitors will support the firm by declining to investigate the matter further. The Office for the Supervision of Solicitors also operates a system known as Lawyer Line, which advises solicitors who are experiencing difficulties resolving a complaint.

The Office for the Supervision of Solicitors does expect that firms will implement Rule 15 procedures and has warned that it takes seriously failures to comply with the spirit as well as the letter of the rule.[32] The rule itself only places an obligation to have a procedure, not an "effective" one.[33] These attempts by the Office for the Supervision of Solicitors to facilitate an appreciation of the positive messages about effective complaint handling is a move in the right direction. However, it must be accepted that, with over 8,000 firms[34] to communicate with, the Office for the Supervision of Solicitors has a difficult task. Equally, something must be done at firm level, if the number of complaints to the Office for the Supervision of Solicitors is to be reduced.

To this end, the Law Society is proposing to introduce radical reforms to the system. The aim is for the Office for the Supervision of Solicitors to cease to deal with complaints about inadequate professional service, and to act solely as a regulator. Its role in

---

[32] There was evidence that firms were complying with the letter of the rule but not with its spirit (*Sixth Annual Report of the Legal Services Ombudsman 1995*, at p.18).

[33] This will charge when the revised Rule 15 is implemented.

[34] In 1997, there were 8,842 firms of solicitors in England and Wales.

complaint handling would be limited to those complaints which have not been resolved properly by firms. The compensation level for inadequate professional service would be increased to £5,000. In addition, the Office for the Supervision of Solicitors would be able to recover handling costs if it became involved in complaints. Rule 15 is also to be amended, to require solicitors to operate a written complaints-handling procedure, and to ensure that complaints are handled in accordance with it.[35]

These measures, if adopted, are an attempt both to persuade and coerce solicitors into taking client care seriously. Responsibility for dealing with complaints will be on individual firms. If this strategy fails, the Government is planning to introduce more external control over complaint-handling.[36]

It is hard to deny the advantages of having complaints dealt with as closely as possible to the original decision-maker, and the emphasis on Rule 15 is part of a general trend towards informal rather than formal mechanisms. There are advantages for the profession, particularly in terms of time and cost savings. However, unless there is a change in culture, complaints will not be dealt with satisfactorily, and both consumers and solicitors will continue to be sceptical about the value of in-house procedures. It has been noted that some firms, particularly small ones, react to Rule 15 with cries of outrage, suggesting that it involves a vast bureaucratic burden. In effect, all that is being asked of them is the level of consumer care expected from any high street store.

The Legal Services Ombudsman highlights the necessity of changing the culture. In one case, the firm had devised complaint-handling procedures that were "so Byzantine in their complexity" that they obstructed rather than promoted the satisfactory resolution of complaints. The procedure required that the client must put the complaint to the solicitor twice before referring it to the Office for the Supervision of Solicitors. There was a clause permitting the solicitor to retain client papers if there were a complaint. Moreover, clients had to pay the costs of solicitors defending themselves against a complaint, if it were eventually determined in the solicitor's favour.[37] This firm seems to have missed the point that a complaints-handling

---

[35] Solicitors' Practice (Costs Information and Client Care) Amendment Rule 1999, dated March 3, 1999, which is to come into force on September 3, 1999.

[36] The Access to Justice Bill will contain powers to set external standards for complaint-handling by the legal profession.

[37] *Seventh Annual Report of the Legal Services Ombudsman 1997*, at p.15.

process should be a means of restoring communications and providing practical remedies.[38]

It is probably unrealistic to expect firms to expend a great deal of time, which is perceived as dead time, on complaints unless the profession becomes convinced that successful handling of complaints is positive and good for business in general. Without this culture change, clients will continue to question the independence of the internal procedure. There is also the danger that if the Office for the Supervision of Solicitors becomes too closely involved with these procedures, its own independence will be called into question

Rule 15 was made "deliberately...undemanding and unprescriptive".[39] Its importance was to give a signal to the profession that complaints should be dealt with within the firm. The message from the Law Society is that to ignore this aspect of client care would be foolish in a highly competitive environment. It is the most efficient way of dealing with complaints and it is good for business. Effective in-house procedures are also the only way to reduce the number of complaints which are swamping the Office for the Supervision of Solicitors.

Client care initiatives

The Office for the Supervision of Solicitors is engaged in a number of initiatives to improve client care. These are an attempt to persuade solicitors to see the Office for the Supervision of Solicitors as a "force for practical help", rather than "just a reactive regulator".[40] All new law firms are now to be visited by monitoring staff from the Office for the Supervision of Solicitors in the first few months of their existence.[41] There is also a compliance team to encourage the implementation of Rule 15, which, over seven years since its implementation, has "yet to take root".[42]

The Office for the Supervision of Solicitors has also begun to target solicitors who are failing to address client complaints. More than 70 firms, which had client complaints referred back, were targeted in this

---

[38] J. Hayes, "Protecting the Public and Serving the Profession," Paper presented to the *Legal Professions in Transition* conference (1994). Centre for Law and Business and Centre for Social Ethics and Policy. University of Manchester.

[39] *Supervision of Solicitors. The Next Decade*, at p.26, Law Society Consultation Paper. July 1995.

[40] *Seventh Annual Report of the Legal Services Ombudsman 1997*, at p.12.

[41] *New Law Journal*, May 1, 1998, at p.614.

[42] *Seventh Annual Report of the Legal Services Ombudsman 1997*, at p.12.

way in the first year of the operation of the client care scheme.[43] Another scheme involves solicitors acting as local conciliation officers[44] making direct, personal approaches to solicitors who are seen to be generating too many complaints. It has been found that 20 per cent of firms give rise to 80 per cent of complaints. The Law Society has recognised that something must be done to target such firms.[45]

Another initiative "Think like clients" was started in July 1997 with the publication of a 120-page client care guide. The Office for the Supervision of Solicitors also established "Lawyer Line" in May 1997. This is a confidential telephone service aimed to help solicitors, who have had a complaint made against them, to resolve the matter. There were 520 calls taken in 1996–97. The Office for the Supervision of Solicitors also issues a quarterly *Bulletin*, which is published in the *Law Society Gazette*. This new development is used as a means to communicate with the profession and keep firms up to date with developments and guidance.[46]

These approaches may serve a useful purpose in encouraging firms to adopt good practices in client care. Research has shown that solicitors saw the ideal relationship between the regulatory body and themselves as that of the positive parent/child relationship. This involved both parties working together towards mutual, positive goals. Solicitors generally acknowledged the necessity for the regulatory body, but any hint of coercion from the regulator was resented.[47] There is still a query, however, as to whether the profession has "the stomach for client care". The Legal Services Ombudsman notes the way the adversarial approach often infiltrates the solicitors' dealings with their own clients. This leads to defensiveness, a refusal to admit mistakes, and an escalation in client dissatisfaction.[48] This approach will have to be changed if the profession is to achieve an acceptable level of satisfaction from complainants.

---

[43] *First Annual Report of the Office for the Supervision of Solicitors 1996/97*, at p.10.

[44] These solicitors work on an ad hoc basis for the Office for the Supervision of Solicitors. Twenty-five of them have now been trained (*First Annual Report of the Office for the Supervision of Solicitors 1996/97*, at p.10).

[45] *Law Society Gazette*, April 8, 1999, at p. 22

[46] *First Annual Report of the Office for the Supervision of Solicitors 1996/97*, at p.10.

[47] A. Palmer, "Solicitors Experience of Complaints Handling" in *Governing the Profession*, Proceedings from the Annual Research Conference (1998), at p.23, Research and Policy Planning Unit. The Law Society.

[48] *Seventh Annual Report of the Legal Services Ombudsman 1997*, at p.15. The Lord Chancellor, too, has told Solicitors to stop treating complaints against them like another piece of litigation (*Law Society Gazette*, April 14, 1999 at p.3).

Barristers

Until recently, the Bar had no equivalent to either Rule 15 or the Office for the Supervision of Solicitors to deal with complaints against barristers. The Bar's professional regulations focused primarily on disciplinary matters, and there was no procedure for awarding compensation or other forms of redress to a complainant. It was only in the more serious cases, where the complaint formed the basis of a charge before a disciplinary tribunal, that the possibility arose of the barrister repaying or foregoing fees, but this power was used only rarely.

As we saw in Chapter 4, a disciplinary procedure does have an important deterrent effect in reducing the incidence of shoddy work, dishonesty or other misconduct. However, such a procedure is concerned with disciplining barristers and, as it is not consumer-focused, it is not concerned with providing consumers with redress. Barristers can be admonished or advised as to future conduct, but the disciplinary process provides no formal method of compelling them to apologise to the client. The lack of consumer focus is illustrated by the fact that, although consumers are informed of the progress and outcome of the disciplinary procedure, they have no right to take part in the disciplinary proceedings. They are therefore not entitled to attend or be represented at the disciplinary hearings, nor to see any relevant documents or transcripts.

The procedures operated by the Bar have a clear professional focus, their objective being to examine allegations of misconduct, and to provide an appropriate penalty if proved. Because of this, there are procedural safeguards, and it is understandable that consumer satisfaction is not an important issue. Such a system, however, is inappropriate for dealing with more minor complaints, for example, poor service or lack of courtesy, which are not of a disciplinary nature. In these cases, complainants want some redress. This failure of the procedure to provide redress was regarded as a deficiency by the Legal Services Ombudsman, who first referred to it in his second annual report,[49] and in subsequent annual reports. Taking heed of this, the General Council of the Bar included the issue of procedures for dealing with poor or inadequate service within the remit of the Bar Council's Standards Review Body, which was set up in 1993.[50] The Review Body reported in 1994[51] and recommended that each

---

[49] *Second Annual Report of the Legal Services Ombudsman 1992* at p.19.
[50] This was set up under the chairmanship of Lord Alexander of Weedon Q.C.
[51] *Blueprint for the Bar: Report of the Bar Standards Review Body* (1994).

set of chambers should have its own complaints procedure to deal
with complaints against barristers or staff.[52] It also recommended that
the Bar Council should enhance the present disciplinary procedures
with complaints procedures. To this end, it was recommended that a
Barristers' Complaints Bureau should be established to handle
complaints against barristers. All complaints against barristers should be
directed to it, whether or not they raised questions of discipline. The
Barristers' Complaints Bureau would have powers to investigate
complaints of poor work or unsatisfactory service and order
compensation of up to £2,000. It would also be able to direct that
fees be reduced, forgone or repaid. Although the report was clear that
the Bar still had the right of self-regulation, the "hallmark of the
professions," it was felt that it could no longer "assume continued
freedom from more direct controls".[53]

These proposals were welcomed by the Legal Services Ombudsman.
He did however find it "ironic" that, just at the time when the
Solicitors Complaint Bureau was "coming under fire from both sides,"
the Bar Council was proposing to set up a new complaints system
with very similar powers.[54] The National Consumer Council was of
the opinion that such a body might be more successful than the
Solicitors Complaints Bureau. There were fewer complaints about
barristers because of the smaller size of the Bar and the more restricted
role of barristers in relation to their clients.[55]

As a result of the report, a Working Group was set up to see how
the recommendations could be implemented. The Working Group
issued a consultation paper in May 1995, and its final report was
published in the following August. The report endorsed the
recommendations of the Review Body, except that, rather than
recommending a Barristers' Complaints Bureau, it proposed to have a
complaints commissioner working with a complaints committee. In
addition, it proposed that compensation for poor service should not be
available for matters which would attract immunity from court action.
This was in direct contrast to the Review Body, which had said that
the immunity in relation to conduct in court should not apply to the
complaints system.[56] It felt that to recognise the immunity would
"emasculate the procedure" and give the appearance that "lawyers

---

[52] This proposal was never implemented. Given the small size of the Bar, perhaps such
a procedure is unnecessary.
[53] *Blueprint for the Bar: Report of the Bar Standards Review Body* (1994), at p.3.
[54] *Fourth Annual Report of the Legal Services Ombudsman 1994*, at p.2.
[55] *The Solicitors Complaints Bureau: a consumer view* (1994), at p.110, National Consumer
Council.
[56] *Blueprint for the Bar: Report of the Bar Standards Review Body* (1994), at p.75.

were raising technical legal defences to protect themselves by a form of special pleading".[57]

Despite this dilution of the Review Body's proposals, opposition to the Working Group report began to grow during the autumn of 1995. The profession was opposed to the idea that barristers should pay compensation to lay clients for poor service. Members of the criminal bar in particular felt that there would be vast numbers of unreasonable compensation claims from dissatisfied clients, whom barristers had defended without success.[58] This opposition culminated in an open meeting for the profession in November 1995, at which the Bar modified the proposals. The modifications were that compensation would only be paid where actual financial loss could be shown, and not in the case of inconvenience or distress. In addition, the level of inadequate professional service would have to be "significantly" below what might be expected of a reasonably competent barrister, before an award would be made.

Even with these modifications, the open meeting rejected the complaints scheme, by 188 votes to 104. Barristers were then invited to take part in a postal ballot on the proposed scheme, which resulted in a majority approval of 2,004 votes, with 1,616 against. Perhaps the majority of barristers appreciated the "political reality" referred to by the (then) chairman of the Bar Council. He warned that if the scheme were rejected, a "far more stringent" one, over which the profession would have little or no control, would be "imposed by statute".[59]

Bar Council complaints system

The new system came into operation in April 1997. A new post was established of Complaints Commissioner, who is appointed by the Bar Council to supervise the running of the complaints system. The Commissioner has wide powers to accept or reject complaints, initiate conciliation, or determine how complaints should be dealt with. The last function is exercised in conjunction with a new Professional Conduct and Complaints Committee of the Bar Council, which determines how complaints are to be dealt with. For those complaints which involve possible professional misconduct, the procedure remains the same.[60]

---

[57] *ibid.*, at p.74.
[58] "Mutiny over Bar Reforms" *The Lawyer* September 26, 1995.
[59] Peter Goldsmith, Q.C., *Counsel*, November/December 1995, at p.3.
[60] The disciplinary procedure is discussed in Chapter 4.

All complaints about barristers will now be examined initially by the Complaints Commissioner, Michael Scott, who is not a lawyer. He decides if the complaint should be investigated. Where he decides that there will not be an investigation, the complainant can refer the matter to the Legal Services Ombudsman.[61] If the Commissioner decides that the case should be dealt with by conciliation, he writes to the barrister and the complainant suggesting an informal resolution. If this is not possible, or the complainant does not want to attempt it, the complainant must write again asking for a formal investigation.

Where the Commissioner decides that there is to be a formal investigation, the Bar Council writes to the barrister, the instructing solicitor and other relevant witnesses asking for their comments. The complainant is normally shown the barrister's comments and asked to make any further comments. The Commissioner will then decide whether or not the complaint should be taken further, and if he decides not to do so, the complainant is informed. Again, at this stage, the complainant can refer the matter to the Legal Services Ombudsman.

Where a complaint is considered further, the matter is examined by the Professional Conduct and Complaints Committee. The committee can dismiss it, giving reasons for doing so, or find that the barrister may be guilty of misconduct, and/or may be guilty of inadequate professional service. Professional misconduct procedures and penalties are discussed in Chapter 4. Complaints involving poor service are referred to adjudication panels, which are chaired by the Commissioner. These adjudication panels consist of two barristers and two lay representatives, one of which is the Commissioner, who, although the chair, does not have a casting vote. Where the panel is equally divided on a decision, the finding is that most favourable to the barrister. This means in effect that barrister members of the panels can veto any proposal to award financial redress. In the case of poor service, the standard of proof is that of the civil courts, on the balance of probabilities, which is unlike the case for professional misconduct, where the matter has to be proved beyond reasonable doubt.

Where there is a finding of inadequate professional service, and this has caused inconvenience, distress or loss to the client, the barrister can be required to apologise, refund or reduce fees, or pay compensation up to £2,000. These remedies are only available where the complainant is barrister's lay client. Compensation can only be awarded where the client has suffered actual loss, for example wasted travelling expenses, or the cost of rectifying mistakes. If there is no

---

[61] This is discussed in Chapter 6.

financial loss, there can be no compensation, and it is thus not available for distress or inconvenience. However, in these circumstances it is possible for a reduction or refund of fees.

Complaints against barristers have increased by nearly 30 per cent since the introduction of the complaints procedure. There were 550 complaints in 1997, compared with 431 in 1996. This represents one complaint for every 21 practising barristers.[62] In 60 per cent of the cases, the complaint was dismissed, but "surprisingly few" were frivolous. Of the 40 per cent which were sent to the Professional Conduct and Complaints Committee, half were dismissed. There were three major areas giving rise to complaints. Firstly, prisoners complained about the incompetence of their barristers, having exhausted the appeal system. Matrimonial disputes also gave rise to a number of complaints. Finally, there were neighbourhood disputes, where the complaints against the barrister became part of the overall dispute.[63] Just over 10 per cent of the complaints resulted in disciplinary action. In only two cases was an award of compensation made. Both of these resulted in a reduction in counsel's fees.

In 184 cases, complainants referred their case to the Legal Services Ombudsman, which represents 33 per cent of the cases dealt with by the Bar procedure. Reasons for referrals to the Ombudsman included dissatisfaction because conduct issues had been overlooked or been given insufficient weight. There were also complaints about the inability or reluctance of the Bar Council to recommend payment of compensation for poor service. In some cases, there was dissatisfaction because complainants had not been advised of the outcome of their complaint.[64]

Evaluation of the Bar complaints procedure

The previous Legal Services Ombudsman welcomed the new system, calling it "an important milestone in the development of the relationship between the Bar and barristers' lay clients".[65] The present Ombudsman feels that the admission of a lay person into "the self-regulatory citadel" was a "striking symbol of change".[66] However,

---

[62] This compares favourably with solicitors, where there was one complaint for every three practising solicitors. Complaints rose to 631 in 1998, of which 491 were from lay clients.

[63] "Bar complaints one year on" *New Law Journal* May 22, 1998, at p.738.

[64] *Seventh Annual Report of the Legal Services Ombudsman 1997*, at p.20.

[65] *Sixth Annual Report of the Legal Services Ombudsman 1996*, at p.16.

[66] *Seventh Annual Report of the Legal Services Ombudsman 1997*, at p.19.

despite its being a "big step forward", there are still some problems. For example, because of the composition of the adjudication panels, barristers in effect have a veto on the imposition of financial redress. When the previous Ombudsman raised this with Bar Council, he was told that it would not be "palatable" to members of the Bar for panels with a lay majority to determine the level of compensation or fee reductions to be imposed on barristers.[67] The Bar Council did concede that they might be prepared to review this in the future. Perhaps the introduction of the new procedure will gradually "change barristers' perception not only of the nature of complaints themselves but also of their relationship with their lay clients".[68]

Another problem is the exemption in relation to those aspects of barristers' work that attracts immunity from suit. The Review Body was clear that the system should cover all aspects of barristers' work, but that recommendation was dropped by the Bar.

The scheme also differs from the Review Body's proposals in that compensation cannot be paid for distress or inconvenience. The standard of service will have to be "significantly" below what can be reasonably expected before there can be a finding against the barrister. These changes to the original proposals are disappointing. The Complaints Commissioner himself has argued that the restrictions on compensation should be removed.[69] However, it is probably better to have a complaints system with this limited financial redress, rather than to continue with the previous procedures, which were a little more than an internal Bar Council disciplinary system".[70]

This new system represents a step in the right direction, and it is incumbent upon the Bar to make sure it works. The Bar does not, however, appear to be heeding the warning of the previous Legal Services Ombudsman. He counselled against "treading too warily" and adopting "too restrictive an approach" in deciding whether barristers should reduce, refund or waive fees. If this were done, there would be a serious loss of goodwill and credibility, and it would take some time to restore confidence".[71]

The present Ombudsman is of the opinion that the changes "appear to be more symbol than substance".[72] Consumer dissatisfaction with the process is illustrated by the fact that one-third of complainants referred their case to the Ombudsman, after it had been through the

---

[67] *Sixth Annual Report of the Legal Services Ombudsman 1996*, at p.11.
[68] *ibid.*, at p. 11
[69] *The Lawyer* May 19, 1998.
[70] *Fifth Annual Report of the Legal Services Ombudsman 1995*, at p.14.
[71] *Sixth Annual Report of the Legal Services Ombudsman 1996*, at p.24.
[72] *Seventh Annual Report of the Legal Services Ombudsman 1997*, at p. 7

Bar procedure.[73] In only 10 per cent of referrals was the Ombudsman dissatisfied with the way the complaint was handled. The Ombudsman is clear that the Bar Council "operates an efficient complaints-handling system". It is well managed, has thorough investigations, operates within reasonable timescales, and gives considered and appropriate decisions. The problem is that it does not leave the consumer satisfied.[74] What the system needs is to make the complainant more central to the process. There is still too much emphasis on the disciplinary aspects of a complaint, rather than focusing on the needs of complainants. It needs to start using its powers, particularly those in relation to compensation, more effectively. Barristers could perhaps help themselves by heeding the advice of the Complaints Commissioner: "saying sorry is not an admission of guilt".[75]

Conclusion

The first Legal Services Ombudsman believed that the present system for the protection of consumers of legal services (self-regulation, plus recourse to an independent, statutory ombudsman) had a number of benefits. He did, however, caution that it would only be a satisfactory system if the professional bodies were able to achieve a reasonable level of consumer satisfaction. There are three conditions for consumer satisfaction: complaints have to be resolved speedily; professional bodies have to achieve greater credibility; there has to be provision for effective redress.[76]

Both the Law Society and the Bar Council are aware of the need to ensure consumer satisfaction, and both branches of the profession have new systems in place for dealing with consumer complaints. The leadership in the legal profession "talk the language of client care".[77] There is a move away from the disciplinary model to a consumerist model. The task is to ensure that this approach has the support of the rest of the profession. There needs to be a change of culture, so that complaint handling is seen as a worthwhile investment of time and effort. Any progress which has been made has been slow, and

---

[73] This is compared with referrals from the Office for the Supervision of Solicitors, where there were only 6 per cent.
[74] *Seventh Annual Report of the Legal Services Ombudsman 1997*, at p.19.
[75] "Bar complaints one year on" *New Law Journal* May 22, 1998, at p.738.
[76] *Fifth Annual Report of the Legal Services Ombudsman 1995*, at p.6.
[77] A. Abraham, "Regulating the Regulators: the Ombudsman's Perspective" in *Governing the Profession* (1998), at p.75, Proceedings from the Annual Research Conference. Research and Policy Planning Unit. The Law Society.

"characterised by resistance, denial . . . compromise and fudge".[78] The profession needs to realise that quality of service is "more important to most people than professional purity".[79]

The Office for the Supervision of Solicitors has been in operation for over two years. It started well, is more consumer-friendly than its predecessor, and has adopted streamlined procedures to deal with complaints more efficiently. Despite this, there are still unacceptable delays, and it is being overwhelmed by the huge increase in the numbers of complaints. Many believe that, as it is part of the Law Society, it is therefore unlikely to be different from the Solicitors Complaints Bureau, which it replaced.[80] It is proving to be as unpopular with the public and the profession as the Solicitors Complaints Bureau.[81]

One strategy for dealing with the rising tide of complaints is to require complaints to be dealt with, as far as possible, by solicitors' firms. In that way, only the intractable cases would be dealt with by the professional body.[82] As we have seen the Office for the Supervision of Solicitors has placed great emphasis on the primary level, in-house, procedures operated by individual firms. Such an approach enhances client loyalty, and is also more cost-effective than a referral to the Office for the Supervision of Solicitors. There is evidence that 80 per cent of complaints to the Office for the Supervision of Solicitors originate in 20 per cent of firms. In-house complaint-handling would ensure that these firms carry the cost of this, rather than the profession as a whole.[83]

Despite the advantages of this approach, there are some difficulties. There is evidence that firms are not complying with the spirit of Practice Rule 15. There are still too many in the profession wanting the process to be less conciliatory and more contentious. Solicitors "could then be certain of being able to put their case forward on proper judicial terms instead of the dubious consideration which is

---

[78] A. Abraham, "Regulating the Regulators: the Ombudsman's Perspective" in *Governing the Profession* (1998), at p.75, Proceedings from the Annual Research Conference. Research and Policy Planning Unit. The Law Society.

[79] *ibid.*, at p.75.

[80] A. Arora and A. Francis, *The Rule of Lawyers* (1998), at p.3, Fabian Society Discussion Paper Number 42.

[81] "Supervision at arm's length," Editorial, *New Law Journal* August 15, 1997, p.1229.

[82] An independent report into the workings of the Office of the Legal Services Ombudsman has also recommended that priority should be given to the "front end of the whole process", with practitioners resolving effectively complaints they receive (*Consumer Satisfaction in a Super-Escalated Complaint Environment.* A report by the Customer Management Consultancy Ltd to the Office of the Legal Services Ombudsman (1999) The Lord Chancellor's Department, Research Programe).

[83] *Law Society Gazette*, March 31, 1999, at p. 15.

given at present".[84] Such an attitude indicates the efforts which must be made if the culture is to be changed, for the benefit of consumers. Even with a positive approach to complaint handling, there are problems with internal procedures. For many firms, the complaint handler is not far enough removed from the original decision, and this makes an impartial investigation difficult.

The Legal Services Ombudsman is not surprised that the public has very little confidence in the complaint-handling system, as solicitors themselves seemed to lack confidence in it. This is indicated by the fact that some members of the profession think that it is "fair game for attack in the columns of the legal and national press".[85] She has placed the responsibility for bringing about the necessary changes in culture and approach on the Law Society and individual solicitors. It is their responsibility to make sure that the new system works. If it does not, she has warned that there are "plenty of players waiting in the wings who are only too keen to replace self-regulation with something . . . . . many solicitors would like even less".[86] This may be the Law Society's last chance to bring about the culture change within the profession which is needed to ensure that consumers have confidence in the system.[87]

As for the Bar, there is no doubt that the creation of a complaints system, with a lay person in charge, and with the power to award compensation was a breakthrough for consumers. The problem is that the benefits for consumers have yet to become a reality. There are too many constraints in the procedure, which prevent consumers receiving a remedy. The exclusion of jurisdiction for acts which relate to a barrister's immunity in court prevents many complaints. The Complaints Commissioner himself feels that this immunity "may well need looking at".[88] The restrictive rules on compensation are also problematic. Since its operation, only two awards of compensation have been made.

Criticisms of self-regulation have dominated debates about complaints against lawyers in the last decade. They are not going to go away. In March 1997, there was an Early Day Motion[89] before the House of Commons calling for an independent complaints procedure

[84] A. Rosen, "Who judges solicitors?" *New Law Journal* February 24, 1995.
[85] A. Abraham, *New Law Journal* October 24, 1997.
[86] *ibid.*
[87] *Fifth Annual Report of the Legal Services Ombudsman 1995*, p.7.
[88] "Bar complaints one year on" *New Law Journal* May 22, 1998, p.738.
[89] This was laid on behalf of CASIA (Complaints Against Solicitors Action for Independent Adjudication) by Gerry Sutcliffe, M.P. for Bradford South. Its focus was solicitors.

for consumer complaints.[90] A recent Fabian Society report has spoken of the "fundamental flaws and weaknesses" of the system, which can only be addressed by a "wholesale rethink of the complaints system. This report recommended the creation of an independent body, modelled on the General Medical Council, and concluded that independent regulation was inevitable.[91]

There is no doubt that the system is being closely watched. The next few years are crucial. Unless the professional bodies can provide appropriate levels of satisfaction, there will be a "major reappraisal of the procedures for dealing with complaints about lawyers".[92] Many believe that if the Law Society does not establish a "clear and apparent division" between itself and the Office for the Supervision of Solicitors then the Government will do it for them.[93] The pressures for a major shake-up in the system are already becoming irresistible. Appraisal of the system by politicians, consumer groups and the media is already taking place.

The Government had no plans at the end of 1997 to create a new complaints handling body, and was prepared to wait and see how effective the Office for the Supervision of Solicitors would be.[94] However, in its recent White Paper[95] it signalled its intention to keep the area of complaints handling under review. Ensuring that effective complaints procedures were in place to deal with client complaints were part of the Government's plans to maintain and improve lawyers' standards of service.

The Government has also introduced a clause in the Access to Justice Bill which allows for the creation of a legal complaints commissioner, whose remit would be to set targets for complaint-handling and make recommendations for complaints systems. These would only be activated where the Lord Chancellor considered that intervention was needed. This is a significant development, as it allows for the Lord Chancellor to have direct input into complaints handling by the legal profession. The powers would be used as a last resort, and the expectation is that their existence would encourage the profession

---

[90] All other self-regulation and any disciplinary action was to be left with the Law Society. See "Abolition of self-regulation?" *New Law Journal* April 18, 1997, at p.554; "Independent complaints procedure?" *New Law Journal* July 11, 1997, at p.1022.

[91] A. Arora and A. Francis, *The Rule of Lawyers* (1998), Fabian Society Discussion Paper Number 42.

[92] *Sixth Annual Report of the Legal Services Ombudsman 1996*, at p.1.

[93] Editorial, *New Law Journal* August 25, 1997.

[94] Geoff Hoon, Minister in the Lord Chancellor's Department, responding to a request for a statutory complaints procedure for solicitors. See "Cleaning up the Act" *Law Society Gazette* December 10, 1997, at p.12.

[95] *Modernising Justice*, White Paper, Cm.4155 (1998), para.2.32.

to put its own house in order.[96] The Government believes that these measures are a reasonable compromise between self-regulation by the profession and an independent system.[97]

The previous Legal Services Ombudsman felt that more information was needed about how well the system was operating, before self-regulation was completely abandoned.[98] The present Ombudsman is not arguing for the fundamental change which the Fabian Society report[99] proposes. However, she does warn that if the profession wants to silence the call for an independent complaints handling body, they have a long way to go and little time to get there.[1]

Even with an effective self-regulatory complaints handling process, there will still need to be an independent element in the system, if it is to command public confidence. The Office of the Legal Services Ombudsman, which was established to monitor the complaints mechanisms of the professional bodies, offers such an element. Any reform of the self-regulatory mechanisms must also take into account the work and influence of the Legal Services Ombudsman. This will be the subject of the next chapter.

---

[96] *Law Society Gazette*, April 14, 1999, at p. 15.
[97] *Law Society Gazette*, March 24, 1999, at p. 1.
[98] *Fourth Annual Report of the Legal Services Ombudsman 1994*, at p.9.
[99] A. Arora and A. Francis, *The Rule of Lawyers* (1998), Fabian Society Discussion Paper Number 42.
[1] *Seventh Annual Report of the Legal Services Ombudsman 1997*, at p.3.

Chapter 6

The Legal Services Ombudsman

If consumers are dissatisfied with the way in which the professional bodies have dealt with their complaints, there is one final port of call. This is the Legal Services Ombudsman,[1] who has responsibility for overseeing the way in which professional bodies deal with complaints.

Ombudsmen have become an increasingly popular consumer remedy[2] in the private sector, with the ability in most cases to decide disputes between consumers and the organisation concerned, and to make binding awards. Private ombudsman schemes were mostly introduced on a voluntary, self-regulatory basis, by the relevant industries.[3] Ombudsmen's origins, however, lie in the public sector, where they have the power to investigate grievances caused by maladministration on the part of central government departments, local government and the health service.[4] These public sector ombudsmen make recommendations rather than binding awards, and those public authorities covered by the legislation have no choice but to submit to their jurisdiction. In some ways, the Legal Services Ombudsman is in a hybrid category, between the traditional public sector ombudsmen and the self-regulatory schemes of the private sector. The Office of the Legal Services Ombudsman was set up by statute,[5] is publicly funded, and is accountable through the Lord

---

[1] Some of the information for this chapter was obtained during research carried out at the Office of the Legal Services Ombudsman, by the author and Rhoda James. See also R. James and M. Seneviratne "The Legal Services Ombudsman: Form versus Function?" (1995) 58(2) *Modern Law Review* 187–207.

[2] Part of their popularity, as an alternative dispute resolution mechanism is the fact that their services are free, and they adopt an inquisitorial, rather than an adversarial, method of investigation.

[3] For a fuller discussion of private sector ombudsman schemes see R. James, *Private Ombudsmen and Public Law* (1997) [Dartmouth].

[4] For a fuller discussion of public sector ombudsman schemes see M. Seneviratne, *Ombudsmen in the Public Sector* (1994) [Open University Press].

[5] Courts and Legal Services Act 1990, s. 21.

Chancellor to Parliament.[6] The jurisdiction of the Ombudsman, however, is over the legal profession, which operates mainly in the private sector.

Background

The Legal Services Ombudsman was created by the Courts and Legal Services Act 1990. The scheme was introduced as part of the reform of complaint handling by lawyers, which was initiated after the concerns which are outlined in Chapter 5. The aim was to provide independent supervision of the way the professional bodies handled complaints against members of their own profession. Before this, the solicitors' profession had been subject to some scrutiny in the form of the Lay Observer. This was an independent person, appointed by the Lord Chancellor, who was empowered to examine any allegation from a member of the public concerning the Law Society's treatment of a complaint about a solicitor.[7] The Lay Observer could report on an investigation, but could not re-investigate the original complaint. He or she could make recommendations to the Law Society, and was also empowered to refer an issue of quality of service to the Solicitors' Disciplinary Tribunal, where a complaint raised issues of both conduct and quality of service.

The Government at the time felt that the Lay Observer's powers were inadequate, in that there were only limited powers to take cases to the Solicitors Disciplinary Tribunal, and no powers of referral to the Solicitors Complaints Bureau. Nor could there be a re-investigation of the case, or award of compensation.[8] It was also anomalous that there was no equivalent of the Lay Observer to review the Bar's complaints process. The Legal Services Ombudsman was introduced to go some way towards rectifying these omissions. The ombudsman proposal contained in the Green Paper[9] was widely welcomed during the consultation process with support coming from both the profession and the public.

The White Paper[10] which followed said that the ombudsman was to be independent of Government and of the profession, and was to

---

[6] The status of the Legal Services Ombudsman is analogous to that of a non-departmental public body, funded from money voted to the Lord Chancellor's Department.

[7] Solicitors Act 1974, s. 45(1).

[8] *The Work and Organisation of the Legal Profession*, Green Paper, Cm.570 (1989).

[9] *ibid.*

[10] *Legal Services: A Framework for the Future*, Cm.740 (1989).

have two main functions: the investigation of the way complaints had been handled by the relevant professional body; and the investigation of the original complaint about the provision of legal services. In Parliament, MPs generally supported the introduction of the ombudsman on the grounds that the Law Society's rules for dealing with complaints were so complicated that supervision by an ombudsman was required.[11] It was also felt that it would increase public confidence in the legal system.[12]

The principal intention in introducing the ombudsman was to provide some comprehensive scrutiny of the handling of complaints against members of the legal profession. This role was emphasised during the debates on the Bill,[13] and this was reflected in the way in which the powers of the Ombudsman were framed in the legislation. The investigation of the original complaint can only occur as part of this process.[14] The powers and jurisdiction of the Ombudsman were thus framed in the context of the Lay Observer's existing powers rather than being devised afresh. This dual role was described by the first Legal Services Ombudsman as encompassing that of "guardian of the guardians" and as a "second port of call" for complainants.[15]

Powers and jurisdiction

Given the proliferation of the ombudsman remedy, and its establishment as an alternative dispute resolution mechanism, it is perhaps unsurprising that the Government should have given this title to the new office which was to be created. Whether it is an appropriate title may be debatable. The powers of the Legal Services Ombudsman are something of a departure from the traditional ombudsman model. Although ombudsman schemes display quite widely differing features, most ombudsmen are able to receive complaints from individuals, to investigate those complaints, and then to recommend or direct a remedy, if the complaint is found. The Legal Services Ombudsman, however, stands at one remove from the individual's complaint. His or her function is to investigate any allegation, which relates to the manner in which a complaint about a

---

[11] H.C. Deb., vol. 170, cols. 1500, 1522, April 18, 1990.

[12] Standing Committee D, col. 165, May 22, 1990.

[13] ibid. cols. 167, 168, 173.

[14] The White Paper had envisaged that this second function would be subordinate to that of overseeing the complaints handling process.

[15] First Annual Report of the Legal Services Ombudsman 1991, at p.6.

lawyer has been handled by the relevant professional body.[16] Secondly, the Ombudsman may investigate the original matter of the complaint, if he or she is also investigating the way the professional body has handled it.[17] So, the principal power is to investigate allegations about the way in which the professional body has dealt with the individual's original complaint about their lawyer, not the complaint itself. This means that consumers with grievances against their lawyers cannot take their complaints directly to the Legal Services Ombudsman. In practice, in the vast majority of cases, the original complaint is not investigated by the Ombudsman.

Even where the Legal Services Ombudsman does elect to investigate the original complaint, it means that there are more stages in the process than is the case with other ombudsmen. It is true that individuals with a complaint against a bank or insurance company, for example, have to take their complaint through the internal procedures of their particular bank or insurance company in the first instance. However, if they are not satisfied with the company's response, they can go directly to the relevant ombudsman. Consumers with a complaint against their lawyer have a much longer route to the Ombudsman, since the legislation ensured that it is still the respective professional bodies who have the prime responsibility for dealing with the complaint. The Legal Services Ombudsman thus stands at a further remove from the original complaint. This pyramid structure and convoluted process carries with it considerable scope for delay, a factor recognised by the post-holders.[18]

The Ombudsman has a discretion whether or not to investigate at either stage, but if he or she decides not to investigate then he or she has to make the reasons known to the complainant, as well as to the lawyer and the professional body concerned.[19] The Ombudsman must also do this if he or she decides to discontinue an investigation. There are some circumstances specified in the Act where the Ombudsman is not allowed to investigate. Normally he or she cannot investigate where the matter is still being investigated by the professional body. However, if the complaint being made is that the professional body has acted unreasonably in failing to start an investigation, or has failed to complete it in a reasonable time, the Ombudsman may do so. He or she may also investigate, where the complaint is still with the professional body, if satisfied that an investigation is justified.[20] The

---

[16] Courts and Legal Services Act 1990, s. 22(1).
[17] *ibid*. s. 22(2).
[18] See, for example *Sixth Annual Report of the Legal Services Ombudsman 1996*, at p.24.
[19] Courts and Legal Services Act 1990, s. 22(4).
[20] *ibid*. s. 22(5) and (6).

Ombudsman cannot investigate if an appeal is pending against the professional body's decision on a complaint, or where the appeal period has not expired. Nor can the Ombudsman investigate any matter which has been the subject of a decision in court, or by the Solicitors Disciplinary Tribunal, or the Disciplinary Tribunal of the Council of the Inns of Court.[21]

Advocate's immunity

One important exclusion is that which relates to negligence cases. The Ombudsman cannot investigate an allegation relating to a complaint about an aspect of conduct for which the lawyer has immunity from any action in negligence or contract.[22] As we saw in Chapter 2, this immunity prevents an advocate, whether a barrister or solicitor, from being sued in negligence in respect of the conduct and management of a case in court. This is a controversial area, but it is one which the first Ombudsman took up at the beginning of his tenure in office. In his first Annual Report, the Ombudsman[23] indicated that this immunity seemed to rule out a significant proportion of complaints made to him about the Bar Council's handling of complaints.[24] As this was far more than he would wish to see excluded, he sought the advice of leading counsel on the wording of the Act. In particular, he wanted to know whether he could investigate an allegation about the way in which the Bar Council had handled a complaint about a barrister's conduct in court. The advice was to the effect that the Ombudsman *could* investigate where the allegation concerned the Bar Council's methods and procedures in the handling of a complaint, even where the complaint itself related to an advocate's negligence. Further, that the Ombudsman's jurisdiction over the original complaint could extend to conduct in court where it was a matter of breach of the professional disciplinary code, or where the behaviour might be thought to be rude or offensive.[25]

This was the approach subsequently adopted by the Ombudsman, and an illustration is given in the Third Annual Report of the kind of behaviour by a barrister which the Ombudsman is able to deal with. The Ombudsman describes it as follows:

---

[21] *ibid.* s. 22(7).

[22] *ibid.* s. 22(7).

[23] Michael Barnes was the first Legal Services Ombudsman. He held the office until September 1997.

[24] *First Annual Report of the Legal Services Ombudsman 1991*, at p.24.

[25] *Second Annual Report of the Legal Services Ombudsman 1992*, at p.11.

"A complainant from the West Midlands had been represented by London counsel at a trial in Wolverhampton. He was sent down for four years. He blamed his barrister. I could see why. A conference had been arranged when the complainant was on remand in Shrewsbury. Counsel never made it. Although learned in the law, geography was not his strong suit. Labouring under the misapprehension that Shrewsbury was near Luton, he was halted by an accident on the M1 and forced to return to London for what he obviously thought was a more important conference with a Q.C. on another case. When some time afterwards the case came to trial, the Wolverhampton one-way system got the better of him and despite reaching the town at 8.30 a.m. (or so he said) he was still hunting for a car parking space at 10.30. Late for the pre-trial conference at court, he later gave the complainant, and a court clerk, the impression that he was nodding off during the judge's summing up. In self-defence, he insisted that appearances can be deceptive: he was in fact having a hay fever attack. Either way, I was satisfied that, overall, the complainant had had a poor deal".[26]

In this case, the Ombudsman concluded that the complainant had been deprived of any confidence in the quality of his representation, and should be paid £1,000 by way of compensation for the attendant distress. The Ombudsman was not, in this case, making a judgment about whether or not the conviction was sound, but was assessing whether there had been professional misconduct, including behaviour in court.

Remedies

When the Ombudsman upholds an allegation, there are a number of remedies available. He or she can recommend that that the professional body reconsider the complaint or exercise any of its disciplinary powers. There can also be a recommendation that compensation be paid by the professional body, or by the lawyer against whom the original complaint was made.[27] In the latter case, this is only available where the original complaint has been investigated. Compensation is to cover any loss suffered by the complainant, as well as inconvenience and distress. The Green Paper[28] had only discussed the payment of compensation by the professional body. But in the White Paper,[29] it was argued that, where the loss, distress or inconvenience arose from the original complaint, the compensation should be paid by the practitioner concerned. Where

---

[26] *Third Annual Report of the Legal Services Ombudsman 1993*, at p.13.
[27] Courts and Legal Services Act 1990, s. 23.
[28] *The Work and Organisation of the Legal Profession*, Cm.570 (1989), at p.18.
[29] *Legal Services: A Framework for the Future*, Cm.740 (1989), at p.35.

the complainant suffered as a result of the complaints procedure operated by the professional body, it was appropriate that that body should pay.

There are no limits on the amount of compensation which the Ombudsman may award. This is unlike the complaint systems operated by the Office for the Supervision of Solicitors, which has a limit of £1,000, and that operated by the Bar Council, where the limit is £2,000. This situation could encourage complainants, hoping for a more generous award than that provided for by the professional body scheme, to refer their complaint to the ombudsman. It might produce a more coherent system if the Legal Services Ombudsman were limited in the same way, or if the professional bodies had no limit. The National Consumer Council has suggested an award limit of £5,000,[30] and the previous Ombudsman suggested that there was a strong case for a £2,000 limit for solicitors, and possibly even an increase to £5,000.[31] The present Ombudsman's position is that the maximum award should be linked to the small claims court limit.[32]

The Ombudsman's awards are not binding, although there are proposals to increase the Ombudsman's powers to allow for binding determinations.[33] The only sanction for non-compliance with a recommendation at present is that of publicity. The Act requires the lawyer or the professional body to notify the Ombudsman within three months of the recommendation, as to what action they have taken or propose to take, to comply with the recommendation.[34] If this is not done, the Act requires the professional body or lawyer to publicise their reasons for non-compliance, at their own expense. The final sanction is publicity by the Ombudsman, the expense of which is to be reimbursed by the miscreant.[35] The National Consumer Council had wanted recommendations to be binding, but the Government at the time did not believe that it was appropriate for a statutory scheme to have mandatory awards. The Ombudsman's powers were to be persuasive only. It was however in the interests of "a member of the

---

[30] This was within the context of a new complaints council. See National Consumer Council *The Solicitors Complaints Bureau—A Consumer View* (1994).

[31] *Fourth Annual Report of the Legal Services Ombudsman 1994*, at p.9. This would also be in line with the new limit for the small claims court.

[32] The Lord Chancellor is inclined to raise the Office for the Supervision of Solicitors' limit to £5,000, and is consulting the Law Society about this.

[33] This is to be a discretionary power, and, if an award is to be binding, there would have to be a hearing. It is unclear why the Government feels that this power is necessary. Statistically, there are only a handful of practitioners who have not complied, and these mainly relate to those who are no longer in practice. This reform was not canvassed by the Ombudsman.

[34] Courts and Legal Services Act 1990, s. 23(7).

[35] *ibid.* s. 23(8)–(10).

public who had a grievance about the handling of a complaint," that they should be "powerfully persuasive".[36] The Government felt that the publicity option was "the reasonable, middle way".[37]

It was this aspect of the Ombudsman's powers which seemed to cause most concern to MPs and peers during the passage of the Bill. It was criticised because it could impose considerable liability, and this called into question whether or not it was truly a voluntary system.[38] Others thought it unusual to require people to publish information against themselves[39] and were concerned that the Ombudsman could require publication in a way which could be highly damaging.[40] The fact that there was no appeal against the Ombudsman's decision was felt to make the provision even more onerous.[41] The view was that the provision came very close to making the recommendations binding and that the sanction might be more damaging than if the matter were dealt with by a court.[42]

In the House of Lords, the Lord Chancellor defended the provision, maintaining that it was not a unique power, and that it had not caused difficulties elsewhere.[43] There was a need to ensure that a recommendation was not ignored by the practitioner or professional body and that the Ombudsman's recommendations were respected. One of the criticisms of the Lay Observer had been that there was no power to enforce recommendations. It was felt that to delete the provision about publicity would severely compromise the Ombudsman's powers and seriously damage his or her whole jurisdiction.[44] The Attorney-General also emphasised the fact that there had been general dissatisfaction with the powers available to the Lay Observer, and that it would be too easy for professional bodies to avoid recommendations. He felt that there were safeguards against unfairness, because the Ombudsman would have to give reasons for the decisions. If the decisions were irrational, or arrived at by a manifestly unfair procedure, they would be amenable to judicial review.[45]

Despite the fact that it was felt by some that this provision was an

---

[36] Standing Committee D, col.177, May 22, 1990, The Attorney-General.
[37] H.L. Deb. Vol. 516, col. 1674, March 15, 1990, Lord Chancellor.
[38] H.L Deb., Committee, vol. 514, col. 1294, January 25, 1990, Lord Coleraine.
[39] H.L. Deb., vol., 516, col., 264, February 20, 1990, Lord Renton.
[40] *ibid.* Lord Boardman.
[41] Standing Committee D, col. 172, May 22, 1990, Mr Lawrence.
[42] *ibid.* col. 173, May 22, 1990, Mr Fraser.
[43] Both the Building Societies Ombudsman and the Local Government Ombudsman have provisions for publicity, where there is non-compliance with recommendations.
[44] H.L. Deb., vol. 514, cols. 1294, 1295, January 25, 1990, Lord Chancellor.
[45] Standing Committee D, col 177, May 22, 1990, Attorney-General.

"effective way of creating bad relations between the ombudsman and the branches of the legal profession,"[46] compliance with the recommendations has not been a serious problem. The professional bodies have always complied with a recommendation, and less than 3 per cent of lawyers have failed to comply. In the first three years of the scheme, there were seven cases of failure to comply, which were duly publicised. The number did increase over the next three years: eight in 1994;[47] five in 1995;[48] and six in 1996.[49] Despite this, the first Legal Services Ombudsman did not feel that lack of compliance should be a disciplinary offence for the practitioner concerned. The system is based on informality. A disciplinary sanction could jeopardise co-operation by the profession. He also considered that the fact that his recommendations were not binding might make it more appropriate for people seeking "substantial compensation" to proceed through the courts.[50] The present Ombudsman is of the same view. She feels that it would not be appropriate to make refusal to comply a disciplinary offence. In view of this, it is surprising that the Government is proposing to allow the Ombudsman the discretion to make binding awards.

Who can make an allegation to the Ombudsman?

Anyone who is affected by what is alleged in relation to the complaint may make a complaint to the Ombudsman. Complaints may also be brought by a relative, or personal or other representative, where the person affected has died, or is unable to bring the complaint himself or herself.[51] There is no requirement that the complainant has to be a client of the lawyer, who is the subject of the original complaint. The professional bodies are generally reluctant to entertain complaints from non-clients. This is on the basis that solicitors do not owe the same duties of care to third parties. The Office for the Supervision of Solicitors, for example, will only investigate third party complaints if the issue relates to serious professional misconduct. Even then, they require sufficient evidence before they will embark on an investigation, and they usually prefer that it is the third party's solicitor who brings the complaint. The Ombudsman adopts a different

---

[46] H.L. Deb., vol. 514, col. 1675, March 15, 1990, Lord Renton.
[47] *Fourth Annual Report of the Legal Services Ombudsman 1994*, at p.29.
[48] *Fifth Annual Report of the Legal Services Ombudsman 1995*, at p.4.
[49] *Sixth Annual Report of the Legal Services Ombudsman 1996*, at p.4.
[50] *Second Annual Report of the Legal Services Ombudsman 1992*, at p.13.
[51] Courts and Legal Services Act, s. 22(9).

approach. Solicitors have a general professional obligation to non-clients, and therefore it is possible for third parties to have legitimate complaints, which should be heard.[52]

The reluctance by the former Solicitors Complaints Bureau to entertain complaints about someone else's solicitor meant that beneficiaries of wills, who were not executors, were unable to use the Bureau to complain about the solicitor dealing with the will. The Ombudsman was successful in persuading the Bureau to be more flexible in this respect, arguing that beneficiaries do have standing, and that it is legitimate for them to complain about delay and the cost of administering the estate.[53] However, in his Fifth Annual Report, the first Ombudsman still spoke of his concern about the Bureau's reluctance to intervene in these cases, and of their tendency to seek refuge behind technical arguments, rather than using common sense to achieve a resolution. One example he quoted concerned the mother of two infant beneficiaries under a trust established by a deceased relative's will. The Bureau refused to take action when she complained about the solicitors acting for the trustees, on the grounds that she was not a client.[54]

There is no provision for practitioners to make allegations to the Ombudsman about the professional body's handling of a complaint about them. The Ombudsman cannot therefore investigate such allegations. There is nothing in the Act to prevent the Ombudsman dealing with allegations from lawyers about other lawyers. Sometimes lawyers make allegations on behalf of their clients. Some allegations are the result of a practitioner's complaint about a conduct matter to the professional body. These kinds of allegations are treated in the same way as allegations from consumers.

Procedure

Allegations must be made in writing, although, as with other ombudsmen, consumers commonly make the initial contact by telephone. There used to be a requirement that they be made within three months of the professional body's decision, and there was no discretion to accept late complaints. This was a short time limit in

---

[52] First Annual Report of the Legal Services Ombudsman 1991, at p.7.
[53] The Solicitors (Non-Contentious Business) Remuneration Order 1994 now gives beneficiaries of estates the right to obtain a remuneration certificate where the only executors are solicitors. This only partially addresses the problem.
[54] Fifth Annual Report of the Legal Services Ombudsman 1995, at p.20.

comparison with other ombudsmen.[55] Since January 1, 1999, this time limit for allegations has been abolished. This is now a matter which is entirely at the Ombudsman's discretion.[56] Even before this, there was some flexibility in the time limit. For example, sometimes the complainant had not received a definitive letter of decision from the professional body at the time of contacting the Ombudsman. By communicating with the professional body again in order to receive a definitive decision letter, complainants were able to bring themselves within the time limit. A flexible approach was taken in relation to the date of the final decision of the professional body's appeal process. Even when the three-month limit operated, the short time limit did not cause serious problems and only a handful of complaints appeared to be rejected as out of time.

The initial inquiry to the Legal Services Ombudsman is usually by telephone. Before a case is accepted, the office support staff need to ensure that the complainant has used the complaints procedures provided by the professional bodies. If the complainant has not, he or she is referred to the relevant body. Cases which are clearly not relevant to the Legal Services Ombudsman Scheme are referred to other ombudsmen or elsewhere.[57] Provided that the complainant has been dealt with by the relevant professional body, and it appears that the complaint comes within the terms of reference of the scheme, an application form and information leaflet are sent out to elicit the relevant details about the complaint. The form itself is very clearly set out, and there appear to be no particular difficulties experienced by complainants in completing it.

About 40 per cent of initial inquiries to the Ombudsman are not pursued. In most cases, this is because complainants do not return a completed complaint form. A small number are rejected when the form is returned, because they are clearly outside the Ombudsman's remit. For the others, a case file is opened; the professional body's file is requested; and a letter is sent to the complainant explaining the position. An investigating officer examines the professional body's file and the complaint file in detail, before deciding whether to investigate

---

[55] The Parliamentary Ombudsman and the Local Government Ombudsman, for example, have a limit of 12 months. Many of the private sector ombudsman schemes have a six-month time limit, and some have discretion to accept complaints beyond this time.

[56] This change was included in new directions from the Lord Chancellor's Department—the Legal Services Ombudsman (Jurisdiction) Amendment Order 1998, September 29, 1998.

[57] A feature of all ombudsman schemes is that they find themselves having to "field" all sorts of inquiries and complaints, and have to refer the member of the public to other mechanisms.

the matter further. If this is to be done, the applicant and lawyer are informed. Some cases are put on "fast-track". This category includes complaints which appear to have no merit, where it is unlikely that there will be a recommendation. Also in this category are the cases where the complaint is that the professional body has taken too long to deal with the original complaint. Straightforward, simple cases, which do not need a full report are also put on "fast-track", to prevent their being subject to unnnecessary delay.

After conducting the investigation, the investigating officer forms a "provisional view" as to whether there should be a recommendation or not, and drafts a report. Where the view is that there should be no recommendation, the draft report is forwarded directly to the Ombudsman, who checks it, amends it where necessary, and signs the final report. If the provisional view is that there will be a recommendation, the report (and file) is passed to the Legal Adviser for checking, before going to the Ombudsman for consideration.

When there is a recommendation that compensation be paid by the lawyer involved in the original complaint, the lawyer is sent a letter explaining that the Legal Services Ombudsman is "minded" to award compensation, together with a draft of the Ombudsman's preliminary view. The lawyer then has 28 days to comment on this. Lawyers usually make submissions, indicating the reasons for their belief that the Ombudsman's assessment is wrong. Sometimes lawyers accept that they are at fault, but feel that the amount of compensation is too high. The draft report is not sent to complainants. The Ombudsman does not consider this to be a breach of natural justice, a view which has been judicially endorsed, in the case of the Parliamentary Ombudsman.[58] When the final report is signed, a copy is issued to all parties.

The procedures used to process complaints are thorough, but time-consuming. There is naturally concern that it should not take longer than necessary, and the Ombudsman aims to complete as many as possible within six months. In 1997, 30 per cent of reports were issued within this time-scale. A further 25 per cent were dealt with within nine months, and only 10 per cent took longer than 12 months to be completed. This was an improvement in overall turn-around times from the previous year. The further improvements, which were anticipated,[59] have taken effect. Last year, 67 per cent of

---

[58] *R v. Parliamentary Commissioner for Administration, ex p. Dyer* [1994] 1 All E.R. 375.
[59] *Seventh Annual Report of the Legal Services Ombudsman 1997*, at p.28.

cases were completed within six months, 95 per cent within nine months, and 99 per cent within a year.[60]

Inevitably, there will be complainants who are not satisfied by the final report, but it has to be recognised that there are some grievances for which there may be no remedy and which are restricted by the terms of the scheme. The scale of this can be seen in the figures for 1997, when the Ombudsman was satisfied with the way the complaint had been handled by the professional body in 70 per cent of the cases.[61] This is not out of line with previous years. Sometimes complainants enter into further correspondence with the Ombudsman, because they are not happy with the decision. Only very rarely would this further correspondence reveal fresh evidence, which would justify re-opening the case. In most cases, a response is sent explaining the powers and jurisdiction of the Ombudsman and repeating the reasons for the decision.[62] Some dissatisfied complainants contact the Lord Chancellor's Department, but the Lord Chancellor never interferes with the Ombudsman's decisions.

Conduct of the investigation

The Act has given the Ombudsman significant powers for conducting investigations. He or she may require any person to furnish such information or produce such documents as he or she considers relevant to the investigation. The Ombudsman has the same powers as the High Court to compel witnesses to attend, and give evidence, and to order the production of documents. Contempt of the Ombudsman can be treated in the same way as contempt of the High Court.[63] Despite these wide powers, there is no guidance in the Act as to what constitutes grounds for complaint, nor what matters should be considered in assessing a complaint. It was left to the first Ombudsman to devise appropriate procedures for dealing with complaints.

Although it is possible to examine witnesses, in practice reliance is

---

[60] This information was obtained by the author in a communication with the Ombudsman's office.

[61] *Seventh Annual Report of the Legal Services Ombudsman 1997*, at p.27.

[62] Recent research has found that many complainants had great difficulty in understanding the remit of the Ombudsman (*Consumer Satisfaction in a Super-Escalated Complaint Environment*. A report by the Customer Management Consultancy Ltd to the Office of the Legal Services Ombudsman (1999) The Lord Chancellor's Department, Research Programe).

[63] Courts and Legal Services Act, s. 25.

placed on written evidence, together with occasional telephone conversations with the parties. Since the inception of the scheme there have been four cases where personal interviews were conducted. Such practices have obvious resource implications. The investigation is usually conducted on the basis of the contents of the professional body's file, and only in rare cases will further information be sought. Even where there is an investigation into the original complaint, the information and evidence on the professional body's file is generally accepted, although it may be re-interpreted. In addition, the practitioner's file may be requested. Generally practitioners are willing to comply with such requests and the Ombudsman has not had to use the powers of compulsion contained in the Act.

The evidence is assessed on the balance of probabilities, but, as in all schemes which rely on written representations, it can be difficult to decide questions of fact. The Ombudsman's staff have to assess the plausibility of explanations, and to seek evidence from the professional body's and lawyers' files. The absence of a note on the solicitor's file would not enhance a solicitor's case, particularly if it were seen as unreasonable not to have made a note. This is particularly the case in a dispute about costs. The previous Ombudsman took the view that if information on costs was not given in writing to the client, it should be assumed that the solicitor failed to give it.

The Ombudsman's office has devised procedures to ensure that the investigation process is consistent with the rules of natural justice. For example, the lawyer concerned in the case is informed as soon a case is accepted for investigation. If the Ombudsman's report is to recommend that an award of compensation be made against a lawyer, he or she is given an opportunity to make representations before this is done. The conduct of the lawyer is assessed in accordance with standards of good practice, and professional conduct standards are taken into account. All the reports containing a recommendation are checked, to ensure that there is nothing contentious, unfair or misleading in them. Decisions of the Legal Services Ombudsman are subject to judicial review, but there have been no reported cases. Although complainants and practitioners sometimes threaten judicial review, in the few cases when this has happened, either leave was not granted, or the applicants withdrew after the leave stage.[64] The Ombudsman is the final decision-maker and the Act requires him or her to sign every report.

---

[64] Recent research has revealed that 80 per cent of solicitors were happy with the Ombudsman's decision. See *Law Society Gazette*, October 28, 1998, at p.6.

Investigation of the original complaint

Although the Ombudsman has discretion to investigate the original complaint, as well as the way the professional body has dealt with it, the Act gives no guidance about when it would be appropriate to do so. In practice this discretion is exercised in a minority of cases. There are no accurate figures for this, but it used to happen in 10 to 20 per cent of cases. The practice of investigating the original complaint is now more common, and in 1998, almost one-third of these were investigated. The Ombudsman will only investigate the original matter if it is clear that the professional body's decision on that matter is seriously deficient. Even in these situations he or she may refer the case back to the professional body for reconsideration by that body. This is likely to be done if it is a matter involving professional misconduct, because the Ombudsman has no disciplinary powers, although he or she can recommend compensation for distress or inconvenience caused by misconduct. If the Ombudsman feels that the professional body has overlooked an important aspect of the complaint, or if the evidence does not appear to support the professional body's conclusion, it may be referred back, as the professional body has the resources and systems for handling detailed investigations. There are thus a limited number of situations where the Ombudsman feels it is appropriate to investigate the matter to which the complaint relates.

The Ombudsman is content that the jurisdiction allows, rather than compels, a reinvestigation of the original complaint. Reinvestigation is unnecessary in many cases. If there were an obligation to re-examine, there would have to be a major increase in resources for the office. However, there are some situations where reinvestigation is desirable, but cases are referred back to the professional body. This is partly because the Ombudsman's office lacks the resources to be able to carry out an adequate investigation.[65] Greater funding is needed to enable a reinvestigation of some highly complex cases in detail.

Staffing

The Legal Services Ombudsman cannot be a lawyer[66] a provision which was subject to some criticism during the passage of the Bill.

---

[65] *Solicitors Journal*, June 12, 1992, at p.563.
[66] Courts and Legal Services Act, s. 21(5).

One M.P. thought that it was "nonsense" that the ombudsman could not be a person "who is most knowledgeable and experienced about legal services". It was felt that the very skills the Ombudsman would require—analysing evidence, speed reading documents, sifting, collating of and finding flaws in arguments—are those possessed by lawyers.[67] The rationale for the use of a non-lawyer is that the Ombudsman is acting "in the interests of an ordinary member of the public". It was thus felt to be entirely appropriate that a person who is not a lawyer should investigate the way a complaint was handled by a professional body.[68]

The first Legal Services Ombudsman, Michael Barnes, had a marketing and advertising background. He had been the chair of the Electricity Consumers Council, a member of the National Consumer Council, a member of the Advertising Standards Authority, and the Director of the U.K. Immigrants Advisory Service. He therefore had close links with the voluntary sector and, as he explained in one interview, he brought to the job "a complaint handling and a consumerist background, combined with a knowledge of Westminster and Whitehall".[69] The present Ombudsman, Ann Abraham, who took up office in September 1997, was previously the chief executive of the National Association of Citizens Advice Bureaux. Prior to this, she was a housing manager in two London local authorities and she worked for 10 years at the Housing Corporation. Her particular interest was in housing for people with special needs. Until recently she was a board member of Centrepoint Housing Association. Like her predecessor, she brings a consumerist perspective to the post.

The Act allows the Ombudsman considerable autonomy and, because of this independence, the focus and perspective of the Legal Services Ombudsman scheme has depended to a large extent on the personal qualities of the individual holding the post of Ombudsman at any one time. There is no doubt of the first Ombudsman's considerable achievements in establishing the office, and he was respected by the profession and by consumers.[70] He saw his role as essentially bringing to the complaint handling process the views of "an independent and . . . fair-minded person".[71] The present Ombudsman sees her role as bringing a sense of humanity to the provision of legal

---

[67] Standing Committee D, col. 167, May 22, 1990, Mr Lawrence.
[68] Standing Committee D, col. 177, May 22, 1990, Attorney-General.
[69] *Legal Action*, November 1991, at p.7.
[70] See *Seventh Annual Report of the Legal Services Ombudsman 1997* at p.2.
[71] *First Annual Report of the Legal Services Ombudsman 1991*, at p.6.

services, and making the consumer central to the complaint handling process.[72]

The Ombudsman's office has a small staff of twenty-three, including the Ombudsman herself. These consist of the secretary, legal adviser, casework manager, investigating officers and support staff. The first Ombudsman had little input in the decision about the office establishment, and no remit to decide the gradings of particular posts. These decisions were made by the Lord Chancellor's Department. Since the legislation provided that the Ombudsman should not be professionally qualified, it was felt by the Lord Chancellor's Department that he or she should have a senior staff member who would be professionally qualified and would act as legal adviser. Part of his or her remit is to vet all reports which contain a recommendation, before they are placed before the Ombudsman. Senior staff in the office are involved in devising policy in relation to Ombudsman decisions.

The employees in the Ombudsman's office are of high calibre, and the small staff are achieving some impressive standards. Although investigating officers need not be graduates, they must have similar intellectual ability. Some are law graduates. There is no bar on their being legally qualified, but the Ombudsman is concerned to achieve a balance, and aware of the dangers of having a large proportion of staff who are members of the legal profession.

Caseload

As can be seen from Table 1 below, the numbers of new inquiries received annually since the inception of the scheme remained fairly static during the first three years. Since then, there has been a steady increase, although the 1995 numbers remains the highest, at 2,092. The numbers of complaints to the Ombudsman represents between 8–10 per cent of the total number of complaints made to the three professional bodies covered by the scheme.[73] As can be seen from Table 1, in the majority of cases, the Ombudsman is satisfied with the way the complaint has been handled by the professional body.[74] It is

---

[72] *Seventh Annual Report of the Legal Services Ombudsman 1997*, at p.9.

[73] As well as the Law Society's Office for the Supervision of Solicitors and the General Council of the Bar, the Council for Licensed Conveyancers and the Institute of Legal Executives are within the Ombudsman's remit.

[74] In 1997, the percentage of reports where the complaints handling was satisfactory was 67 per cent in the case of solicitors and 90 per cent in the case of barristers. *Seventh Annual Report of the Legal Services Ombudsman 1997*, at p.6.

only in a minority of cases, usually less than 30 per cent, that the Ombudsman makes a recommendation for a remedy. Sometimes the Ombudsman may not disagree with the decision on the complaint,

Table 1: Caseload

Year	1991	1992	1993	1994	1995	1996	1997
Number of Inquiries	1238	1263	1235	1598	2092	1855	⋆
Completed Reports	170	761	580	839	1041	1388	1519
Outcomes:							
Recommendation ⋆⋆	31	125	146	178	199	321	349
Formal Criticism	23	110	106	95	70	90	143
Satisfactory	116	535	339	579	781	989	1055

⋆ The present Ombudsman believes that it is not meaningful to give figures for initial inquiries. Many of these are not pursued by complainants. In practice, if a completed application form is received from a complainant, the matter will be investigated, unless it is outside the Ombudsman's remit.
⋆⋆ Some reports contain more than one recommendation.

(**Source:** *Legal Services Ombudsman Annual Reports*)

but issues a formal criticism of the way the professional body handled the complaint.

Not surprisingly, there are more allegations about solicitors than about barristers, a function of the much larger number of solicitors in practice, and their more direct involvement with clients.[75] Some of these allegations relate to cases where the Office for the Supervision of Solicitors found substance to the complaint, but the action taken was felt by the complainant to be inadequate. The biggest category of complaints about solicitors concern cases of divorce or family proceedings and this is followed by house sales/purchase, property disputes and the administration of wills. The reasons for complaints are usually poor service, either in general, or specifically relating to delay or inaction, disregarding instructions, failure to keep the client informed, documents withheld or lost, and failure to reply to letters or phone calls.

Allegations about barristers are fairly small in number. Some

---

[75] Allegations about solicitors account for between 85 and 95 per cent of the total cases dealt with each year by the Legal Services Ombudsman.

complaints have to be rejected by the Ombudsman because they relate to the barrister's immunity in respect of the conduct of a case in court. Nevertheless, there are valid complaints about the failure to provide a proper standard of service and about poor communication. Recurring themes which emerge from complaints involving barristers include the fact that conduct issues are overlooked or given insufficient weight by the Bar Council. There are also complaints about the reluctance of the Bar Council to recommend compensation for poor service.[76]

Recommendations for a remedy

Where the Ombudsman is not satisfied with the way the professional body has handled the complaint, he or she can recommend a number of remedies. He or she can ask the professional body to reconsider the complaint. Alternatively, there can be an award of compensation, to be paid either by the professional body or by the lawyer who was the subject of the original complaint. Table 2 below shows the

Table 2: Recommendations

Year	1991	1991	1993	1994	1995	1996	1997
Professional Body to reconsider	15	69	84	68	71	127	106
Compensation— professional body	1	10	20	49	56	81	101
Compensation— lawyer	15	46	42	61	72	113	142
Total recommendations	31	125	146	178	199	321	349

(**Source:** *Legal Services Ombudsman Annual Reports*)

distribution of the various remedies over the last seven years.

Where the Ombudsman recommends that the professional body should reconsider the complaint, and this is done, the process often does result in a worthwhile benefit for complainants. A revised decision to the benefit of the complaint is made in about half of these

---

[76] *Seventh Annual Report of the Legal Services Ombudsman 1997*, at p.21.

reconsidered cases. However, where the request for reconsideration does not lead to further investigation, or where the decision remains the same, the complainant receives no benefit from the Ombudsman's recommendation. For example, in the first four years of the office, there had been 225 cases where the Solicitors Complaints Bureau had been asked to reconsider complaints. Of the 155 cases where the results of these reconsiderations were known, 59 were favourable to the complainant, 31 of these being some monetary benefit.[77]

Table 2 above shows the number of awards of compensation, to be paid either by the professional body or the lawyer. Although there is no limit on the size of awards, in practice, these are not large. The Ombudsman has tended to bear in mind the self-regulatory framework within which the professional bodies complaints systems operate in assessing what might be realistic. The first Ombudsman took the view that he was "constrained by the amounts that the courts have seen fit to award" as compensation for distress or inconvenience.[78] Although the Lord Chancellor's Department has not given much guidance on this, the Ombudsman tends to award £100-£250 for nominal inconvenience and £250-£500 for clearer cases of inconvenience, involving longer delay or having to write letters. Amounts between £500 and £1,000 will only be awarded where there has been significant delay, and some other more positive hardship for the complainant, for example, being deprived of a sum of money for a period of time, or having to instruct another firm of solicitors. Awards of over £1,000 are unusual, and the larger awards tend to be given for loss, rather than for inconvenience or distress.

Table 3 below shows the amounts which have been awarded. It is very rare for the professional bodies to cause actual loss, the usual problem in these cases being delay and the awards against professional bodies are consequently fairly small. In all the cases, the amounts recommended to be paid by the professional bodies was less than £500.

Compensation is only awarded against the practitioner in cases where the original complaint has been investigated.[79] When there is an award for actual loss against practitioners, the aim is to put the person in the position he or she would have been in had the fault not occurred. However, the Ombudsman has to be realistic about the amount of compensation lawyers could be expected to pay. The

---

[77] *Fourth Annual Report of the Legal Services Ombudsman 1994*, at p.10.

[78] *Second Annual Report of the Legal Services Ombudsman 1992*, at p.13.

[79] It is understood that the Bar Mutual Indemnity Fund will pay compensation awards made against a barrister. The Solicitors Indemnity Fund have not adopted this practice, on the basis that such an award is not a legal liability.

Table 3: *Compensation Awards*

Year	1991	1992	1993	1994	1995	1996
Number of awards	16	56	62	110	128	194
Size of award:						
Up to £500		50	50	84	109	172
£500-£1,000	16★	3	6	15	8	16
£1,000-£2,000		3	4	5	9	2
£2,000-£3,000			2	3	1	
£3,000-£4,000				2		2
£4,000-£6,000					1	2
Over £6,000				1		

★ All 16 awards ranged between £250 and £1,500.

(**Source:** *Legal Services Ombudsman Annual Reports*)

credibility of the scheme could be affected if the awards were so high that lawyers refused to comply. Notwithstanding this, the ombudsman has made an award of £59, 809 in one case,[80] where the complainant had no other avenue of redress. This case concerned an allegation of negligence in connection with the drawing up of a will. The solicitors concerned failed to comply with the recommendation.

In 1991, there were only 16 cases where awards for compensation were made. The amounts were within a range of £250 and £1,500. Fifteen of these cases involved solicitors and the payments related to inconvenience or distress caused by lack of communication or delay.[81] In 1992, compensation awards were made against solicitors in 45 cases, barristers in one case, and the Solicitors Complaints Bureau in ten cases.[82] In 1993, compensation awards were made against lawyers in 42 cases, and against professional bodies in 20 cases.[83] In 1994 there were 49 recommendations that the professional body should pay compensation, and 61 recommendations that the lawyer should pay compensation. There was one case, mentioned above, where the amount of compensation recommended was £59,809.[84] In 1995 there

---

[80] *Fourth Annual Report of the Legal Services Ombudsman 1994*, at p.23.

[81] *First Annual Report of the Legal Services Ombudsman 1991*, at p.3.

[82] *Second Annual Report of the Legal Services Ombudsman 1992*, at p.3.

[83] *Third Annual Report of the Legal Services Ombudsman 1993*, at p.3.

[84] *Fourth Annual Report of the Legal Services Ombudsman 1994*, at p.3.

were 56 recommendations that the professional body should pay compensation, and 72 compensation recommendations for individual lawyers.[85] In 1996, the professional body was recommended to pay compensation in 81 cases, and 113 recommendations that individual lawyers pay compensation. There was also a proposal to recommend compensation for loss of £32,871. This resulted in negotiations between the parties being re-opened and a settlement of £25,000 being agreed.[86]

In 1997, there were 142 recommendations for payment of compensation by the individual lawyer. Solicitors accounted for 137 of these. In 20 of these cases, the compensation was for loss, and the highest award was for £6,801, the lowest was £10, and the average was £730. There were 117 cases where compensation was recommended for distress and inconvenience. The average award was £357, and the lowest was £50. The highest award, of £5,000, was recommended where costs information for the work done by solicitor was "singularly lacking" and the complainant was shocked to receive bills totalling £30,000.[87] In the five cases where barristers were recommended to pay compensation, the average award was £320, the highest being £400, and the lowest £200. These were all for distress and inconvenience. There were 101 recommendations that the professional body pay compensation. All of these were against the Office for the Supervision of Solicitors. The highest award was £400, the lowest £50, and the average £175.[88]

Professional negligence

Despite the occasional high award, on the whole, awards are fairly modest, and are indicative of the fact that the Ombudsman tends to operate in the area of shoddy work and poor service, rather than professional negligence. The fact that the Ombudsman can award compensation for loss raises the question of the relationship between the Ombudsman scheme and professional negligence. Both the Green Paper[89] and the White Paper[90] discussed the jurisdictional problems for professional bodies where a complaint involves an allegation of negligence. While allowing that these bodies should not involve

---

[85] *Fifth Annual Report of the Legal Services Ombudsman 1995*, at p.3.
[86] *Sixth Annual Report of the Legal Services Ombudsman 1996*, at p.4.
[87] *Seventh Annual Report of the Legal Services Ombudsman 1997*, at p.14.
[88] *ibid.* at pp. 6, 28.
[89] *The Work and Organisation of the Legal Profession*, Cm.570 (1989), at p.17.
[90] *Legal Services: A Framework for the Future*, Cm.740 (1989), at p.35.

themselves in cases concerning large amounts of money or complex issues, the Government felt that a simple remedy was being denied in many cases. It was therefore proposed that the Ombudsman should be given explicit power to re-investigate small negligence cases.[91]

Interestingly, therefore, the Act specifically allows the Ombudsman to entertain a complaint even though the individual might be entitled to bring proceedings in court.[92] So, the availability of an alternative remedy does not preclude the consumer from seeking redress from the Ombudsman, an approach which is entirely consistent with the philosophy of providing an ombudsman as a cheap and informal grievance remedial process. There is, however, some uncertainty in this area. It is not clear what is meant by "small" in this context. It could be taken to mean cases involving sums below £1,000, which was the limit for the small claims procedure in the county court at the time the Ombudsman's scheme was established. The Lord Chancellor's Department has advised that the Ombudsman should not be concerned with the amount being claimed but should decide whether it was an appropriate case to be dealt with by the Legal Services Ombudsman.

The Ombudsman does not have a compensation limit. However, where he or she is asked to decide whether to investigate a complaint where the loss runs into five or six figures, the scheme is "in effect being asked to act as a free alternative dispute resolution mechanism for professional negligence claims against lawyers".[93] Despite the wording of the Act, it was probably not Parliament's intention that the Ombudsman should provide an effective alternative dispute resolution mechanism for these matters, regardless of the amount of compensation claimed. The Ombudsman's office has insufficient resources to provide a feasible alternative to the courts in handling anything but the most simple negligence cases.[94] The Ombudsman will only investigate where it is clear that he or she will not be prevented by the complexity of the law or the facts from conducting a fair investigation, and reaching a fair and authoritative decision. There is no direct correlation between the size and complexity of the claim, but often a valuable claim, especially one which has not justified the risk of court proceedings, will turn out to involve complexity.[95] Cases which are complicated, legally or factually, are therefore not investigated.

[91] *ibid.* at p.35.
[92] Courts and Legal Services Act 1990, s. 22(10).
[93] *Fourth Annual Report of the Legal Services Ombudsman 1994*, at p.21.
[94] *ibid.* at p.25.
[95] *ibid.* at p.21.

Nevertheless the problem remains of drawing a distinction between shoddy work/poor service and negligence, a matter which was discussed in Chapter 2. The Ombudsman has taken issue where the professional body has demonstrated an eagerness to classify complaints as negligence matters, and therefore beyond jurisdiction. Since 1991, the Solicitors Complaints Bureau (and now the Office for the Supervision of Solicitors) can deal with minor negligence cases, where there is a clear quantifiable loss of under £1,000. The Solicitors Complaints Bureau was too ready to say that they had no power to deal with such complaints, and that complainants should seek independent legal advice.[96] For example, one complaint concerned an application for a licence by a restaurant. The solicitor failed to inform the client about displaying a notice before the application, and as a result, the application was delayed until the following month. This resulted in between £400 and £600 loss of profits. The Solicitors Complaints Bureau said that the only course of action was to sue in negligence, and to take independent legal advice with a view to commencing proceedings. The Ombudsman felt that as the Bureau could make awards of up to £1,000, and that as this was not a complex case, it was just the kind of "small negligence" case that should be settled by the professional body.[97]

The Office for the Supervision of Solicitors also appears to be retreating behind legalistic barricades, in rejecting complaints on the grounds that the issue is one of negligence. In one case, the complaint was the solicitor's delay in accounting to the client for the £15,000 proceeds of sale from his business lease. The Office for the Supervision of Solicitor said that this was a contract or negligence claim, and therefore they could not deal with it. The Ombudsman disagreed with this conclusion, on the grounds that a professional body should be concerned about the claim that a firm had grown too attached to a client's money.[98] In another case, where the other side's solicitor failed to give information about a boundary dispute in a conveyancing matter, the Ombudsman felt that the solicitor had a professional obligation to the complainant, and that it was not a purely negligence matter.[99]

Even where complainants mention negligence in their complaint, the professional body should investigate if it is clearly about delay, or some other aspect of poor service.[1] Nor should the professional body

---

[96] *Second Annual Report of the Legal Services Ombudsman 1992*, at p.9.
[97] *Fifth Annual Report of the Legal Services Ombudsman 1995*, at p.28.
[98] *Seventh Annual Report of the Legal Services Ombudsman 1997*, at p.16.
[99] *Sixth Annual Report of the Legal Services Ombudsman 1996*, at p.29.
[1] *ibid.* p.8.

always decline to investigate where the complainant is claiming compensation in excess of the compensation limit. The professional body can make reductions in fees as a remedy, and this could be in excess of the compensation limit.[2]

"Guardian of the guardians" and influence on good practice

An important aspect of the Ombudsman's role is the supervision of the complaints mechanisms of the professional bodies, and the regulator of good practice within the profession. This is clearly of some importance if the Ombudsman is to fulfil expectations expressed by the Government during the passage of the Bill. The Ombudsman's impact in relation to the way in which lawyers deal with their clients[3] has been discussed in Chapters 4 and 5. In addition, the Ombudsman is specifically empowered by the Act to make recommendations to the professional bodies about their complaints procedures.[4] The professional body is required "to have regard to" such a recommendation.[5] There are three mechanisms, which can be used to exert influence on the complaints bodies and the professions. Recommendations specifically on complaints procedures may be made under section 24 of the Act. The Ombudsman can also have informal meetings with the professional bodies. Finally, there are the formal comments in the Ombudsman's Annual Reports.

Understandably, the Ombudsman lays great stress on this regulatory role seeing it as ultimately of greater benefit to the consumer interest than decisions made in individual cases. Recommendations or comment on practice can be made on the basis of the case work experience. Issues raised by consumer complaints can be used to seek to influence the profession on the way in which it treats its clients. As the Ombudsman receives over a thousand referrals each year about the way complaints are handled by the profession, he or she is in "an especially privileged position to assess the human consequences of

---

[2] *Seventh Annual Report of the Legal Services Ombudsman 1997* at p.15.

[3] This was acknowledged in the *First Annual Report of the Legal Services Ombudsman*, which noted that the expectation was that the Legal Services Ombudsman "would be able to identify the general issues reflected in complaints and thereby help to chart a path for the maintenance and improvement of professional standards" (p.21).

[4] In this context, it is worth noting that the Government is introducing a proposal to allow the creation of a Legal Complaints Commissioner, with power to make recommendations on complaints systems.

[5] Courts and Legal Services Act, s. 24.

developments in the profession".[6] This important role has been acknowledged by the Secretary-General of the Law Society. He spoke of the benefits of the Ombudsman in bringing to the surface "valuable issues about the manner in which the profession treats clients and how the professional body treats both".[7]

Section 24 powers have been used sparingly. One such occasion, in 1991, was a recommendation to the General Council of the Bar that complainants should be informed of the barrister's response to their complaint.[8] The Bar agreed to accept the recommendation in principle and the (then) Professional Conduct Committee agreed as a general point to provide complainants with more information. Section 24 recommendations may not be the most appropriate weapon in improving complaints procedures. When the first Ombudsman sought to deal with the more fundamental point about deficiencies in the Bar's complaints procedures, he chose to influence the Bar through informal meetings rather than exercise his formal powers under the Act. Clearly, in that case his pressure was enough to cause the Bar to take action, albeit perhaps rather belatedly.

An early concern of the Ombudsman was the way the (then) Solicitors Complaints Bureau dealt with complainants who alleged loss as a result of negligence on the part of their solicitor. The Bureau practice was to tell the complainant that they had no jurisdiction in such cases and that the complainant should instruct another solicitor with a view to taking action in court. The Ombudsman did not feel that this was a helpful response, and raised it at a meeting with the Bureau in March 1991. Reassurances were given,[9] but the anticipated improvements in the system did not materialise immediately.[10] Concern was again expressed by the Ombudsman, and given the fact that the matter was not raised in the following year, it appears that the Ombudsman's interventions achieved some improvement for consumers. As noted in the previous section, however, this is an area where the Ombudsman has to be particularly vigilant, to ensure that the professional body does not evade its responsibilities in these cases.

Case examples, and the lessons to be learnt from them are also a useful way of disseminating good practice. The annual reports of the Ombudsman contain details of cases, which give an indication of the

---

[6] *Seventh Annual Report of the Legal Services Ombudsman 1997*, at p.9.

[7] J. Hayes, "Protecting the Public and Serving the Profession," Paper presented to the *Legal Profession in Transition* conference (1994), Centre for Law and Business and Centre for Social Ethics and Policy, University of Manchester.

[8] *First Annual Report of the Legal Services Ombudsman 1991*, at p.3.

[9] *ibid.* at p.9.

[10] *Second Annual Report of the Legal Services Ombudsman 1992*, at p.9.

types of complaints, and the approach adopted by the Ombudsman. The Ombudsman also issues free broadsheets, which are distributed to practitioners. It did appear that the Ombudsman's impact on the profession was not as great as it should be. Research in the mid-1990s indicated that only 18 per cent of solicitors in a survey admitted to reading the Ombudsman's newsletters or annual reports.[11] This indicated a limited appreciation of the Ombudsman's role by individual solicitors, and a failure to use an important mechanism for improving practice.

This may now be changing. More is being done to inform the profession of the work of the Ombudsman, and to disseminate good practice. The *Law Society Gazette* now publishes a monthly insert on the Ombudsman's decisions.[12] This has created more dialogue between the Ombudsman and the profession. The Ombudsman now also publishes a summary of the annual report, which is sent to all solicitors' firms. This is helping to raise the profile of the work of the Ombudsman among solicitors.

Successive annual reports have been critical of the office procedures of the Bureau.[13] This, in conjunction with criticism from other quarters,[14] fuelled the call for a reform of the system. The result was the formation of the Office for the Supervision of Solicitors, which is discussed in Chapter 5. When the Law Society and Bar Council made their recent changes to their complaint handling procedures, the Ombudsman was consulted. It appears, however, that despite the section 24 powers, the professional bodies do not have to seek the Ombudsman's approval for any changes they may make.

Evaluation of the scheme

As an ombudsman, the Legal Services Ombudsman would be expected to fulfil the criteria of independence, effectiveness, fairness and public accountability.[15] These are values normally associated with adjudicative procedures, and are relevant to the operation of the

---

[11] See R. James and M. Seneviratne, "Solicitors and Client Complaints" (1996) 6(3) *Consumer Policy Review* 101–105.

[12] This started in March 1998.

[13] See, for example *Second Annual Report of the Legal Services Ombudsman 1992*, at p.10; *Third Annual Report of the Legal Services Ombudsman 1993*, at p.8.

[14] See, for example, National Consumer Council, *The Solicitors Complaints Bureau—A Consumer View* (1994).

[15] These are the criteria agreed by the British and Irish Ombudsman Association for full membership of the Association. See R. James, "Self-Regulation for Regulators—the Ombudsman Association" [1994] *Consumer Law Journal* 71.

scheme as an alternative dispute resolution mechanism. Another criterion for evaluation is the extent to which the Ombudsman is able to exert influence on the profession in relation to good practice, both in the way in which the professional bodies operate their complaints mechanisms, and indeed on the way in which the members of the legal profession deal with their clients. One of the strengths of an ombudsman system, as opposed to the courts, is that an ombudsman has the opportunity to bring about improvements in administration and policy in the organisations within his or her jurisdiction, rather than simply being confined to decision making in individual cases. As has been seen this was identified as a function of the Legal Services Ombudsman by the Lord Chancellor in presenting the Bill to Parliament and the Ombudsman has accepted this role.

INDEPENDENCE AND ACCOUNTABILITY

The Ombudsman is appointed by,[16] and is accountable to, the Lord Chancellor. The main mechanism for implementing this accountability is through the annual report which he or she formally presents to the Lord Chancellor who in turn lays it before Parliament.[17] The accountability is thus a formal one, in the main, rather than on a day-to-day basis, and it seems that the Lord Chancellor's Department maintains a hands-off approach in its dealings with the Ombudsman. The one area where the Department exerts real control is in budget approval and staffing. There seems to be no evidence that the Department wants a greater role in monitoring performance, and its main concern seems to be ensuring financial constraint.

As to independence, the Ombudsman seems to have been successful in keeping independent of Government. So far as the profession is concerned, it is interesting that the first Legal Services Ombudsman saw himself as supporting the consumer as the disadvantaged party in any dealings with the legal profession. Other Ombudsmen adopt a different approach and would not see themselves as a consumer's champion but rather as an independent arbiter.[18] The present Ombudsman sees herself as an "extra, protective tier" to the professional regulatory system. As such, she is holding in the "balance the competing interests of profession and public," but from a

---

[16] Courts and Legal Services Act 1990, s. 21(1).
[17] *ibid.* s. 21(6) and Sched. 3, para.5(1).
[18] See R. James, *Private Ombudsmen and Public Law* (1997) [Dartmouth], and M. Seneviratne, *Ombudsmen in the Public Sector* (1994) [Open University Press].

lay perspective.[19] The Legal Services Ombudsman is entirely independent of the professions, and to emphasise this, he or she cannot be a solicitor or barrister. While there are some solicitors on the staff, they are limited in number, and the dangers of employing a greater proportion are recognised.

FAIRNESS AND EFFECTIVENESS

The office procedures have been designed to ensure fairness as far as possible. The process seems fair and consistent. The Ombudsman makes the final decision in each case, which should ensure consistency. In addition, all recommendation reports are checked by the Legal Adviser. The procedures are designed to ensure that the requirements of natural justice are met in relation to both the complainant and the lawyer concerned.

It should be borne in mind that the number of decisions with recommendations is only a small proportion of the whole because most complaints are held to have no merit under the terms of the scheme. In some cases, for example, even though the Ombudsman may be critical of the way the complaint has been handled, he or she may still not find in favour of the complainant because there is no problem with the actual decision of the professional body. Where awards are made, there is a danger that the effectiveness of the scheme could be jeopardised if too many lawyers decided to opt for publicity rather than providing the recommended remedy to the consumer. The vast majority of lawyers accept and pay up. But it must be remembered that, in framing the awards, the Ombudsman has to bear in mind what he or she can realistically expect lawyers to pay. If there are too many "publicity options" there will be a consequent diminution of the credibility of the scheme. Where there are large awards,[20] lawyers, not unexpectedly, refuse to pay. Not only does this diminish the credibility of the scheme, but it also means that consumers who have been found to have made a justifiable complaint, and deserve a remedy, go unrecompensed.[21]

The speed with which cases are dealt with is also an important aspect of fairness and effectiveness. Delay seems to be inherent in many ombudsman schemes but the Legal Services Ombudsman has adopted some measures to deal with the problem, including the fast

---

[19] *Seventh Annual report of the Legal Services Ombudsman 1997,* at p.9.
[20] As we have seen, these are mainly to cover financial loss.
[21] The Government is proposing to give the Ombudsman the discretion to make binding awards.

track and priority classification for certain complaints and the use of short reports where appropriate. Given that delay is a common cause of complaint to the Ombudsman about professional bodies, it is particularly important that delay does not become a feature of the Ombudsman scheme itself. Delay also strikes at one of the supposed advantages of ombudsman schemes, which is that they are supposed to be not only a cheap alternative to the courts, but a speedy one as well.

The main question, however, in relation to the effectiveness of the Ombudsman as a complaints mechanism relates, not to the way in which the office operates,[22] but to the powers which are given by the Act to deal with grievances. One is bound to question the extent to which the Ombudsman can be considered an effective consumer redress mechanism when it can only deal with the consumer's principal complaint in a small percentage of cases.[23] At the very least, the Ombudsman may not meet consumer expectations in this regard. Despite clear information given in the Ombudsman booklets, consumers probably expect him or her to deal with their original complaint in each case since it is unlikely that, if they have had satisfaction through the self-regulatory mechanisms, they would then wish to invoke the Ombudsman remedy. Presumably most consumers who take their case to the Ombudsman, actually want a reversal of the professional body's decision in their case, and expect that their original complaint will be investigated.[24]

---

[22] One of the conclusions from research conducted by the author and R. James was that the first Legal Services Ombudsman and his staff had made an impressive job of bringing into being an effective and efficient operation. See R. James and M. Seneviratne, "The Legal Services Ombudsman: Form versus Function?" (1995) 58(2) *Modern Law Review* 187–207.

[23] Other ombudsman schemes in the public and private sector normally have a requirement that, before a complaint can be investigated by the Ombudsman, the authority or organisation concerned must have had an opportunity to deal with the complaint internally. Ombudsmen, therefore, traditionally become involved where a complainant is dissatisfied with the outcome of the internal process. Where the Legal Services Ombudsman differs from the norm is that the primary function is to investigate the manner in which the professional body has dealt with the complaint, and most of the investigations do not go beyond this. Other schemes are not established primarily to investigate the internal complaint handling process. Their main function is to investigate the substance of the original complaint. It may be that the way that the organisation has dealt with the grievance forms a part of that complaint, but it is not a precondition for using the scheme

[24] This has been confirmed by recent research, which indicates that complainants did not understand the remit of the Ombudsman, and expected their original complaint to be dealt with (*Consumer Satisfaction in a Super-Escalated Complaint Environment*. A Report by the Customer Management Consultancy Ltd to the office of the Legal Services Ombudsman (1999). The Lord Chancellor's Department Research Programme).

Conclusion

The advantages of ombudsman schemes have been well documented.[25] They provide consumers with cheap, speedy and informal mechanisms for resolving their grievances. The Legal Services Ombudsman, however, is different from other ombudsmen, in that his or her function is not primarily to resolve the consumer's grievance. The main function, as outlined in the Parliamentary debates, is to oversee the professional bodies' mechanisms for dealing with dissatisfied customers. The Ombudsman exists to provide independent supervision of the self-regulatory mechanisms of the legal profession. It is only when the original complaint is investigated (and this happens in less than one-third of cases) that he or she acts like other ombudsmen. Should the jurisdiction, therefore, be amended to impose a duty to look at the original complaint? This would mean taking on the role of the traditional ombudsman, but it would require vastly more resources, bearing in mind that at present, only a minority of cases involve a reinvestigation of the original complaint.

The Legal Services Ombudsman's office is an performing excellent role, on a limited budget. This role and the effectiveness of the office has to be seen in the context of the other avenues of redress open to the consumer of legal services. It may be that the system as set up is satisfactory if the self-regulatory mechanisms of the professional bodies are working well.[26] However, from the Ombudsman's comments in successive annual reports, and the issues addressed in Chapter 5, it seems that the self-regulatory mechanisms are not working well. The upheavals of recent years within the Law Society and the Bar are further evidence of this. Self-regulation can only survive its present form, if the profession can deliver higher levels of consumer satisfaction and deal effectively with complaints.

If the professional bodies fail to achieve consumer satisfaction, should their role as the second tier complaints mechanism be removed? The Ombudsman could then be approached directly, after the consumer has not obtained satisfaction with the provider of the service, the individual lawyer. A complaint to the professional body would no longer be a preliminary stage to an approach to the Ombudsman. If this were to happen, it would completely change the nature of the Ombudsman's operation. It is unlikely that the office would be publicly funded, as there would have to be a huge increase in resources to deal with the thousands of complaints which

---

[25] See R. James, *Private Ombudsmen and Public Law* (1997) [Dartmouth].
[26] This is certainly the view of the first Legal Services Ombudsman.

professional bodies now receive. It is, however, an issue to be addressed, if the Ombudsman is to be judged as an effective consumer redress mechanism.

Even within the present system, Parliament has failed to give the Ombudsman adequate powers to perform the supervisory function and to provide really effective independent monitoring. The Ombudsman only sees cases where complainants have the energy and commitment, often after many years, to put their case. The Ombudsman's knowledge of how the professional bodies operate in relation to complaints come from a patchy experience, and the cases he or she see are only a very small proportion of those dealt with by the professional bodies. Perhaps there should be a power for own-initiative investigations, making unannounced inspections of the professional bodies, seeing files at random. Further, he or she lacks enforcement powers when dissatisfied with the way the professional bodies are operating. The main weapon is the section 24 recommendation, but the professional bodies only need to "have regard" to this. The Ombudsman can exhort the professional bodies to change their practices but has no power to compel.

If the Ombudsman does not have adequate powers, does it matter? The Ombudsman has been given the important role of standing above the providers of legal services, and monitoring their performance. If the Ombudsman is to oversee the way in which lawyers deal with their clients, he or she must have adequate powers to fulfil that role. Without these powers, this, albeit specialised, version of the ombudsman remedy will not fulfil its potential as a means of protecting the consumer interest.

Chapter 7

Conclusion

The opening up of the market to new providers of legal services has not been matched by a relaxation of the mechanisms which regulate the work of the legal profession. The reforms of the last decade were designed to allow for more professionals to provide legal services by making inroads into the traditional restrictive practices operated by the profession. They did not result in "full-blooded deregulation" and "free-floating entrepreneurialism".[1] The aim of the reforms was to increase choice, but maintain standards. Despite the introduction of the market and competition into the delivery of legal services, there is still as much regulation of the profession as previously.

The reasons for regulation of the market for legal services have been discussed in Chapter 1. To summarise, it is inherent in the nature of professional-client relations that there is asymmetry of information. Most individual consumers lack the experience, information and expertise to judge the quality of legal services. They have to rely on the very lawyers who have a financial interest in the sale of such services. They also have little control over the quantity of the services they receive, but must again rely on the judgment of those with a financial interest in increased consumption. Because they may be unable to assess quality, poor quality may not be noticed, and good service which fails to achieve results might be criticised.

If consumers are dissatisfied, it may be difficult for them to impose an effective sanction. Unlike corporate or institutional clients, they are not "repeat players," and therefore the loss of future business is not a major concern for providers.[2] Private law remedies are also of limited use for most consumers. There is an additional reason why legal services need to be regulated. Poor quality legal services can have

---

[1] *Seventh Annual Report of the Legal Services Ombudsman 1997*, at p.8.
[2] R. Baldwin, "A Model of Self-Regulation?" in *Governing the Profession* (Proceedings from the Annual Research Conference 1998), at p.5 [The Law Society, Research and Policy Planning Unit].

detrimental effects on third-party interests, as well as the system of justice itself. Confidence in the legal system depends upon the competence of those operating the system. Regulation is not therefore simply to protect the individual consumer, but the public interest in general.

Traditionally, it was the profession itself which was seen as appropriate for protecting the interests of consumers and the public at large. To a large extent, this is still the case, and most regulation of the legal profession is self-regulation, albeit within a statutory framework. Despite the general deregulation rhetoric of the previous Government, it placed on the professional bodies the clear duty to ensure standards of competence and professional conduct, in order to protect the interests of clients.[3] The present Government too, while accepting that it will do what it can to raise standards, believes that it is "predominantly for the legal profession to put its own house in order".[4]

It is not difficult to see why self-regulation is a preferred option for regulation, not only for the professions, but also for other industries. It is less costly for Government, is more amenable to change, and it does not have the same implementation problems associated with coercive mechanisms of control. It is not surprising that it has become one of the hallmarks of a profession, as it is also a mechanism for eliminating disreputable practitioners, thereby increasing the status of the profession.

Despite these advantages, there are problems with self-regulation, particularly in relation to the legitimacy of self-regulatory regimes. The public is less trusting of professionals than it was in the past, and it is therefore increasingly difficult for the legal profession to present a credible case for its role as the guardian of standards and the public interest. The traditional concept of professionalism has been challenged. Fifty years ago, the professions automatically had the respect of the public and clients. They "operated in a climate of deference".[5] This is no longer the case, and the public is increasingly sceptical of self-regulation.

There is some doubt about whether professional bodies can both represent their members, and at the same time regulate their conduct.

---

[3] *The Work and Organisation of the Legal Profession*, Green Paper, Cm.570 (1989), paras. 4.1, 4.2.
[4] Lord Chancellor, Access to Justice Bill, second Reading, December 14, 1998, col.1107. It is, however, making provision in the Bill for external standard setting for complaints if the legal profession fails to put house in order.
[5] M. Mears, "Foreword" in *Keeping Clients. A Guide for Solicitors* (1997) Office for the Supervision of Solicitors.

One of the major tasks of a professional body is to look after the interests of its members, and it is felt by some that this conflicts with the role of protecting the public. There is inconsistency between the roles of protecting the public and maintaining standards, and at the same time furthering the interests of the profession. This tension between these two roles undermines their effectiveness. This inconsistency has been recognised by the Office of Fair Trading in connection with the self-regulatory mechanisms operated by trade associations. Because they are dependent on their member firms for income and have a primary role of representing the interests of their members, they are "difficult vehicles for regulation". Because of the conflict between the two roles, it is suggested that "some division in these functions is necessary if effective regulation is not to be inhibited".[6]

It has been argued that the rights of any profession to both represent and regulate its members are outmoded, outdated and outweighed by the need for consumer protection and confidence in the legal system.[7] Even within the profession itself there is scepticism about whether the professional bodies can perform these dual roles effectively. A member of the Bar Council has spoken of its dichotomy of function which "leaves many barristers feeling isolated and disenchanted .... usually at the moment of greatest need.[8] A former president of the Law Society has questioned whether the combined roles are any longer tenable, maintaining that commercial pressures have made "the conflict between the representative role and the regulatory one impossible to sustain". As there is bound to be an increase in commercial pressures, self-regulation will become even more suspect in the eye of the consumer.[9]

Even those who believe that a professional body can both protect the public and serve the profession at the same time, recognise that this can only be done if it displays "great determination and willingness at times to alienate" its own members.[10] The two roles can only be reconciled if professional bodies no longer see themselves as protectors of particular monopolies or privileges. This involves a change in the culture of the profession. Client care must become

---

[6] Office of Fair Trading, *Raising Standards of Consumer Care: Progressing beyond codes of practice* (1998), Consultation document.

[7] A. Arora and A. Francis, *The Rule of Lawyers* (1998), at p.3, Discussion Paper 42 [Fabian Society].

[8] M. Beaumont, in *Counsel*, November/December 1998, p.12.

[9] Tony Holland, "The end of lawyers' self-regulation?", *The Times*, 1998

[10] J. Hayes, Secretary-General of the Law Society, "Protecting the Public and Serving the Profession" in *Legal Professions in Transition* Conference (1998), at p.1, Centre for Law and Business and Centre for Social Ethics and Policy, University of Manchester.

paramount, and the "following of sound business practice" must no longer be regarded as "alien to the values of the profession.[11]

This appeal for a change in culture highlights another tension in the legal profession. There is a precarious balance between professional values and commercial pressures.[12] They are not necessarily in direct conflict. The profession can only survive if it provides good quality services and value for money. Quality of service depends on competence and client care. It is generally in the interests of consumers that firms are more business-minded. But the values of professionalism means that the profession has to provide remedies when recalcitrant members are guilty of misconduct or incompetence. Such values can be an obstacle to competition. The pressures of competing in the market may lead some practitioners to question the reason for professional regulation.[13] There must be a serious question as to whether a viable professional culture can co-exist with a culture of commercialism.

This challenge to professionalism also arises because the traditional homogeneity of the profession is disappearing, if it has not already disappeared. This change in the nature of the legal profession has been considerable over the last two decades. The profession has increased dramatically in size, has more women members, is younger in profile, and covers a wider range of class backgrounds. This heterogeneity is further reinforced by the widely different range of clients it serves. For the solicitor's branch of the profession, the gulf between the small high street firm and the large city firm, with their different client bases and disparity of incomes, has widened to such an extent that they almost appear to be two different professions. With such a disparate profession, appeals for it to put its own house in order become less realistic.

Alongside the move towards commercialism in the profession, there is also the demand for more consumer protection. This has been a feature of the supply of goods and services since the 1970s, which has resulted in more legislative interference in consumer affairs. There is no doubt that we live in a consumer oriented society, where consumers expect high standards of service, and where the culture is one of complaining if those expectations are not met. If the legal profession is unable to deal adequately with these complaints, then the

---

[11] J. Hayes, Secretary-General of the Law Society, "Protecting the Public and Serving the Profession" in *Legal Professions in Transition* Conference (1998), at p.1, Centre for Law and Business and Centre for Social Ethics and Policy, University of Manchester.

[12] *Seventh Annual Report of the Legal Services Ombudsman 1997*, at p.8.

[13] Some large city firms consider the Law Society as irrelevant to the way they practise ("A Better way of Regulating" *Law Society Gazette*, March 3, 1999, at p.22).

warning is that the Government will do so, but that the profession will still have to bear the cost.[14] As the Legal Services Ombudsman has warned, if there were a head-on fight between professionalism and consumerism, there is "little doubt that consumerism will win the day".[15]

Given the tensions in the legal profession, what regulatory mechanisms are appropriate? Baldwin has noted the vast array of bodies concerned with the regulation of the legal profession, and the "highly complex set of arrangements for controlling a number of aspects of legal services provision".[16] Many of these have been addressed in this book. Some have remarked that it is the "multi-layered nature of the regulatory process that provides its very strength".[17] Others have also observed the difficulties in using one particular enforcement mechanism for controlling lawyer misconduct, and that a "multi- door" enforcement system is preferable.[18] The emphasis is on informal controls and changing cultures.

Despite the scepticism about self-regulation, it does have some support from consumer organisations. For example, the National Consumer Council is not opposed to self-regulation, provided it is effective and accountable. Self-regulatory schemes must have characteristics which address some of the criticisms of this form of regulation. These include external involvement in their design and operation. In addition, the operation and control of such schemes should, as far as possible, be separate from the institutions of the industries concerned. There should be clear statements of principles and standards, and there must be accessible and well-publicised complaints procedures, with adequate and meaningful sanctions.[19]

So far as the legal profession is concerned, the reforms of the past decade have preserved self-regulation, but with a more powerful watchdog, in the form of the Legal Services Ombudsman. The first Ombudsman referred to this as a "joint regulation model"[20] for

---

[14] A. Andrew, Law Society Council member for west London, *Law Society Gazette* April 16, 1998, at p.8.

[15] A. Abraham, "Prophet or High Priestess?" (1998) *Counsel* December

[16] R. Baldwin, *Regulating Legal Services* (1997) Lord Chancellor's Department Research Series No.5/97.

[17] A. Paterson, "Professionalism and the Legal Services Market" (1996) *International Journal of the Legal Profession* 137.

[18] D. B. Wilkins, "Who Should Regulate Lawyers?" (1992) 105 *Harvard Law Review* 799–887, at p.851.

[19] National Consumer Council, *Self-Regulation* (1986), at p.15.

[20] M. Barnes, "Monitoring and Evaluating Methods of Regulation" in *Proceedings from the Annual Research Conference 1994: Profession, business or trade: Do the professions have a future?* (1994), at p.61, The Law Society's Research and Policy Planning Unit, London: The Law Society.

consumer complaints. It involves a two-tier system of complaint handling, where complaints are first made to the relevant professional body. If the consumer is dissatisfied with the way that the professional body has handled the complaint, it can be referred to the Legal Services Ombudsman, an independent, statutory ombudsman, who provides the second tier of the process. The advantage for the profession of this two-tier system is that it gives the profession a high degree of control over the way complaints are handled. The disadvantage is that the profession must bear the cost of this, and the costs are high. This, of course, is an advantage for the public, as the cost is not borne by the taxpayer. There is also an incentive for the profession to deal with complaints effectively and efficiently, in order to keep the costs at a reasonable level.[21]

There can be no doubt that the creation of the Office of the Legal Services Ombudsman has been a force for good. It has provided a much needed independent contribution to the maintenance and development of high standards of service and conduct in the legal profession. It has given some legitimacy to the complaint mechanisms of the professional bodies, by providing independent supervision of their operation. The lessons from the casework have been filtered back to the profession, which in turn has helped to raise standards.

The first Legal Services Ombudsman believed that the joint-regulation model was a good one, but only if the self-regulation stage was consumer-friendly, fair and efficient, and able to achieve an acceptable level of complainant satisfaction. It is particularly important therefore that the professions establish complaints systems which enjoy public confidence. They must be, and be seen to be, independent, accessible, easy to understand, impartial, effective and flexible in the range of sanctions which can be imposed.[22]

As we have seen, the complaints-handling mechanisms of the professional bodies are failing to inspire such confidence. Public perception is that the procedures for complaints against the legal profession are lawyer-focused not consumer-focused.[23] This appears to be a general criticism of professional regulation, which in many cases is not delivering the benefits claimed, particularly because "the consumer interest is not at the heart of the regulatory framework".[24] This undermines the legitimacy of the system. Despite the considerable change which has recently taken place in the complaints

---

[21] *Fifth Annual Report of the Legal Services Ombudsman 1995*, at p.6.

[22] C. J. Whelan and C. G. Veljanovski, "Professional negligence and the quality of legal services—an economic perspective" (1983) *Modern Law Review* 700.

[23] *Seventh Annual Report of the Legal Services Ombudsman 1997*, at p.20.

[24] *Leave it to the professionals?* (1998), p.1, Consumers' Association, Policy Report.

handling systems of the professional bodies, there are still high levels of consumer dissatisfaction. Notwithstanding the valiant efforts of the professional bodies, there is still too much delay in dealing with complaints. There is still a failure to achieve credibility in the eyes of complainants. Moreover, there are still problems with adequate redress, particularly in relation to the Bar, where the conditions for obtaining compensation are so rigorous that hardly any awards have been made.

The Legal Services Ombudsman's conclusion from all this is that some progress has been made by the professional bodies, but that they have a long way to go to satisfy the pre-requisites of an effective complaints-handling procedure. If self-regulation is to survive into the twenty-first century, the professional bodies are warned that they will need to "put on some speed if they are to make it in time for the Millennium".[25] The profession as a whole has yet to acknowledge the positive aspects of complaints procedures, as a tool for management information, and as a mechanism for turning dissatisfied clients into loyal ones. The increase in the number of complaints does not necessarily signal a decline in standards. Our consumer-orientated society encourages complaints. What is important is how complaints are dealt with. More and more, legal practitioners will be considered as out-of-touch with their clients' expectations unless they view complaint handling as a normal part of their service provision.

If the professional bodies fail to deliver client satisfaction, who will? There have been a number of proposals for reform. Among the most radical is the establishment of a new regulatory body to take over the functions of the professional bodies in relation to all regulatory matters. This would leave the professional bodies to perform purely representational functions on behalf of their members. This proposal is modelled on the regulatory framework for the medical profession, where the British Medical Association is the representative body for the profession, and the General Medical Council regulates conduct and handles complaints.[26] There is no reason in principle why regulation and supervision should necessarily lie with the body that represents and promotes the legal profession's interests.[27]

A less radical proposal would keep the regulatory functions with the professional bodies, but remove complaint handling to another body. This was recommended in the mid-1980s, when the Law Society was devising new procedures to deal with complaints of inadequate

---

[25] *Seventh Annual Report of the Legal Services Ombudsman 1997*, at p.3.
[26] A. Arora and A. Francis, *The Rule of Lawyers* (1998), at p.14 [Fabian Society, Discussion Paper no.42].
[27] A.L. Newbold and G. Zellick, (1987) *Civil Justice Quarterly*,25–43, at p.26.

professional services. The recommendation was that an independent statutory body should be established to investigate and adjudicate on complaints against solicitors, and that complaints and discipline should be administered separately from the Law Society.[28] This solution is the one favoured by the National Consumer Council. Even less radical would be for complaints about inadequate professional services, which constitute the majority of client complaints, to be dealt with by an independent body. Such a body could refer disciplinary matters to the appropriate professional body.

Another solution would be to augment the Legal Services Ombudsman's powers, to bring the office in line with traditional ombudsman schemes. The Ombudsman would then be charged with investigating complaints, rather than investigating allegations that the professional body has not dealt properly with the original complaint against a lawyer. Such a proposal has serious resource implications, and it would presumably have to be financed by the profession. A less dramatic alteration would be to allow the Ombudsman to make investigations on his or her own initiative, and thus provide a more direct supervisory role.

The professional bodies have always been resistant to proposals which impinge upon their self-regulatory powers, and they would probably resist any proposal which took control over complaint handling from them.[29] After all, they would probably still be obliged to finance it. If they are to avoid what has been called an "overwhelming" case for reform,[30] they will have to make self-regulation more credible and effective. The Ombudsman has made some suggestions as to how the profession might achieve this. To restore public confidence, complaints must be taken seriously at a local level. The Office for the Supervision of Solicitors must deliver on its promises. Barristers should try to see things from the complainant's point of view. Lawyers should stop making excuses, and legalistic and defensive responses to complaints. The Ombudsman believes that the profession still "has a fundamental part to play in the future of complaints resolution".[31]

---

[28] Coopers and Lybrand *Exposure Draft* 1985, and Coopers and Lybrand *Final Report* 1986.
[29] However, it may be that the profession is not as wedded to self-regulation as it used to be. The Law Society is currently leading a debate on the future shape of regulation. It has issued a discussion paper which analyses the advantages and disadvantages of moving away from a system of self-regulation (*Regulation of Solicitors—A Strategic Discussion Paper* (1999) The Law Society
[30] A. Arora and A. Francis, *The Rule of Lawyers* (1998), p.14 [Fabian Society, Discussion Paper no.42].
[31] A. Abraham, "Regulating the Regulators: The Ombudsman's Perspective" (1998), at

The regulatory framework which exists for the legal profession has undergone radical transformation in the last decade, and is still in the process of being transformed. The profession is "engaged in a fundamental restructuring whose outcome is indeterminate".[32] The result may achieve an appropriate balance between self-regulation and deregulation,[33] and may provide appropriate mechanisms for protecting the interests of consumers. It may provide the mechanisms to ensure that self-regulation is subject to public scrutiny, is operated in the interests of society as a whole, and is more responsive to the public interest. If that could be achieved, we will have a commercially orientated profession, which is also attentive to the needs of the public and individual consumers. In the words of the Legal Services Ombudsman, we will have "humane professionalism".[34]

p.77, *Governing the Profession* Proceedings from the Annual Research Conference 1998, The Law Society, Research and Policy Planning Unit.

[32] R. Abel, "Ten Years On: Changes in the Regulatory Framework" (1998) *Governing the Profession* Proceedings from the Annual Research Conference 1998, The Law Society, Research and Policy Planning Unit, at p.10.

[33] A. Crawley and C. Bramall "Professional Rules, Codes, and Principles Affecting Solicitors (Or What Has Professional Regulation to do with ethics?)" in *Legal Ethics and Professional Responsibility* (R. Cranston ed., 1995) [Oxford: Clarendon Press].

[34] *Seventh Annual Report of the Legal Services Ombudsman 1997*, at p.9

Index